STECK-VAUGHN

PRE GED® TEST PREPARATION

REASONING THROUGH

LANGUAGE ARTS

Houghton
Mifflin
Harcourt

- Instruction at manageable reading levels and practice of basic skills aligned to the 2014 GED® Test content areas

- Emphasis on critical thinking skills

- Pretest and posttest assessments identify strengths and weaknesses

- Complete answers and explanations

Houghton
Mifflin
Harcourt

CONTENTS

To the Learner v
Pretest 1
Pretest Evaluation Chart 13

UNIT 1 READING SKILLS 14

Lesson 1   Main Idea 16

Lesson 2   Details 18

Lesson 3   Inference 20

Lesson 4   Sequence of Events 22

Lesson 5   Compare & Contrast 24

Lesson 6   Cause & Effect 26

Lesson 7   Conclusions 28

Lesson 8   Author's Evidence & Purpose 30

Lesson 9   Setting 32

Lesson 10   Character 34

Lesson 11   Application 36

Lesson 12   Synthesis 38

Unit 1 Review: Reading Skills 40
Unit 1 Mini-Test 42

UNIT 2 FICTION 44

Lesson 13   Adventure 46
The Call of the Wild
by Jack London

Lesson 14   Mystery 51
The Hound of the Baskervilles
by Sir Arthur Conan Doyle

Lesson 15   Fantasy 56
Alice's Adventures in Wonderland
by Lewis Carroll

Lesson 16   Classic 61
The Tell-Tale Heart
by Edgar Allan Poe

Unit 2 Review: Fiction 66
Unit 2 Mini-Test 68

UNIT 3 INFORMATIONAL TEXTS 70

Lesson 17   Informational Science 72
Eating Five to Stay Alive!

Lesson 18   Scientific Research 77
Ways of Fighting Germs

Lesson 19   Scientific Concepts 82
Photosynthesis: Making Energy for Life

Lesson 20   Biographies 87
Frederick Douglass: Abolitionist Leader

Lesson 21   Informational Social Studies 92
Thomas Paine: Bold Voice of Protest

Lesson 22   Historical Court Cases 97
Plessy v. Ferguson (1896)

Lesson 23   Brochures &
Advertisements 102

Lesson 24   Forms & Documents 107

Lesson 25   Manuals & Handbooks 112

Lesson 26   Legal Documents 117

Unit 3 Review: Informational Texts 122
Unit 3 Mini-Test 124

CONTENTS

UNIT 4 WRITING 126

Lesson 27 The Writing Process 128

Lesson 28 Writing Prompt 141

Unit 4 Review: Writing 146
Unit 4 Mini-Test 149

UNIT 5 LANGUAGE SKILLS 150

Lesson 29 Contractions, Homonyms,
& Confused Words 152

Lesson 30 Subject-Verb Agreement 155

Lesson 31 Pronouns 157

Lesson 32 Informal Language 163

Lesson 33 Misplaced &
Dangling Modifiers 165

Lesson 34 Coordination &
Subordination 168

Lesson 35 Parallelism 171

Lesson 36 Revising Sentences 173

Lesson 37 Transition Words 176

Lesson 38 Capitalization 179

Lesson 39 Sentence Fragments &
Run-on Sentences 184

Lesson 40 Apostrophes with
Possessives 188

Lesson 41 Commas 190

Lesson 42 End Punctuation 194

Lesson 43 Punctuation in
Clause Separation 196

Unit 5 Review: Language Skills 200
Unit 5 Mini-Test 202

Posttest Answer Sheet 204
Posttest 205
Posttest Evaluation Chart 230
Answers and Explanations 231
Glossary 268

How to Use This Book

The purpose of this book is to help you develop the foundation you need to pass the GED® Reasoning Through Language Arts test. In this book, you will read selections from many types of texts. You will read fiction texts, such as adventure, mystery, and fantasy stories, and you will read informational texts, such as science and social studies texts, biographies, brochures, manuals, and legal documents. You will learn reading strategies and critical thinking skills that you will need to answer reading comprehension questions. You will also learn the five steps of the writing process and the language skills that you will need to write an extended response and to edit and revise passages.

Pretest and Posttest

The Pretest is a self-check to see which skills you already know. When you complete all the items in the Pretest, check you work in the Answers and Explanations section in the back of the book. Then fill out the Pretest Evaluation Chart. This chart tells you where each skill is taught in the book. When you complete this book, you will take a Posttest. Compare your Posttest score to your Pretest score to see that your skills have improved.

Units and Lessons

This book consists of five units. The first unit focuses on critical thinking skills that will help you comprehend and analyze different types of texts. The second unit focuses on reading fiction texts and applying what you have learned about characters, setting, mood, and sequence of events. The third unit focuses on reading and comprehending informational texts, such as science, social studies, and workplace texts. The fourth unit focuses on the five steps of the writing process to be applied to writing the extended response. The fifth unit focuses on the many language skills you need to edit and revise passages on the GED® test and to write clearly and effectively.

Each unit is organized into lessons. Each lesson in Unit 1 introduces an essential critical thinking skill and helps you apply each of these to the texts you read. Each lesson in Units 2 and 3 introduces and helps you evaluate a different type of text. Each lesson in Unit 4 introduces and helps you apply the five steps in the writing process. Each lesson in Unit 5 focuses on a language skill such as sentence structure, punctuation, and capitalization.

Reading

Each lesson in Units 1–3 presents you with a passage to read actively. *Active reading* means doing something before you read, while you read, and after you read. By reading actively, you will improve your reading comprehension and critical thinking skills. Many lessons have a list of **vocabulary** words listed down the left-hand side of the first page. You should preview the meaning of these words. As you are reading the passage, you will see some words in bold type. These are the vocabulary words that were in the list on the first page. When you see one of these words, try to figure out its meaning from the way it is used in the passage. Then if you are still not sure of the meaning, look up the word in a dictionary. You may want to keep a vocabulary notebook with pages titled *A, B, C,* etc. You can record new words and their meanings in this notebook. Increasing your vocabulary will help you succeed on the GED® Reasoning Through Language Arts test.

Each lesson also points out skills that apply to the passage during reading. After reading, you will have the opportunity to do a variety of activities that apply to what you have just read. There are fill-in-the-blank, short answer, and multiple-choice questions to complete. Answering the questions will help you decide how well you have understood what you've read and provide another way for you to connect with the passage.

The Writing Process and Language Skills

Writing is a process, a series of steps. A five-step writing process is presented in Unit 4. The first step of this process will help you generate ideas and organize them before you begin to write. Then you will follow additional steps to write, revise, edit, and publish—or share—your work. In Unit 5 you will learn many of the language skills that will help you revise and edit your writing to improve it. Clear, mistake-free writing is not only important on the GED® test, but in the workplace as well.

Unit Reviews and Mini-Tests

Unit Reviews let you see how well you have learned the reading and writing skills covered in each unit. Mini-tests follow each of the Unit Reviews. These timed practice tests allow you to practice your skills with questions similar to those that you will see on the GED® test.

Answers and Explanations

Answers and explanations to the exercises are listed at the back of this book on pages 231–267. Some exercise items have more than one possible correct response. In such cases, a sample response is given.

Directions

Use this Reasoning Through Language Arts Pretest before you begin Unit 1. Don't worry if you can't easily answer all the questions. The Pretest will help you find out the areas in which you are already strong and which ones need further study.

For the Reading Comprehension section, read each selection and answer the questions that follow. For the Extended Response section, read the selections carefully and then respond to the writing prompt. For the Language Skills section, read each set of instructions and choose or write the best answer.

Check your answers on pages 231–233. Then enter your scores on the Evaluation Chart on page 13. Use the chart to determine which content areas to work on and where to find them in the book.

When you are ready to begin, turn the page and read the first selection of the Pretest.

Reading Comprehension: Fiction Selection

▶ **Read the following selection and then answer the questions.**

From *Stories of Gods and Heroes*

by Thomas Bulfinch

Bacchus, on a certain occasion, found his old schoolmaster and foster-father, Silenus, missing. The old man had been drinking, and in that state wandered away, and was found by some peasants, who carried him to their king Midas. Midas recognized him, and treated him hospitably, entertaining him for ten days and nights with an unceasing round of jollity. On the eleventh day he brought Silenus back, and restored him in safety to his pupil. Whereupon Bacchus offered Midas his choice of a reward, whatever he might wish. He asked that whatever he might touch should be changed into gold. Bacchus consented, though sorry that Midas had not made a better choice. Midas went his way, rejoicing in his new-acquired power, which he hastened to put to the test. He could scarce believe his eyes when he found a twig of an oak, which he plucked from the branch, become gold in his hand. He took up a stone; it changed to gold. He touched a sod; it did the same. He took an apple from the tree; you would have thought he had robbed the garden of Hesperides. His joy knew no bounds, and as soon as he got home, he ordered the servants to set a splendid repast on the table. Then he found to his dismay that whether he touched bread, it hardened in his hand; or put a morsel to his lips, it defied his teeth. He took a glass of wine, but it flowed down his throat like melted gold.

In consternation at the unprecedented affliction, he strove to divest himself of his power; he hated the gift he had lately coveted. But all in vain; starvation seemed to await him. He raised his arms, all shining with gold, in prayer to Bacchus, begging to be delivered from his glittering destruction. Bacchus, merciful deity, heard and consented. "Go," said he, "to the River Pactolus, trace the stream to its fountain-head, there plunge your head and body in, and wash away your fault and its punishment." He did so, and scarce had he touched the waters before the gold-creating power passed into them, and the river-sands became changed into *gold,* as they remain to this day.

▶ **Write the answer to each question.**

1. Who is Silenus? _____

2. According to this myth, why does the River Pactolus have gold in its sands?

   _____

3. What does the expression "He has the Midas touch" mean?

   _____

▶ **Circle the letter of the best answer for each question.**

4. What inference can you draw from Bacchus's reaction to Midas's choice of a reward?

   A. Bacchus thinks that Midas should not have asked for anything.

   B. Bacchus knows he will have trouble granting the wish.

   C. Bacchus thinks it shows Midas's wisdom.

   D. Bacchus realizes it will lead to trouble for Midas.

5. What words could you use to describe Midas in this myth?

   A. kind but shallow

   B. wise and good

   C. greedy and uncaring

   D. lazy but charming

6. Using context clues, what does the word *consternation* mean in the passage?

   A. constant suffering

   B. dismay

   C. conflict

   D. chaos

7. Of the events listed below, which happens first?

   A. Midas brings Silenus back to Bacchus.

   B. Midas orders his servants to set a splendid repast on the table.

   C. Midas turns an oak branch to gold.

   D. Midas recognizes Silenus.

8. Which statement expresses a main idea of the myth?

   A. The more money a person has, the more he or she wants.

   B. Money truly bestows happiness on a person.

   C. People should be kind to others in the hope of being rewarded.

   D. Something that may seem to be a gift can become a curse.

Reading Comprehension: Informational Selection—Social Studies

▶ **Read the following excerpt from a letter written by First Lady Dolley Madison to her sister on August 23, 1814, during the War of 1812. Then answer the questions.**

James Madison was the fourth president of the United States. By the time James and Dolley Madison moved into the White House, the building was mostly complete and had begun to be viewed as a symbol of U.S. leadership. Dolley Madison concentrated on decorating and furnishing the interior of the White House, and she often entertained politicians, diplomats, and local residents at dinner parties there.

Tuesday, Augt. 23d. 1814

Dear Sister

My husband left me yesterday morning to join General Winder. He inquired anxiously whether I had courage or firmness to remain in the President's house until his return on the morrow, or succeeding day, and on my assurance that I had no fear but for him, and the success of our army, he left <u>beseeching</u> me to take care of myself, and of the Cabinet papers, public and private. I have since received two dispatches from him, written with a pencil. The last is alarming, because he desires I should be ready at a moment's warning to enter my carriage, and leave the city; that the enemy seemed stronger than had at first been reported, and it might happen that they would reach the city with the intention of destroying it. I am accordingly ready; I have pressed as many Cabinet papers into trunks as to fill one carriage; our private property must be sacrificed, as it is impossible to procure wagons for its transportation. I am determined not to go myself until I see Mr. Madison safe, so that he can accompany me, as I hear of much hostility towards him. Disaffection stalks around us. My friends and acquaintances are all gone, even Colonel C. with his hundred, who were stationed as a guard in this enclosure. French John (a faithful servant), with his usual activity and resolution, offers to spike the cannon at the gate, and lay a train of powder, which would blow up the British, should they enter the house. To the last proposition I positively object, without being able to make him understand why all advantages in war may not be taken.

▶ **Write the answer to each question.**

9. Why was President Madison absent from the White House when Dolley Madison wrote this letter?

   _____

10. Why do you think Dolley Madison does not want to blow up the British if they enter the White House?

    _____

11. Using context clues, what does the word *beseeching* mean as it is used in the passage?

    _____

▶ **Circle the letter of the best answer for each question.**

12. When Dolley Madison writes, "Disaffection stalks around us," she is *most likely* trying to convey

    A. the proximity of the enemy as they approach Washington.

    B. her fears for her own safety.

    C. the lack of support she feels from people around her.

    D. the lack of affection in her marriage.

13. What is the *most likely* reason President Madison writes his dispatches to his wife in pencil?

    A. As a result of his nervousness, he is making many mistakes that he must erase.

    B. He is writing these messages in a hurry without pausing to take out his inkwell and pen.

    C. He is injured and cannot hold a pen.

    D. He does not want his words to have the permanence of ink.

14. Which conclusion can you draw from Dolley Madison's letter?

    A. She feels anger at her husband for deserting her at a time of such danger.

    B. She possesses courage and is willing to sacrifice for the good of the country.

    C. The British forces were overestimated by American intelligence during the War of 1812.

    D. President Madison was an uninvolved leader who relied on reports from others for his information about the war.

Reading Comprehension: Informational Selection—Workplace

▶ Read the following selection from an employee handbook and then answer the questions.

What Are the Benefits of Job Sharing and Part-Time Employment?

Fulton Lumber Personnel Policies

This section provides information for employees who are considering part-time employment or job sharing. We believe that offering employees a variety of personnel options helps to achieve a family-friendly workplace. Employees should consider the following information when thinking about reducing their work hours.

Part-Time Employment

A part-time, permanent employee works between 16 and 32 hours each week on a prearranged schedule. Part-time, permanent employees are eligible for health and insurance benefits, as well as family leave and retirement once they have built up enough hours.

Job Sharing

Job sharing is a form of part-time employment. Most job-sharing teams are at the same job classification. The schedules of two or more part-time employees are arranged to cover the duties of one full-time position (40 hours a week). However, job sharing does not necessarily mean that each job sharer must work half-time, or 20 hours a week.

Who Benefits?

Both employees and managers benefit from part-time work schedules. Employees can spend more time with their children, pursue educational opportunities, care for an aging or ill family member, or continue working when illness or physical limitations prevent working full-time. Managers can retain highly qualified employees, improve recruitment, increase productivity, and reduce absenteeism.

▷ **Circle the letter of the best answer for each question.**

15. What would happen if an employee who is job sharing could only work 18 hours?

    A. The employee would not receive benefits.

    B. The employee and the job sharer would be fired.

    C. The employee would be demoted.

    D. The other job sharer would work 22 hours.

16. Which statement supports Fulton Lumber's opinion that job sharing and part-time work mean a family-friendly workplace?

    A. Job sharers and part-time employees have benefits and flexible hours.

    B. Job sharing and part-time employment improve recruitment and productivity.

    C. Employees have to work 20 hours.

    D. Job sharers and part-time employees have prearranged schedules.

17. Which *best* describes the tone of the handbook?

    A. humorous

    B. intimidating

    C. sarcastic

    D. business like

▷ **Write the answer to each question.**

18. When is a part-time employee eligible for retirement?

    _____

    _____

19. List two benefits of part-time work schedules for employees.

    _____

    _____

20. List two benefits of part-time work schedules for managers.

    _____

    _____

Extended Response—Opposing Perspectives

▶ **Read the following selections and then answer the questions.**

On Woman's Right to the Suffrage

Before August 18, 1920, American women did not have the right to vote in presidential elections. Susan B. Anthony, who fought for this right for women, was fined for casting an illegal ballot in the 1872 presidential election. Very angry, she went on a speaking tour to fight for the women's right to vote. This is the speech she gave during that tour.

Friends and Fellow Citizens: I stand before you to-night under indictment for the alleged crime of having voted at the last presidential election, without having a lawful right to vote. It shall be my work this evening to prove to you that in thus voting, I not only committed no crime, but, instead, simply exercised my citizen's rights, guaranteed to me and all United States citizens by the National Constitution, beyond the power of any State to deny. . . . The preamble of the Federal Constitution says:

"We, the people of the United States, in order to form a more perfect union, establish justice, insure domestic tranquility, provide for the common defense, promote the general welfare, and secure the blessings of liberty to ourselves and our posterity, do ordain and establish this Constitution for the United States of America."

It was we, the people; not we, the white male citizens; nor yet we, the male citizens; but we, the whole people, who formed the Union. And we formed it, not to give the blessings of liberty, but to secure them; not to the half of ourselves and the half of our posterity, but to the whole people—women as well as men. And it is a downright mockery to talk to women of their enjoyment of the blessings of liberty while they are denied the use of the only means of securing them provided by this democratic-republican government—the ballot. . . .

The only question left to be settled now is: Are women persons? And I hardly believe any of our opponents will have the hardihood to say they are not. Being persons, then, women are citizens; and no State has a right to make any law, or to enforce any old law, that shall abridge their privileges or immunities. Hence, every discrimination against women in the constitutions and laws of the several States is today null and void, precisely as is every one against negroes.

Elihu Root was a delegate to the New York State Constitutional Convention of 1894. He opposed women's suffrage, believing it would be a detriment to women. He gave the following address to the New York Constitutional Convention in 1894.

It is not that woman is inferior to man, but it is that woman is different from man; that in the distribution of powers, of capacities, of qualities, our Maker has created man adapted to the performance of certain functions in the economy of nature and society, and women adapted to the performance of other functions. One question to be determined in the discussion of this subject is whether the nature of woman is such that her taking upon her the performance of the functions implied in suffrage will leave her in the possession and the exercise of her highest powers or will be an abandonment of those powers and on entering upon a field in which, because of her differences from man, she is distinctly inferior. Mr. President, I have said that I thought suffrage would be a loss for women. I think so because suffrage implies not merely the casting of the ballot, the gentle and peaceful fall of the snowflake, but suffrage, if it means anything, means entering upon the field of political life, and politics is modified war. In politics there is struggle, strife, contention, bitterness, heart-burning, excitement, agitation, everything which is adverse to the true character of woman. Woman rules today by the sweet and noble influences of her character. Put woman into the arena of conflict and she abandons these great weapons which control the world, and she takes into her hands, feeble and nerveless for strife, weapons with which she is unfamiliar and which she is unable to wield. Woman in strife becomes hard, harsh, unlovable, repulsive; as far removed from that gentle creature to whom we all owe allegiance and to whom we confess submission, as the heaven is removed from the earth.

Extended Response—Opposing Perspectives

The speeches by Susan B. Anthony and Elihu Root on the previous pages took either side of the debate over a woman's right to vote. Susan B. Anthony was for women's suffrage, while Elihu Root was against it.

21. On your own paper, write a response to these two speeches. In your response, analyze both speeches to determine which position is better supported. Try to use relevant and specific evidence from both speeches to support your response. Keep in mind that the better-supported position is not necessarily the position you agree with, or, because these are historical speeches, the position that eventually won. Give yourself 45 minutes to write your response.

Language Skills

▶ Write *C* if the sentence is correct. Write *E* if there is an error in capitalization or punctuation and correct the error.

_____ **22.** Who do you consider to be a hero these days.

_____ **23.** Many people think of actors athletes, or singers as heroes.

_____ **24.** Some people think football players are heroes but I think my Aunt Ann is a hero.

_____ **25.** She goes to school during the day, and works as a nurse's aide at night.

_____ **26.** My Aunt is a hero to me because she helps people tirelessly.

▶ Circle the correct plural or possessive noun to complete each sentence.

27. Sometimes **(parents, parents', parent's)** cannot get their children to behave.

28. They appreciate getting an **(experts, experts', expert's)** advice.

29. Experts say it is wise to show **(childrens, children's, children)** an example of good behavior.

▶ Write the correct homonym or contraction to complete each sentence.

Did you _____ that diamonds are the hardest substance on
        (30.) no   know

Earth? You can only _____ a diamond with a sharp blow in a
        (31.) break   brake

certain spot. Diamonds can be used to drill a _____ through
                                    (32.) hole   whole

metal. In fact, _____ difficult to think of anything that a
              (33.) its   it's

diamond _____ cut _____.
        (34.) ca'nt   can't   (35.) threw   through

▶ Circle the correct adjective or adverb to complete each sentence.

36. It is a fact that widows and widowers do not live as **(well, good, best)** as married people.

37. Their illnesses are **(worse, worst, bad)** than those of married people.

38. They often recover from illnesses more **(slow, slowly, slower)**.

39. They are also likely to die **(soon, sooner, soonest)**.

▶ **Circle the correct verb form to complete each sentence.**

40. All the supervisors on this floor **(agrees, agree)** that too many employees are arriving late.

41. There **(is, are)** several reasons for this situation.

42. Ms. Gomez and her staff **(has, have)** come up with some possible solutions.

▶ **Write *S* next to each correctly written sentence (complete thought), *F* next to each fragment (incomplete thought), and *RO* next to each run-on (two or more complete thoughts that run together without correct punctuation and/or a connecting word).**

_____ 43. One good way to save money.

_____ 44. You should take some time to learn basic car repair.

_____ 45. One cost-saving measure is fixing your own flat tire any able-bodied person can do it.

_____ 46. If you are willing to invest time up front.

▶ **Combine each pair of sentences with the connecting word given in parentheses. Use correct punctuation.**

47. **(and)** The sun dries out your skin. It affects the growth of skin cells.

_____

48. **(but)** The sun feels good. It's not good for you.

_____

49. **(if)** You should see a doctor. A mole changes shape or color.

_____

▶ **Circle the word or phrase that *best* completes each sentence.**

50. Some of the best ways to reduce stress are to cut back on obligations, to have clear priorities, and **(understand, to understand)** what makes you anxious.

51. Knowing your stressors, **(it is easier to, you can more easily)** control your environment to avoid anxiety.

52. In **(today's world, the current world of the present day)**, reducing stress is a challenge.

Reasoning Through Language Arts Pretest Evaluation Chart

The chart below will help you determine your strengths and weaknesses in reading comprehension, writing an extended response, and language skills.

▶ **Directions**

Check your answers on pages 231–233. On the chart below, circle the number of each question you answered correctly on the Pretest. Count the number of questions you answered correctly in each row. Write the number in the Total Correct space in each row. Complete this process for the remaining rows. Then add the four totals to get your Total Correct for Pretest.

Skill Area	Questions	Total Correct	Pages
Reading Comprehension: Fiction	1, 2, 3, 4, 5, 6, 7, 8	_____ out of 8	44–69
Reading Comprehension: Informational	9, 10, 11, 12, 13, 14, 15, 16, 17, 18, 19, 20	_____ out of 12	70–125
Extended Response	21	_____ out of 1	126–149
Language Skills	22, 23, 24, 25, 26, 27, 28, 29, 30, 31, 32, 33, 34, 35, 36, 37, 38, 39, 40, 41, 42, 43, 44, 45, 46, 47, 48, 49, 50, 51, 52	_____ out of 31	150–203

Total Correct for Pretest _____ out of 52

If you answered fewer than 47 questions correctly, look at the skill in the skill areas above. In which areas do you need more practice? Page numbers to refer to for practice are given in the right-hand column of the chart.

You already use basic thinking skills to understand whatever you read. However, you probably use other thinking skills as well. Have you ever read something and then applied the information to your own life, drawn a conclusion, made a comparison, or made a choice based on a fact or opinion? When you did so, you used more advanced thinking skills that are often called *critical* or *higher order* thinking skills.

Write the topic of something that you read to make something or to solve a problem.

_____

Write about a time when you had to compare information from different sources to make a decision.

_____

Thinking About Reading

You may not realize how often you use thinking skills in reading in your everyday life. Think about your recent activities.

Check the box for each activity you did.

- ☐ Did you compare items in ads or catalogues to find the best deals?
- ☐ Did you scan a newspaper article to get the main idea?
- ☐ Did you use something you learned in a new situation?
- ☐ Did you gather information from different sources to plan a trip?
- ☐ Did you follow a sequence of written directions?

Write some other activities where you have used thinking skills with materials you have read.

_____

_____

_____

Previewing the Unit

In this unit, you will learn:

- how to find the main idea and supporting details
- how to infer and put events in order
- how to compare and contrast and find cause-and-effect relationships
- how to draw conclusions and evaluate author's evidence and purpose
- how to analyze setting and character
- how to apply and synthesize information from several sources

Lesson	**1**	Main Idea	**Lesson**	**7**	Conclusions
Lesson	**2**	Details	**Lesson**	**8**	Author's Evidence & Purpose
Lesson	**3**	Inference	**Lesson**	**9**	Setting
Lesson	**4**	Sequence of Events	**Lesson**	**10**	Character
Lesson	**5**	Compare & Contrast	**Lesson**	**11**	Application
Lesson	**6**	Cause & Effect	**Lesson**	**12**	Synthesis

MAIN IDEA

On the GED® Reasoning Through Language Arts test, you will see questions about the main idea of a paragraph or reading passage. The **main idea** is the most important idea in the reading. It states the overall topic of the reading. Often, the main idea will be stated in one sentence within the passage. Look for the main idea of the passage below.

> TIP
>
> To find the main idea of a passage, imagine a friend asked you, "What are you reading about?" How would you answer your friend in one sentence? Your answer would be the main idea.

Lara finished patching the crack running through her neighbor's kitchen wall. The earthquake had awoken a leader in the usually shy Lara. Minutes after the quake, she checked her home for gas leaks and then began to assist her neighbors check for gas leaks. She convinced her neighbors to combine and share their food and water. She even set up an old crystal radio set to hear reports from city officials. After the quake, she continued to help her neighbors. She became friends with her neighbors because of the experiences they shared.

1. Which sentence gives the most important information about Lara?

_____

2. State the main idea of the paragraph in your own words.

_____

1. The earthquake had awoken a leader in the usually shy Lara. 2. Your answer should contain the idea that Lara became a leader the day of the earthquake.

To find the main idea, organize the main idea and supporting details in a chart. The main idea is the central idea. The details point to the main idea.

Main Idea

Lara helped with repairs.		She set up a food and water bank.
	Lara became a leader the day of the earthquake.	
She helped her neighbors check their homes for gas leaks.		She set up a radio to get reports.

To find the main idea in a passage, ask yourself:
- What is the most important information in the passage?
- What one sentence is most helpful in understanding the passage?

Think of a time when you listened to a friend talk about an experience. What was the most important idea about that experience?

▶ SKILL PRACTICE **Read the passage and complete the chart with one detail and the main idea. Then answer the questions.**

Preserving photos of the past is a challenge for museum curators. They must control the humidity, light, and temperature to preserve these fragile works of art. To protect museums' collections, curators must also have some idea of how the photos were made. Most museums do not have enough money to test each photograph. Instead, curators must make reasonable guesses and hope their efforts will not destroy the artwork they seek to preserve.

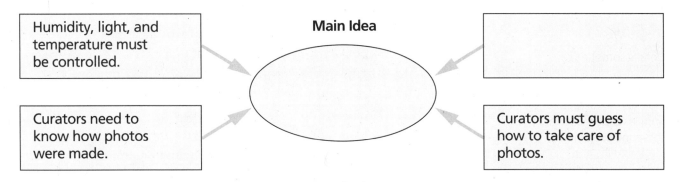

1. Imagine you are talking to a friend. In one sentence, how would you explain what this paragraph is about?

   _____

   _____

2. Which of these ideas supports the main idea of the passage?
   A. Curators must find the best way to display photos for the public.
   B. Some photos must be protected from exposure to normal air.

▶ GED® PRACTICE **Choose the <u>one best answer</u> to the question.**

By the end of the season, I knew a lot about Max. He was the best shortstop I ever saw. He always convinced some friend, usually me, into hitting him ground balls late into the night. He once spent five hours in the batting cage working on his swing. Max was only 16 years old, and he was surely headed for the big leagues.

We were all surprised by the car accident in his senior year. Max shattered his right arm, his throwing arm. Some people said his career was over, but I knew he'd be back. Max was never a quitter.

3. Which of the following is the main idea of the first paragraph?
   A. Max convinced his friends to work with him.
   B. Max worked very hard to be a good baseball player.
   C. Max spent five hours practicing his swing.
   D. Max was headed for the big leagues.

DETAILS

Some questions on the GED® Reasoning Through Language Arts test are based on understanding the details in a paragraph or passage. As you saw in Lesson 1, the **details** in a paragraph support the main idea. They give facts about people, places, things, times, and events. Details give life to a passage and make it more interesting for the reader. Read the passage and look for interesting details.

TIP

Details sometimes involve our five senses. To find details, look for words and phrases that tell what someone sees, hears, feels, smells, and tastes.

Marcus felt exhausted and numb after working the second shift. He had been loading identical cardboard boxes into delivery trucks for twelve hours straight. He remembered to bend his knees with each lift to protect his back, but still his strong shoulders and thighs burned and ached with overuse. During the fifteen-minute breaks at the loading dock, his muscles became stiff and cold. Around midnight, he dozed off while standing up. "Go on home," his boss offered, but he couldn't stop. He needed only one more paycheck to move his family to a new city.

1. Which details tell *when* the action of the passage is taking place?

_____

2. Which sentence explains *why* Marcus is willing to work so hard?

_____

1. The details *twelve hours straight* and *around midnight* tell us that Marcus has worked all day and it is now after midnight. 2. The last sentence explains that Marcus needs money to move his family to a new city.

Details answer the questions *who, what, when, where, why,* and *how.* Use a chart to organize the details.

Who? Marcus is a strong, hard-working father.	Supporting Details	What? He is working an extra shift loading boxes.
When? He has been working all day until after midnight.	Where? He is working at a loading dock.	Why or How? Marcus wants to move his family to a new city.

To find the details in a passage, ask yourself:
- What information helps me understand the main idea?
- What information makes the passage more interesting?

Think of a television show you like to watch. What details about the characters make it interesting?

▶ SKILL PRACTICE **Read the passage and complete the chart by filling in the four missing details. Then answer the questions.**

Sunrise found Detective Leo Stuart ready with a shovel and pickaxe. He began digging ten feet due east of the ancient bronze marker. It did not take long before Stuart's shovel struck something hollow. Within fifteen minutes he had removed the antique hardwood chest from its hiding place in the hillside. The chest was bound by strong iron bands. After much effort, he broke the final band. The chest sprang open to reveal nothing but a dollar bill. Scrawled across the face of the bill was the message, "Too late!" Stuart threw his shovel in frustration.

Who?	Supporting Details	What?
When?	Where?	Why or How? He is searching for something.

1. What details describe the exact place where Detective Stuart begins digging?

   _____

2. Before the chest is open, what detail suggests that the chest will be empty?

   _____

▶ GED® PRACTICE **Choose the one best answer to the question.**

One of the greatest engineering feats was inspired by a mollusk. In 1825, an engineer named Marc Brunei watched shipworms bore holes in the wood hulls of ships. These soft-bodied animals used their shells like a hard shield to push their way farther into the wood. Brunei proposed boring a tunnel under the Thames River in London by building a great shield. As workers dug, they would push the shield into the tunnel opening in the same way shipworms would bore into wood. After many delays, Brunei's plan finally worked. Today, engineers use variations of tunneling shields to build subways all over the world.

3. A shipworm is a kind of mollusk. According to the details in the passage, which of the following is the best description of a mollusk?

   A. an animal that eats wood

   B. a destructive animal that digs holes

   C. a soft-bodied animal that lives in a shell

   D. an animal that engineers use to dig holes

INFERENCE

Some questions on the GED® Reasoning Through Language Arts test will ask you to **infer** ideas that are not actually stated in a passage. When you infer, you apply knowledge you already have to the situation in the passage to figure out the meaning.

> I won my first contest when I was 21. I worked for a month to strengthen my arm so that I could hurl that folded piece of paper as high as possible. My first throw was a disaster, but my second throw had good upward speed. At the top of the arc, the wings opened beautifully and my little sparrow began to glide, slowly spiraling to the ground. To win, I needed to beat fifteen seconds, an impossible length of time, but I did it.

1. What details help you infer that the thrown object was a paper airplane?

_____

2. Do you think the author expected to win the contest?

_____

1. A folded paper object with wings that glides through the air is a paper airplane.
2. No, the writer did not expect to win. In the last sentence, the writer describes fifteen seconds as an impossible length of time.

In the following chart, statements from the passage are followed by inferences. You can organize your thinking in the same way.

Statement	Inference
• Won first contest at 21	• He has won more contests since then.
• Worked for a month	• This event required strength.
• First throw was a disaster, but second had good upward speed	• The first throw lacked speed.
• Wings opened and it began to glide	• The airplane worked.
• Needed to beat fifteen seconds	• The goal was to keep the airplane in the air as long as possible.

To make inferences, ask yourself:
- What is the author suggesting without directly stating it?
- What clues tell me how the author feels about the topic?

When a friend tells you about something that happened, how do you use your experiences to understand it?

TIP

Some questions ask which answer choice can be inferred from the passage. First, rule out any choices that cannot be supported by at least one detail from the passage.

▶ SKILL PRACTICE **Read the passage and complete the chart, writing two new inferences. Then answer the questions.**

The Owens family thinks that their dog Riley is a problem because he begs for food. They begin every meal by giving Riley a scrap of food from their plates. They expect the dog to let them eat in peace, but he keeps begging for more. He will only stop if they shout, "Lie down!" Then Riley will lie down on the floor immediately. Naturally, the Owens give him more food from their plates as a reward. Not surprisingly, he pops up and starts begging again. Riley's owners have tried reasoning with him, but nothing works. Clearly, Riley has no desire to obey.

Statement	Inference
• His owners begin every meal by giving him a scrap of food from their plates.	• His owners have trained Riley to beg by feeding him at the table.
• He will only stop if they shout, "Lie down!" Then Riley lies down on the floor immediately.	•
• His owners have tried reasoning with him, but nothing works.	•

1. The owners believe that Riley is a problem dog. What details help you infer that the author does not agree with the owners?

_____

2. Which of the following can you infer from the passage?
   A. Riley's owners don't understand how dogs learn.
   B. Riley has no desire to obey.

▶ GED® PRACTICE **Choose the one best answer to the question.**

Two hundred thousand healthcare workers provide "in-home supportive services" to low-income elderly and disabled persons throughout California. A recent study recommends protecting in-home healthcare workers through improved training and equipment. The study also suggests that the workers themselves need better access to healthcare services when they become injured on the job. One innovative proposal suggests that there should be written contracts between in-home healthcare workers and their clients.

3. An organization conducted this study and made the recommendations. You can infer that this organization works on behalf of which people?

   A. senior citizens

   B. low-income families

   C. in-home healthcare workers

   D. California elected officials

SEQUENCE OF EVENTS

Some questions on the GED® Reasoning Through Language Arts test relate to the sequence of events, or the order in which events happen. Some authors do not tell the events in order. As you read, think about the order in which the events take place.

TIP

Logic or common sense can help you put many events in order. Also look for words like *first, then,* and *next* to help you order the events.

In 1939, Marian Anderson sang for an audience of more than 75,000 at the Lincoln Memorial in Washington, D.C. First Lady Eleanor Roosevelt arranged for the performance soon after Anderson's request to sing at Constitution Hall was denied because she was African American. Anderson first came to the public's attention when she sang in church choirs in Philadelphia. As word of her amazing vocal talent spread, she was offered many scholarships to study music. As a result of her fame, she toured Europe in 1925 with the New York Philharmonic Orchestra.

1. Of all the performances described in the passage, which came first?

_____

2. What happened after Anderson's request to sing in Constitution Hall was denied?

_____

1. The earliest performances mentioned in the paragraph were in church choirs in Philadelphia. 2. Eleanor Roosevelt arranged for Anderson to sing at the Lincoln Memorial.

Use a sequencing chart to order the events in a passage. Use as many boxes as you need.

Order of Events

1	Anderson sang in church choirs.
2	She was offered scholarships to study music.
3	1925: She toured Europe with the N.Y. Philharmonic.
4	Her request to sing in Constitution Hall was denied.
5	1939: She sang at the Lincoln Memorial.

Have you ever seen a movie that contained a scene in which a character remembered an event from the past? How did you know the scene was from the past?

To find the sequence of events in a passage, ask yourself:
- Are there clue words or dates to help me put the events in order?
- How do the details of one event lead to the next event?

▶ SKILL PRACTICE **Read the passage and complete the chart with three events. Then answer the questions.**

Andrew was surprised to see the shed with the rotting canoe propped against its side. He had been so lost in thought that he hadn't realized that he wasn't heading for the Jacobs' farmhouse. Instead, something had pulled him to the deserted boathouse by the river. He cautiously entered the building and struck a match from his pocket. The flickering light revealed a rusted lantern on a shelf. He lit it with a second match. "I knew you'd come," said a deep voice behind him.

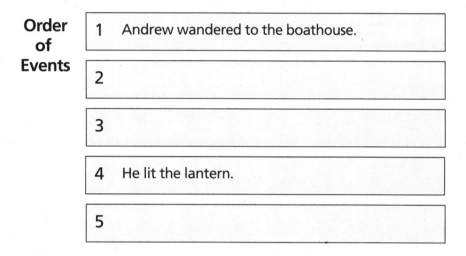

Order of Events

1	Andrew wandered to the boathouse.
2	
3	
4	He lit the lantern.
5	

1. The first sentence says that Andrew was surprised. Based on the passage, what happened before this?

_____

2. What did Andrew do immediately after he entered the boathouse? Why?

_____

▶ GED® PRACTICE **Choose the one best answer to the question.**

A doctor placed two cups in front of a nine-month-old baby. Then she put a shiny toy under the first cup. Immediately, the child picked up the cup to find the toy. Next, while the baby was watching, the doctor moved the toy, placing it under the second cup. As the baby reached for the second cup, the doctor clapped her hands four times high in the air as a distraction. The curious baby watched the clapping and then looked for the toy under the first cup. The baby had forgotten that the toy had been moved.

3. The passage describes an experiment a doctor used to test a child's memory. What did the doctor do just before she distracted the child?

A. She clapped her hands loudly.

B. She placed the toy under the second cup.

C. She placed the toy under the first cup.

D. She allowed the baby to hold the toy.

Check your answers on page 234.

COMPARE & CONTRAST

On the GED® Reasoning Through Language Arts test, you may read passages that use comparison and contrast. Authors often **compare** people, places, or things to show how they are the same. Passages can also show **contrast**—how people, places, or things are different. As you read this passage, think about how the sisters are similar and different.

Billie's daughters, Bea and Jean, believed they were as different as night and day, but they were really two birds from the same nest. Both were nonstop talkers. Bea liked retelling jokes from late-night talk shows, whereas Jean preferred to discuss serious things like the fate of social security. On many occasions, both sisters spent the whole day shopping. Bea generously spent money on gifts for all her friends. Jean enjoyed looking for bargains at yard sales, rarely buying anything.

1. What are two ways that Jean and Bea are alike?

_____

2. What does it mean to be *as different as night and day*?

_____

TIP

In some passages, one paragraph may be used to compare and one to contrast. Make sure you read the entire passage before you answer questions about comparing and contrasting.

1. Both like to talk and shop. 2. *Night* and *day* are opposites. Two things that are as different as night and day have nothing in common.

A Venn diagram can help you compare and contrast two people, places, or things. Label the circles and write the qualities in the correct circle. If both share a quality, write it in the overlapping space.

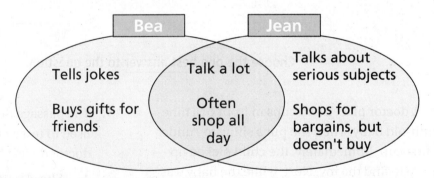

To compare and contrast people, places, and things, ask yourself:
- What are some qualities both share?
- What qualities belong to only one or the other?

Think of two of your favorite desserts. What do they have in common? How are they different?

▶ SKILL PRACTICE **Read the passage and add at least one more statement to each section of the Venn diagram. Then answer the questions.**

The Continental Congress stated only a few requirements for the making of the first American flag. The flag was to have thirteen white stars in a blue field and thirteen stripes, alternating red and white. This simple prescription allowed for much creativity. The first flags had stars with anywhere from four to eight points. These unique flags had additional stripes, symbols, pictures, and colors. In 1914, by executive order, the design of the flag became standard. Now, the size of the flag, its colors, the 50 five-pointed stars, and the thirteen horizontal stripes are uniform.

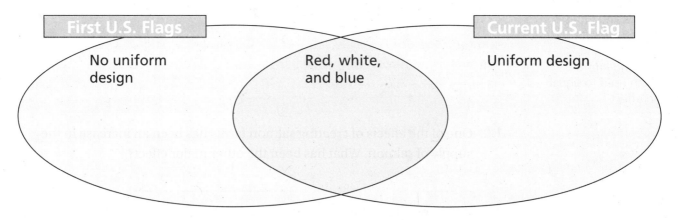

First U.S. Flags
No uniform design

Red, white, and blue

Current U.S. Flag
Uniform design

1. The current design meets the original requirements of the Continental Congress in every way except for one. What is it?

_____

2. Which description is different from the current flag design?
   A. The first flag of the United States had horizontal red and white stripes.
   B. Some early flags had an eagle stitched in the blue field.

▶ GED® PRACTICE **Choose the <u>one best answer</u> to the question.**

Jeremy went to Sanibel to escape the harsh cold of January in Michigan. The thin barrier island off the coast of Florida was a definite change from the loud, crowded city of Detroit. "Nature matters more here," he thought. From his cabin, he could see mangrove trees and the beach sparkling in the sun. Jeremy took a stroll along the shore. Soon he stooped to retrieve a gleaming object. It was simply a shell, a Venus sunray, but at the moment it seemed more precious than fine gold.

3. The purpose of this paragraph is to contrast which of the following?
   A. the island and the mangrove trees
   B. fine gold and the Venus sunray
   C. Detroit and Sanibel
   D. Jeremy and his feelings about nature

CAUSE & EFFECT

On the GED® Reasoning Through Language Arts test, you will be asked questions about cause-and-effect relationships. A **cause** is an event that makes another event, the **effect,** happen. Read the passage and look for causes and effects.

Salmon farms were originally created to relieve the pressure on the wild salmon population. Although these farms have increased the available supply of salmon, they have actually endangered what they were meant to preserve. Many wild salmon are now in danger of starvation. This is because farmers use the wild fish that the wild salmon would eat to feed the farmed salmon. Furthermore, wild salmon are succumbing to diseases that have migrated from the overcrowded fish farms. Wild salmon are also losing territory to the larger, stronger farmed salmon that have escaped from farms into the wild.

1. One of the effects of creating salmon farms has been an increase in the supply of salmon. What has been the other major effect?

   _____

2. What does the author imply is the reason for disease in fish farms?

   _____

1. The other major effect has been that salmon farms have endangered the population of wild salmon. 2. In the fifth sentence, the author implies that the diseases are caused by overcrowding in the fish farms.

Not all causes and effects are stated directly in order. Also, a cause may have more than one effect and an effect may have several causes. Use a chart to organize your thinking.

CAUSE	EFFECT
Farmers use wild fish to feed farmed salmon. →	Wild salmon are in danger of running out of food.
Diseases are spread from fish farms into the wild. →	Wild salmon are dying from diseases.
Some larger farmed salmon have escaped into the wild. →	The stronger farmed salmon have taken over the wild salmon's territories.

To find cause-and-effect relationships, ask yourself:

- What happened in this passage?
- What related event or events caused it to happen?

Have you ever caused something to happen? What happened? What did you do to make it happen?

▶ SKILL PRACTICE **Read the passage and complete the chart by adding one cause and one effect. Then answer the questions.**

Many parents wipe their countertops with the latest antibacterial cleaner. They think they are protecting their family from germs, but they are probably making their children's environment more dangerous. Scientists now know that the overuse of antibiotic medicines and cleaners is allowing more powerful strains of bacteria to flourish. Although many germs are killed, those that survive become stronger. In fact, the use of antibiotic cleaners may be counterproductive. When children grow up with normal amounts of bacteria in their homes, their own ability to fight off disease improves.

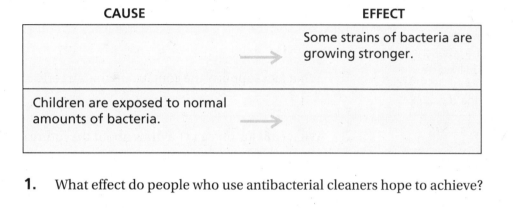

CAUSE	EFFECT
	Some strains of bacteria are growing stronger.
Children are exposed to normal amounts of bacteria.	

1. What effect do people who use antibacterial cleaners hope to achieve?

   _____

2. What actually causes powerful strains of bacteria to flourish?

   _____

▶ GED® PRACTICE **Choose the one best answer to the question.**

To: All Employees
From: Westbrook Management

Because of everyone's great efforts, we had strong sales this holiday season. In spite of a slow economy, we were able to post a 5% increase in sales over last year's holiday season. The marketing department's suggestion of free shipping on all Internet sales caught customers' attention. Our fine workers in shipping and receiving put in many hours of overtime to make sure that we could fill all of our orders. Everyone contributed to our success, and management would like to thank you with the enclosed bonus. Happy New Year to you and your families!

3. According to the memo, what caused the company to be profitable during the holiday season?

   A. a stronger economy

   B. layoffs and budget cutbacks

   C. a smart marketing promotion and hard work

   D. a 5% increase in profits over the previous year's holiday season

CONCLUSIONS

On the GED® Reasoning Through Language Arts test, you will be asked to draw conclusions about the ideas in a passage. A **conclusion** is an idea that follows logically from facts or evidence. Read the passage and draw your own conclusions.

Although millions of Americans play soccer, the sport has yet to find a large television audience in the United States. With its large field of play and spread out action, a soccer game is difficult to watch on a television screen. Soccer has continuous action, making it difficult for American television networks to schedule commercial breaks. Compared to popular televised sports, soccer is low scoring with less physical contact.

1. What fact supports the conclusion that Americans like soccer?

_____

2. What conclusion can you draw about the future of soccer and American television?

_____

1. The fact that millions of Americans play soccer means that Americans do like the sport. 2. One possible conclusion is that soccer probably won't gain popularity with American audiences because it is difficult to watch on TV and is not as exciting as other sports.

You can use this diagram to organize your thinking. The facts (columns) support the conclusion (roof).

CONCLUSION				
Soccer probably won't become popular with American television audiences.				
The large field is hard to see on TV.	F A C T S	Networks need commercial breaks.	F A C T S	Viewers like high scores and physical contact.

To draw a conclusion, ask yourself:

- What facts are presented in the passage?
- How do these facts work together to support a conclusion?

Have you ever drawn a conclusion and explained it to someone? How did you use facts to support your idea?

▶ SKILL PRACTICE **Read the passage and add two more facts that can support the conclusion. Then answer the questions.**

Alan hugged the cliff wall next to the hiking path. He had agreed to make the short climb to the cave entrance because everyone else in the family was going. "The trail is paved and carefully marked. What's going to happen to you?" his sister teased. Sure the trail was paved and marked, but there was no handrail. Why didn't anyone say there would be no handrail? One little misstep and off the edge he would go. It could happen to anyone. "Get away from the edge!" he wanted to yell, but they were too busy laughing and talking. Didn't anyone else see the danger?

CONCLUSION Alan's fear is unreasonable.				
Alan is hugging the cliff wall.	F A C T S		F A C T S	

1. What fact supports the idea that Alan's family doesn't think they are in danger?

_____

2. How do you think Alan's family members feel about his fears?

_____

▶ GED® PRACTICE **Choose the one best answer to the question.**

Cesar Chavez, the famous union leader, was born in 1927. Although he was born on a farm, his family became migrant farm workers during the Great Depression. He attended 65 elementary schools and never graduated from high school. In 1962, he founded the National Farm Workers Association (NFWA), based in California and the Southwest. The NFWA attracted national attention in 1965 when Chavez led the union in a strike and called for a national boycott of table grapes. To highlight the plight of farm workers, Chavez also fasted for 28 days. The strike and boycott lasted until 1970 and ended with the first major victory for migrant workers in the United States.

3. Which of the following conclusions can you draw based on the facts from the passage?

A. The National Farm Workers Association was founded in 1927.

B. Chavez's personal leadership played a big role in the union's success.

C. The strike and boycott did not accomplish their goals.

D. Farm workers now enjoy the same benefits as other unionized workers.

Check your answers on page 235.

AUTHOR'S EVIDENCE & PURPOSE

On the GED® Reasoning Through Language Arts test, you may be asked to explain how an author uses **evidence** to support the **author's purpose,** or the main reason a text was written. Authors usually write to inform, persuade, or entertain the reader. The author's choice of supporting facts, words, dialogue, and descriptive details are all evidence that support that purpose. Read this passage to find the author's purpose and identify evidence to support the purpose.

Every year, thousands of cats and dogs are taken to animal shelters because the number of these neglected animals far exceeds the number of available homes. There they sit alone and frightened. It doesn't have to be this way. Spay or neuter pets to prevent another generation of homeless animals. Consider adopting pets from a shelter instead of buying from a breeder or pet store. If we work together, we can spare our animal friends much suffering.

TIP

If the question asks about a specific part of the passage (opening or closing paragraphs, for example), mark that portion of the passage.

1. What is the author's main purpose for writing this passage?

   _____

2. What words and phrases provide evidence to support the author's purpose?

   _____

1. The author wants to persuade the reader to care about homeless animals and take action. 2. Some evidence that appeals to the reader includes the words *neglected, alone, frightened, homeless,* and the phrase *"if we work together."*

Organize your thinking with a chart. Think about what the author wants you to feel or do and write the author's purpose in the top box. Use the other boxes to write supporting facts, opinions, key words, and phrases.

Author's Purpose
To persuade readers to care about homeless animals and take action.

Supporting Facts and Opinions	Key Words and Phrases
There are more animals than there are homes. People can help by spaying and neutering their pets and by adopting animals from shelters.	The animals are described as *neglected, alone, frightened,* and *homeless.*

Think of a time when you had to convince someone that you were right. What did you do to persuade the other person? What evidence did you offer to convince the person?

To find the author's purpose and evidence, ask yourself:
- What does the author want me to do, feel, or think?
- What does the author feel or think about the subject?

▶ SKILL PRACTICE   **Read the passage and add to the chart. Then answer the questions.**

Our company suffered substantial losses last quarter. To avoid layoffs, we must instigate cost-cutting measures immediately, and we are asking for your cooperation during this difficult time. Too many absent employees hurt our productivity, so we are requesting that all employees give at least one month's notice before using vacation leave. Temporary workers further stretch our budget. Therefore, to reduce our reliance on temporary workers, we ask that all employees schedule any planned absences with their supervisors. Our goal is to have no more than two workers out per department on any given day. Your cooperation is critical in helping us avoid severe budget cuts and possible layoffs.

Author's Purpose	
Supporting Facts and Opinions The company must save money to avoid layoffs.	**Key Words and Phrases** *suffered substantial losses, difficult time*

1. What is the author's purpose?

2. What words or phrases provide evidence to support the author's purpose?

▶ GED® PRACTICE   **Choose the <u>one best answer</u> to the question.**

Mrs. Oliphant was an energetic third-grade teacher. A pair of glasses hung around her neck on a chain. She held them to her eyes with one hand as she read us *King Arthur and the Knights of the Round Table.* I closed my eyes and let her low contralto voice lift me across a great divide. I was Gareth, the kitchen boy, slaying the mighty Black Knight and then kneeling while Sir Lancelot raised his heavy broad sword to knight me. Then I heard the closing of the book, and gently, so gently, Mrs. Oliphant told us to open our eyes.

3. In this passage, the author's purpose is to entertain the readers with his childhood experience of being read to by a teacher. Which words provide evidence this is the author's purpose?

A. third-grade teacher

B. pair of glasses

C. I closed my eyes

D. slaying the mighty Black Knight

SETTING

On the GED® Reasoning Through Language Arts test, you may be asked questions about the setting of a passage. The **setting** tells where and when the action of the passage takes place. As you read, try to picture the action. Look for descriptive clues in the passage below that will help you identify the time of day and the place.

The automatic doors swept aside as Linda entered. She squinted in the bright fluorescent light as she walked toward the information desk. "Excuse me. My friend Celia is here. She had a little accident." Linda stopped short. All the attention had shifted to a father carrying a small, injured child. Linda wandered through a door. Perhaps she could find Celia on her own. The treatment rooms were small and smelled of antiseptic. In an empty room, a television was broadcasting a replay of the evening news. Long pleated pink curtains surrounded the occupied beds. A technician carrying a tray of test tubes pushed past her. She'd never find Celia this way.

1. Where is Linda looking for Celia?

_____

2. What detail tells you the action takes place sometime in the middle of the night?

_____

1. Linda is looking for Celia in the emergency room at a hospital. All the clues point to some type of medical building. 2. There is a rerun of the evening news on television.

Look for sensory details that may provide clues to the setting. You can organize your thinking with a chart.

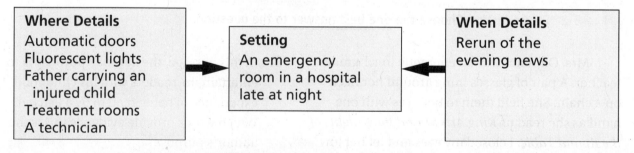

Where Details
Automatic doors
Fluorescent lights
Father carrying an
  injured child
Treatment rooms
A technician

Setting
An emergency
room in a hospital
late at night

When Details
Rerun of the
evening news

To find the setting, ask yourself:
- What clues describe the place, time of day, and time of year?
- What words tell how things look and sound?

Think of a time when you told a friend about an experience from your childhood. What words did you use to describe the setting?

▶ SKILL PRACTICE   **Read the passage and add where and when details to the chart. Then answer the questions.**

Back in those days, NASA scientists weren't sure how astronauts would react to the weightless environment of space, so we became their lab rats. The scientists developed a training program. They started taking the seven of us on rides in the cargo hold of a large Air Force C131 transport. The engines would roar as we climbed in a steep arc, and then, just as we went over the top, we felt up to a minute of weightlessness. They wanted to see if we could do simple tasks like talking, reading gauges, flipping switches, and keeping down our breakfasts.

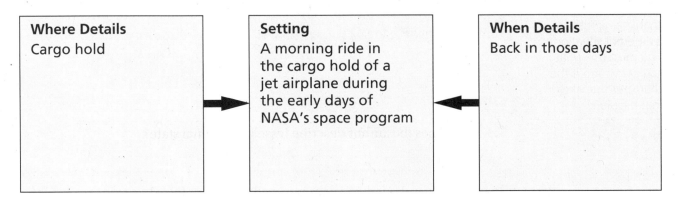

Where Details	**Setting**	**When Details**
Cargo hold	A morning ride in the cargo hold of a jet airplane during the early days of NASA's space program	Back in those days

1. What detail suggests that the training program was also an experiment?

_____

2. Based on details in the passage, riding in the cargo hold was most like which of the following?
    A. going over a hill on a roller coaster
    B. making a sharp turn in a fast car

▶ GED® PRACTICE   **Choose the one best answer to the question.**

Millie was worried that she was going to ruin her shoes. If she got tar on them, she would have to change and might be late getting back to work. Apparently, the city had decided to resurface the street on the same day that she had scheduled a haircut. Some big machine was spraying hot oil and sending bits of black grit flying everywhere. A few men stood around with stop signs doing absolutely nothing. When the light changed, she hurried across the street and into the small shop with no sign of any tar on her shoes.

3. Based on the details in the passage, which of the following is the *most* accurate description of when this event takes place?

    The action takes place
    A. during the late evening.
    B. during the daytime.
    C. on a weekend.
    D. in the future.

CHARACTER

On the GED® Reasoning Through Language Arts test, you will be asked questions about fictional characters. A **character** is a person created by an author through description and speech. As you read the passage below, think about what the character is like.

TIP

On the GED® test, you may be asked to decide how a character would act in a different situation. You must use what you know about the character to make that decision.

Jesse spun the globe and stopped it quickly by pressing his fingertip, ragged fingernail and all, on the slick metal surface. "That's it. That's where I'll be as soon as I save up enough money," he said defiantly. "Anyplace will be better than here. And I'll start my own company and be my own boss. You'll see. I got big ideas, you know, and I won't be sitting around in this dead-end town when I'm fifty or sixty or whatever you are."

"I believe you're pointing at the middle of the ocean," his father responded.

1. How does the author describe Jesse's emotional state?

_____

2. What does the father's comment tell you about Jesse?

_____

1. The passage states that Jesse spoke defiantly. Jesse is likely frustrated and angry.
2. The father's comment suggests that Jesse doesn't really have a plan to leave.

Characters are defined by their physical description, actions, and words, as well as the words and reactions of other characters. You can organize these details on a character chart. (You may not always have something to write in each section.)

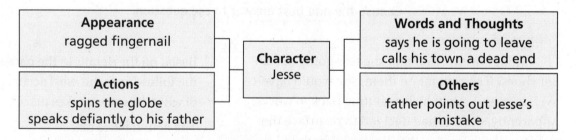

Appearance		Words and Thoughts
ragged fingernail		says he is going to leave
	Character	calls his town a dead end
Actions	Jesse	Others
spins the globe		father points out Jesse's
speaks defiantly to his father		mistake

Have you ever described your family to a friend? What details did you choose to explain what your family is like?

▶ SKILL PRACTICE   **Read the passage and add one appearance detail and one action detail to the chart. Then answer the questions.**

Sheila was born under a curse. She was ordinary looking, fairly small but with efficient, perfect posture. Her dull brown hair was never out of place. She had her teeth cleaned every six months, and she ate exactly the recommended number of servings of fruits and vegetables each day. It would be hard to imagine a more perfect person, except Sheila had been cursed. You see, when Sheila met other people, she instantly knew what their biggest faults were. The faults came to her in a flash, and it was so very, very hard not to tell them.

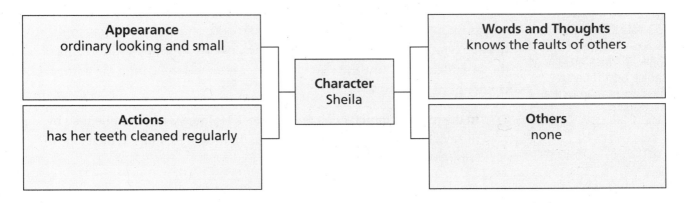

Appearance ordinary looking and small		Words and Thoughts knows the faults of others
	Character Sheila	
Actions has her teeth cleaned regularly		Others none

1. What is Sheila's curse?

   ....

2. Which of the following would Sheila be more likely to do at a party?
   A. compliment the hostess on her decorations
   B. tell the hostess how to make better decorations

▶ GED® PRACTICE   **Choose the one best answer to the question.**

Elio signed up for a computer class, but he didn't go. Instead, he pecked out a letter on an old manual typewriter that he kept under his bed, asking for a refund. Elio believed firmly that computers were just a fad. "It's silly to spend so much time learning to do something that won't be around in ten years," he thought. Elio's boss, however, didn't share his opinion. In fact, his boss told him that if he didn't get with the program, Elio's job wouldn't last another ten days. Elio gently patted the typewriter case and slid it back under the bed.

3. Elio doesn't like microwave ovens because he says "nuked food doesn't taste right." Based on this information and the details in the passage, which word best describes Elio's attitude toward new technology?

   A. admiring

   B. fearful

   C. disapproving

   D. disgusted

Check your answers on page 236.

APPLICATION

Application is an important thinking skill because it allows you to use information you learn by applying it in a new context or situation. On the GED® Reasoning Through Language Arts test, you will be asked to read a passage and then apply the information to a new situation that is stated in a question. Read the short passage below. Then answer the application questions based on it.

Conflict is the foundation for an interesting story. It makes something happen. Generally, conflict in a fictional work is one of four types: man versus man, man versus nature, man versus society, and man versus self. In each type, a main character is pitted against an opponent. The events of the story deal with how the main character resolves the conflict, whether in victory or defeat.

TIP

When you are asked to apply information to answer a question, think, "Which answer choice best reflects the information in the passage?"

1. In the movies, famed detective Sherlock Holmes is often challenged by the evil Professor Moriarty, once a math tutor of Holmes. Which type of conflict is this?

   _____

2. In the book *1984* by George Orwell, the main character strives to maintain his freedom from the government's Thought Police. Which type of conflict is this?

   _____

1. Since Sherlock Holmes battles another person, the conflict is man versus man.
2. The government represents society, so this conflict is man versus society.

To answer an application question, read the question to learn what the new situation is. Then apply the information you learned from the reading passage to answer the question. You can organize your thinking in an application chart.

New Situation	Given Information
Holmes against Moriarty	man vs. man
main character against Thought Police	man vs. society

To apply information, ask yourself:
• What is the new situation presented in the question?
• How does the given information apply to the new situation?

Have you ever used what you already knew to solve a problem? How did you apply your knowledge to the problem?

▶ **SKILL PRACTICE**   **Read the company policy and the new situation that is stated in each question. Then answer the questions and complete the chart.**

New Flex-Time Policies: Managers may allow employees to alter their schedules to meet family needs when these requirements are met: 1) employees work a 40-hour week, 2) costs to the company do not increase, and 3) each office or operation is covered during normal business hours.

1.   The company operates two main shifts: 7 a.m. to 3 p.m. and 3 p.m. to 11 p.m. Walter Ford needs to get his son off to school. Walter is one of five employees that answers customer calls. He asks if he can come in from 9 a.m. to 5 p.m. Is this within the scope of the new policies? Why or why not?

_____

2.   Sue García is the only employee who can answer payroll questions in the employee benefits department, which operates from 9 a.m. to 5 p.m. to be accessible to both shifts. She needs to take care of her elderly mother. She asks if she can come in from 6:30 a.m. to 2:30 p.m. Is this within the scope of the new policies? Why or why not?

_____

New Situation	Given Information
Walter Proposes to work from 9 a.m. to 5 p.m. No cost information provided One of five employees	Company Policy 1. 40-hour work week 2. no increased costs 3. office covered
Sue	Company Policy 1. 40-hour work week 2. no increased costs 3. office covered

▶ **GED® PRACTICE**   **Choose the one best answer to the question.**

Serious head injuries can happen in any sport where the participants are traveling at a high rate of speed. To be effective, a helmet must fit properly and guard against the particular dangers of a sport. For example, a ski helmet must cover more of the head than a bicycle helmet. A ski helmet is designed to protect against collisions with tree branches and the sharp edges of a ski.

3.   An athlete asks if a ski helmet would be a good choice for hockey. Which response best applies the ideas in the passage?

A.   No, it is not designed for hockey.

B.   No, it covers too much of the head.

C.   Yes, if it fits properly.

D.   Yes, all helmets are basically alike.

SYNTHESIS

You **synthesize** information when you 1) put together several ideas from across a passage or 2) use additional information that is presented in a question and combine it with ideas in the passage. Try the second type of synthesis skill with the passage and the first question below.

TIP

Some questions may provide additional information about the passage or the author. Make sure your answer choice is supported by <u>both</u> the passage and the new information.

We were eating breakfast when we heard a rushing sound by the back door. Startled, we looked out the window. The old elm planted by my grandfather had fallen, stopping inches before our house. The tree was old and could have fallen at any time. Our children played outside under that tree nearly every day of their young lives. We gave it water and tended it with laughter and love, and it happily gave us shade and comfort. I believe the tree chose to fall in the early morning to spare us all.

1. The author believes that animals can think and feel. What suggests that the author has the same belief about trees?

_____

2. What ideas did you put together to understand the author's beliefs?

_____

1. The author believes the tree spared the family by falling in the morning. 2. The author thinks the tree decided when to fall. The author also believes that animals have thoughts and feelings. Therefore, the author thinks that both animals and trees have thoughts and feelings.

Organize your ideas in a synthesis chart. Record the main idea from each source and then combine them to create a new main idea.

Passage Main Idea	**Idea with Question**
The author thinks that the tree decided when to fall.	The author believes that animals have thoughts and feelings.

Synthesized Idea
The author believes that animals and trees have thoughts and feelings and can care about people.

To synthesize information, ask yourself:
- Across a passage: What does the information have in common?
- If additional information is given in a question: How does this relate to a key idea in the passage?

Have you ever determined how a friend felt by listening to clues in a conversation?

▶ **SKILL PRACTICE**   **Read the passage and answer the questions below. Then add the ideas to the chart.**

President John F. Kennedy's inaugural address has been praised as one of the best public speeches ever delivered. However, President Kennedy did not write the speech himself. Kennedy gave his speechwriter, Ted Sorensen, clear instructions—keep it short, focus on foreign affairs, set a tone for a new era, and don't attack other politicians.

Passage Main Idea	**Idea with Question**
President Kennedy asked his speechwriter, Ted Sorensen, to write his inaugural address.	

Synthesized Idea

1.   Kennedy asked Sorensen to study Lincoln's Gettysburg Address for its "secrets" of success. Why do you think Kennedy asked him to do that?

_____

_____

2.   What do you think Sorensen did with that information?

_____

▶ **GED® PRACTICE**   **Choose the one best answer to the question.**

Russ had been driving all night in the rain. The red taillights of the cars ahead swam in the glare of the wet windshield. Russ sat up straighter and hunched forward against the steering wheel to stretch out his lower back. The green road signs were impossible to read until he was right up on them. The rain, the windshield wipers, the wet tires on the pavement—the sounds of the night were hypnotic. Russ knew he should check into a motel and sleep for a few hours, but he was running out of time and Jamie was counting on him. The rain was getting heavier now. He turned the radio up even louder and began to sing at the top of his lungs.

3.   The author of this passage once drove from Chicago to Los Angeles without stopping, a feat that he often bragged about to his friends. The author would probably use which of the following words to describe Russ?

A.   foolish

B.   determined

C.   likable

D.   overconfident

▶ **Read the following passage. Then answer the questions.**

When you submit a resume for a job, it is essential that you include a cover letter. Below is a sample letter.

Dear Ms. Livingston:

I was excited to see your online job posting for a customer service representative. I have completed the online application and uploaded my resume, which will show that I have the qualifications and skills to fill the position.

I graduated from Culver Community College with an Associate Degree in Communications. My school experience gave me strong communication skills that will help me handle telephone calls, solve customer problems, and write reports.

While I was in school, I participated in an activity that helped me prepare for this job. On a volunteer basis, I developed public relations materials for the Boys and Girls Club. Since graduating, I have been a customer service representative in Portland for five years and have been regularly given the "employee of the month" award by my department.

Thank you for your consideration.

Sincerely,

Andy Parker

1. What is the main idea of the second and third paragraphs?

_____

2. Based on the letter, which of the following *best* describes Andy Parker's personality?
   A. playful
   B. competent
   C. demanding
   D. self-centered

3. Based on the letter, what happened first?
   A. Andy won the "employee of the month" award.
   B. Andy graduated from Culver Community College.
   C. Andy developed public relations material for the Boys and Girls Club.
   D. Andy saw the online job posting for a customer service representative.

▶ **Directions: Read the newspaper article. Then answer the questions.**

Spring Meadows to Help Build New Community Center

CARVERTON Thursday the Spring Meadows Development Company announced that it will help the town of Carverton build a new community center. Carverton Mayor Kendra Clay said, "We're delighted to have Spring Meadows' support for this exciting new facility that will benefit all of our residents."

The Carverton Community Center will have a gymnasium, a fitness center, an indoor track, an outdoor Olympic-size swimming pool, and an indoor pool. The center will also have meeting rooms and locker areas.

Spring Meadows is a large residential development in Carverton consisting of 200 single-family homes and 300 apartments. To date, 35% of the homes have been sold and 50% of the apartments have been rented.

As part of the agreement between the town and the development company, Mayor Clay announced that Spring Meadows residents would receive a discounted membership to the new community center.

1. What is the author's main purpose for writing this article?

   _____

2. What words and phrases provide evidence to support the author's purpose?

   _____

3. As property manager of Spring Meadows, you would be *most* interested in this article because

   A. Mayor Clay lives in Spring Meadows near the community center.

   B. Spring Meadows residents are building the new center.

   C. There will be meeting rooms in the community center.

   D. Spring Meadows residents will receive a discounted membership.

4. In the third paragraph of the article, the author mentions the percentage of homes and apartments in Spring Meadows that have been rented or sold. Why did the author include this information?

   _____

   _____

   _____

MINI-TEST

This is a 15-minute practice test. After 15 minutes, mark the last number you finished. Then complete the test and check your answers. If most of your answers were correct but you did not finish, try to work faster next time.

▶ **Directions: Choose the one best answer to each question.**

Questions 1 through 3 refer to the following passage.

BENJAMIN FRANKLIN

Benjamin Franklin was born in Boston in 1706. As a boy, he was an apprentice to his brother, a newspaper publisher. At age 20, Franklin started his own newspaper. During his 20s and 30s, Franklin founded a library, a fire company, a college, an insurance company, and a hospital. At 45, he began nearly 40 years of service as a public official. When he was 48, Franklin performed his famous kite experiment that led to the discovery that lightning contained electricity. To this day, this was the most important American discovery. In his late 50s, Franklin reorganized the postal system of the American colonies. In 1776, Franklin helped draft the Declaration of Independence. For most of his 70s, he served as the first American minister to Paris. Finally, at age 81, he helped write the Constitution of the United States. Franklin died in Philadelphia in 1790.

1. Choose the correct sequence of the following events from the passage.

   1 Franklin performed his kite experiment.

   2 Franklin served as the first American minister to Paris.

   3 Franklin started his own newspaper.

   4 Franklin reorganized the postal system.

   A. 1, 2, 3, 4

   B. 4, 3, 2, 1

   C. 3, 1, 4, 2

   D. 2, 4, 3, 1

2. Which detail from the passage is *not* a fact?

   A. Franklin died in Philadelphia in 1790.

   B. To this day, this was the most important American discovery.

   C. Franklin founded a library, a fire company, a college, an insurance company, and a hospital.

   D. At age 20, Franklin started his own newspaper.

3. What conclusion can you draw about Benjamin Franklin?

   A. Franklin was successful in a variety of subject areas.

   B. Franklin was constantly striving to be better than his older brother.

   C. Franklin wished he could devote all of his time to scientific discovery.

   D. Franklin is famous because he wrote the Declaration of Independence and the Constitution of the United States.

Questions 4 through 7 refer to the following article.

HOW CAN YOU BE PREPARED FOR A PET EMERGENCY?

Preparing for a Pet Emergency

(1)   Accidents and injuries are the number one cause of death and disability for dogs and cats in their prime. Prevention of injuries is the best course of action, but if injuries do occur, it's important to be prepared.

Emergency Preparedness Kit

(2)   Prepare an emergency kit for your pet and keep it in a container that is easy to locate and carry. The kit should include basic first aid items, identification and medical information for your pet, a leash, a collar, a crate, a flashlight, a two-week supply of current medications, canned food for three days, a blanket, a radio, and batteries.

Pet Emergency Hospital

(3)   Accidents can occur at very impractical times—such as after 5:00 p.m. when your vet's office is closed. Know the name and location of the nearest 24-hour pet emergency hospital. Keep the phone number along with other vital numbers in your emergency kit.

Pet Identification

(4)   There are several ways to identify your pet, the most common being a tag on the pet's collar that has a name and phone number. You can also ask your vet to implant an identification chip. If there is a disaster (such as a flood or fire), or if your pet is startled by fireworks or thunder, it may run away. Identification could be the saving grace that brings your pet home safely. Also keep a picture of your pet in your emergency kit for easy access if an emergency arises.

4. What is the main idea of this passage?

   A. Be prepared for emergencies with your pet.

   B. Accidents occur at impractical times.

   C. An emergency kit should be easy to carry.

   D. There are several ways to identify your pet.

5. Which detail *best* supports the idea that you should know where the nearest pet emergency hospital is?

   A. Prevention is the best course of action.

   B. Your pet may be startled by fireworks or thunder.

   C. The emergency kit should include extra food and water.

   D. The vet may be closed when your pet is hurt.

6. Based on the passage, why is it important to have your pet's photo handy?

   A. to give it to the vet

   B. to show it to people if your pet is lost

   C. to identify which pet the medications are for

   D. to use as an ID tag for your pet

7. What is the main idea of the section Emergency Preparedness Kit?

   A. Include first aid items.

   B. Make sure you have a crate for your pet, plus food for three days.

   C. Keep at least two-weeks' worth of medications plus a blanket in the kit.

   D. The kit must be easy to carry and locate and should have important items for a pet emergency.

Novels and short stories are works of fiction. They come from writers' imaginations and take us places we might never experience in real life. There are many different types of fiction. An adventure story might describe a character's journey to Antarctica. A mystery story might detail how a crime is solved. A fantasy story might take place in a make-believe land where dragons and monsters fight it out in battle. Fictional writing can take us to worlds far away or just down the block—or even to places that don't really exist. It can let us experience the lives of people from different times, places, and ways of life.

Thinking About Fiction

You may not realize how often you come across works of fiction in your daily life. Think about your recent activities.

Check the box for each activity you did.

☐ Did you read a story to a child?

☐ Did you check out a book of fiction from the library?

☐ Did you read a short story in a magazine?

☐ Did you read some fiction while browsing in a bookstore?

☐ Did you watch a television movie that was based on a work of fiction?

☐ Did you read a book while riding the bus or subway?

☐ Did someone tell you a story he or she made up?

Write about some other experience you have had reading fiction. What did you read? Where were you? Why did you choose the fiction story you did?

_____

_____

_____

_____

Previewing the Unit

In this unit, you will learn:

• what makes adventure and mystery stories so exciting

• how fantasy stories help us suspend reality and enjoy make-believe characters and places

• why people still enjoy classic works of fiction that were written long ago

Lesson 13   **Adventure**

Lesson 14   **Mystery**

Lesson 15   **Fantasy**

Lesson 16   **Classic**

Vocabulary

submerged

ceased

impede

miscalculated

veered

propelled

ADVENTURE

We love adventure stories because they keep us on the edge of our seats. In adventure stories, characters often battle with forces of nature. They climb mountains and fight hurricanes. The passage you are about to read is about a man who is thrown overboard into whirling rapids while boating down a dangerous river. His friends and his dog try to save him. But will they?

From *The Call of the Wild* by Jack London

Later on, in the fall of the year, he saved John Thornton's life in quite another fashion. The three partners were lining a long and narrow poling-boat down a bad stretch of rapids on the Forty-Mile Creek. Hans and Pete moved along the bank, snubbing [stopping the motion of an object with a rope, which is tied around a fixed object] with a thin Manila rope from tree to tree, while Thornton remained in the boat, helping its descent by means of a pole, and shouting directions to the shore. Buck, on the bank, worried and anxious, kept abreast of the boat, his eyes never off his master.

At a particularly bad spot, where a ledge of barely **submerged** rocks jutted out into the river, Hans cast off the rope, and, while Thornton poled the boat out into the stream, ran down the bank with the end in his hand to snub the boat when it had cleared the ledge. This it did, and was flying down-stream in a current as swift as a mill-race, when Hans checked it with the rope and checked too suddenly. The boat flirted over and snubbed in to the bank bottom up, while Thornton, flung sheer out of it, was carried down-stream toward the worst part of the rapids, a stretch of wild water in which no swimmer could live.

Buck had sprung in on the instant; and at the end of three hundred yards, amid a mad swirl of water, he overhauled Thornton. When he felt him grasp his tail, Buck headed for the bank, swimming with all his splendid strength. But the progress shoreward was slow, the progress down-stream amazingly rapid. From below came the fatal roaring where the wild current went wilder and was rent in shreds and spray by the rocks which thrust through like the teeth of an enormous comb.

▶ Identifying Mood Mood is the overall feeling, or emotional atmosphere, of a story. Jack London creates the mood by describing Thornton's struggle in the dangerous river and Buck's efforts to save him. The author uses words such as "fatal roaring" and "wild current." How would you describe the mood of this passage?

   A. suspenseful   B. lighthearted   C. sad

The suck of the water as it took the beginning of the last steep pitch was frightful, and Thornton knew that the shore was impossible. He scraped furiously over a rock, bruised across a second, and struck a third with crushing force. He clutched its slippery top with both hands, releasing Buck, and above the roar of the churning water shouted: "Go, Buck! Go!"

Buck could not hold his own, and swept on downstream, struggling desperately, but unable to win back. When he heard Thornton's command repeated, he partly reared out of the water, throwing his head high, as though for a last look, then turned obediently toward the bank. He swam powerfully and was dragged ashore by Pete and Hans at the very point where swimming **ceased** to be possible and destruction began.

They knew that the time a man could cling to a slippery rock in the face of that driving current was a matter of minutes, and they ran as fast as they could up the bank to a point far above where Thornton was hanging on. They attached the line with which they had been snubbing the boat to Buck's neck and shoulders, being careful that it should neither strangle him nor **impede** his swimming, and launched him into the stream. He struck out boldly, but not straight enough into the stream. He discovered the mistake too late, when Thornton was abreast of him and a bare half-dozen strokes away while he was being carried helplessly past.

▶ Synthesizing Ideas There are many things to keep track of in a story. As you read stories, you have to keep track of the different characters, the situations they encounter, and the places where the action happens. Putting together information from different parts of the story can help you better understand the relationships between characters and the events in the plot. That's what synthesizing is: connecting information from different parts of the story.

For example, earlier in this story Buck jumped off a cliff just because Thornton told him to. Putting this fact together with the events from this passage tells you that Buck would do anything for Thornton.

You can also synthesize information from outside the story, such as information about the author, with facts from the story. Putting together these pieces of information can help you better understand the story, the author, or both.

The author of this story, Jack London, once said that "to live placidly [calmly] and complacently [contentedly] is not to live at all." If you take that information and put it together with information from the passage, which of the following conclusions makes the *most* sense?

A. Jack London lived an exciting life.
B. Jack London led a happy life.
C. Jack London felt he hadn't really lived.

Hans promptly snubbed with the rope, as though Buck were a boat. The rope thus tightening on him in the sweep of the current, he was jerked under the surface, and under the surface he remained till his body struck against the bank and he was hauled out. He was half drowned, and Hans and Pete threw themselves upon him, pounding the breath into him and water out of him. He staggered to his feet and fell down. The faint sound of Thornton's voice came to them, and though they could not make out the words of it, they knew that he was in his extremity. His master's voice acted on Buck like an electric shock. He sprang to his feet and ran up the bank ahead of the men to the point of his previous departure.

Again the rope was attached and he was launched, and again he struck out, but this time straight into the stream. He had **miscalculated** once, but he would not be guilty of it a second time. Hans paid out the rope, permitting no slack, while Pete kept it clear of coils. Buck held on till he was on a line straight above Thornton; then he turned, and with the speed of an express train headed down upon him. Thornton saw him coming, and, as Buck struck him like a battering ram, with the whole force of the current behind him, he reached up and closed with both arms around the shaggy neck. Hans snubbed the rope around the tree, and Buck and Thornton were jerked under the water. Strangling, suffocating, sometimes one uppermost and sometimes the other, dragging over the jagged bottom, smashing against the rocks and snags, they **veered** into the bank.

Thornton came to, belly downward and being violently **propelled** back and forth across a drift log by Hans and Pete. His first glance was for Buck, over whose limp and apparently lifeless body Nig was setting up a howl, while Skeet was licking the wet face and closed eyes. Thornton was himself bruised and battered, and he went carefully over Buck's body, when he had been brought around, finding three broken ribs.

"That settles it," he announced. "We camp right here." And camp they did, till Buck's ribs knitted and he was able to travel.

▶ Applying Ideas You already have many skills that you apply in different day-to-day situations. For example, when you were younger you learned how to add and subtract. Now, you apply that skill in everyday situations, such as adding up the cost of items at a store before you buy. You can do the same with an idea from a story. For example, knowing that a character is careful with money might help you predict what kind of car he or she would buy—probably an economy car rather than an expensive sports car. Being able to use information or ideas in new situations is an important skill to have, not just for reading, but for many things in life.

Based on what you have read about Thornton and Buck, which of the following is *most likely* to happen in this story?
   A.   Thornton punishes Buck for disobeying him.
   B.   Thornton is grateful and hopes that Buck isn't hurt.

Thinking About the Story

Practice Vocabulary

▶ **The words below are in bold type in the passage. Study the way each word is used. Then write each word next to its meaning.**

submerged	ceased	impede
miscalculated	veered	propelled

1. came to an end _____

2. put under water _____

3. driven forward by a force _____

4. interfere with _____

5. changed direction or course _____

6. incorrectly solved a problem _____

Understand What You Read

▶ **Write the answer to each question.**

7. What caused the boat to turn over?

_____

_____

_____

_____

8. Why did Buck swim back to the bank before saving Thornton?

_____

_____

_____

_____

9. Why did the men decide to camp right where they were?

_____

_____

_____

_____

Go on to the next page. 49

Apply Your Skills

▶ **Circle the letter of the best answer for each question.**

10. Which of the following words *best* describes Thornton?

    A. lazy

    B. anxious

    C. unforgiving

    D. tough

11. What is similar about Hans, Pete, and Buck?

    A. They don't give up trying.

    B. They like to make things easy.

    C. They are each very self-involved.

    D. They never delegate tasks to others.

12. Which of the following would Thornton probably enjoy?

    A. working in an office

    B. watching a hockey game on television

    C. camping alone on top of a mountain

    D. skydiving with his trusted friends

Connect with the Story

▶ **Write your answer to each question.**

13. If you were in Thornton's situation, would you react as he did? How would you react? Give reasons for your answer.

_____

_____

_____

14. In the passage, Hans and Pete try to save Thornton by fixing the rope around Buck's neck and shoulders and sending him into the water. However, it causes Buck to almost drown. Have you ever been in a situation where what you did caused a problem you didn't expect? Explain.

_____

_____

_____

LESSON 14

Vocabulary

recurred

puritanical

singular

stealthy

circumspectly

furtive

resumed

profile

MYSTERY

In a mystery, the main character is often a detective whose job it is to solve the mystery. Most of the fun of reading mysteries is putting all the clues together and trying to solve the puzzle yourself. The following excerpt from *The Hound of the Baskervilles* is part of a letter written by Dr. Watson to the famous detective Sherlock Holmes. Mrs. Barrymore and her husband are servants at Baskerville Hall.

From *The Hound of the Baskervilles*

by Sir Arthur Conan Doyle

And now, having brought you up to date. . ., let me end on that which is most important and tell you more about the Barrymores, and especially about the surprising development of last night.

First of all about the test telegram, which you sent from London in order to make sure that Barrymore was really here. I have already explained that the testimony of the postmaster shows that the test was worthless and that we have no proof one way or the other. I told Sir Henry how the matter stood, and he at once, in his downright fashion had Barrymore up and asked him whether he had received the telegram himself. Barrymore said that he had.

"Did the boy deliver it into your own hands?" asked Sir Henry.

Barrymore looked surprised, and considered for a little time.

"No," said he, "I was in the box-room at the time, and my wife brought it up to me."

"Did you answer it yourself?"

"No; I told my wife what to answer and she went down to write it."

In the evening he **recurred** to the subject of his own accord.

"I could not quite understand the object of your questions this morning, Sir Henry," said he. "I trust that they do not mean that I have done anything to forfeit your confidence?"

Sir Henry had to assure him that it was not so and pacify him by giving him a considerable part of his old wardrobe. . . .

▶ Reading Dialogue Dialogue is the conversation between characters. You can learn a lot about characters through the dialogue.

1. Read the dialogue above again. What do the comments by Sir Henry tell you about his attitude toward Barrymore?

_____

2. What in the dialogue tells you that Barrymore is eager to please Sir Henry?

_____

Mrs. Barrymore is of interest to me. She is a heavy, solid person, very limited, intensely respectable, and inclined to be **puritanical.** You could hardly conceive a less emotional subject. Yet I have told you how, on the first night here, I heard her sobbing bitterly, and since then I have more than once observed traces of tears upon her face. Some deep sorrow gnaws ever at her heart. Sometimes I wonder if she has a guilty memory which haunts her, and sometimes I suspect Barrymore of being a domestic tyrant. I have always felt that there was something **singular** and questionable in this man's character, but the adventure of last night brings all my suspicions to a head.

And yet it may seem a small matter in itself. You are aware that I am not a very sound sleeper, and since I have been on guard in this house my slumbers have been lighter than ever. Last night, about two in the morning, I was aroused by a **stealthy** step passing my room. I rose, opened my door, and peeped out. A long black shadow was trailing down the corridor. It was thrown by a man who walked softly down the passage with a candle held in his hand. He was in shirt and trousers, with no covering to his feet. I could merely see the outline, but his height told me that it was Barrymore. He walked very slowly and **circumspectly,** and there was something indescribably guilty and **furtive** in his whole appearance.

▶ Visualizing Characters   Sometimes characters in fiction are described in detail. Sometimes the author says only a little about how they look. Either way, characters become more alive if you can form some mental pictures of them.

To visualize a character, use all the details you can find about how the character looks. What the person does and says also helps create a mental picture.

1. Based on details from the passage above, which of the following is the *best* description of Mrs. Barrymore?
    A. She is large and gives an appearance of being under control.
    B. She is tiny and is always crying so people will feel sorry for her.
    C. She is short and is unexpectedly severe and cold.

2. Based on details from the passage above, which of the following is the *best* description of Mr. Barrymore's behavior?
    A. He is harmlessly walking down a hallway.
    B. He is concerned with making sure the hallway is dark.
    C. He is mysteriously sneaking down a hallway.

I have told you that the corridor is broken by the balcony which runs round the hall, but that it is **resumed** upon the farther side. I waited until he had passed out of sight and then I followed him. When I came round the balcony he had reached the end of the farther corridor, and I could see from the glimmer of light through an open door that he had entered one of the rooms. Now, all these rooms are unfurnished and unoccupied, so that his expedition became more mysterious than ever. The light shone steadily as if he were standing motionless. I crept down the passage as noiselessly as I could and peeped round the corner of the door.

Barrymore was crouching at the window with the candle held against the glass. His **profile** was half turned towards me, and his face seemed to be rigid with expectation as he stared out into the blackness of the moor. For some minutes he stood watching intently. Then he gave a deep groan and with an impatient gesture he put out the light. Instantly I made my way back to my room, and very shortly came the stealthy steps passing once more upon their return journey. Long afterwards when I had fallen into a light sleep I heard a key turn somewhere in a lock, but I could not tell whence the sound came. What it all means I cannot guess, but there is some secret business going on in this house of gloom which sooner or later we shall get to the bottom of. I do not trouble you with my theories, for you asked me to furnish you only with facts. I have had a long talk with Sir Henry this morning, and we have made a plan of campaign founded upon my observations of last night. I will not speak about it just now, but it should make my next report interesting reading.

▶ Drawing Conclusions A conclusion is an opinion or judgment you make after studying all the facts you have. The conclusion is not usually stated directly in what you read.

To draw a conclusion, use two or more stated ideas to come up with an idea that is not explicitly stated in the reading. You can conclude some things based on the facts that you find in the reading.

Which two facts from the passage *best* support a conclusion about Barrymore's actions? Select two of the choices.
   A. He cannot sleep and goes for a long walk to help him sleep.
   B. He is waiting for someone who is outside the house.
   C. He locks or unlocks a door.

Check your answer on page 238.

Thinking About the Story

Practice Vocabulary

▶ The words below are in bold type in the passage. Study the way each word is used. Then match each word with its meaning. Write the letter on the line.

_____	**1.** circumspectly	**A.**	side view of the face
_____	**2.** furtive	**B.**	extremely strict in matters of morals and religion
_____	**3.** profile		
_____	**4.** puritanical	**C.**	secretive
		D.	began again
_____	**5.** recurred		
		E.	with care
_____	**6.** resumed	**F.**	quietly to avoid being noticed
_____	**7.** singular	**G.**	unusual
_____	**8.** stealthy	**H.**	returned

Understand What You Read

▶ Circle the letter of the best answer to each question.

9. Who is writing this letter?

A. Sherlock Holmes

B. Dr. Watson

10. What does Sir Henry give Barrymore?

A. a telegram

B. old clothes

11. What does Dr. Watson hear the first night?

A. Mrs. Barrymore sobbing bitterly

B. a key turning inside a lock

▶ Write the answer to each question.

12. What kind of mood does the author create when he uses the imagery of a long, black shadow?

_____

13. What does Dr. Watson do the morning after he sees Barrymore?

_____

_____

Apply Your Skills

▶ **Circle the letter of the best answer for each question.**

14. How does Barrymore's "guilty and furtive" appearance affect the mood of the passage?

    A. It makes the mood less scary.

    B. It adds to the happy mood.

    C. It creates a dark, frightening mood.

    D. It produces a mood of silliness.

15. How does the description of Barrymore's actions at the beginning of the last paragraph affect the mood of the story?

    A. The description provides relief.

    B. The description makes everything clear.

    C. The description adds hope.

    D. The description increases the tension.

16. After reading the entire passage, which conclusion can you draw about Dr. Watson?

    A. He is a suspicious man.

    B. He has a lot of money.

    C. He is a sound sleeper.

    D. He has much scientific knowledge.

Connect with the Story

▶ **Write your answer to each question.**

17. Have you ever known someone you did not know well but just did not trust? What was it about that person that made you not trust him or her? Explain.

_____

_____

_____

18. Have you or someone you know had an experience solving a mystery? Was the mystery solved? Explain.

_____

_____

_____

FANTASY

Vocabulary

passage

longed

ventured

curious

fancy

sharply

respectable

anxiously

In fantasy, an author brings to life places, characters, and creatures that are completely made up in his or her imagination. These stories are called fantasies because they involve fantastical (unreal or unbelievable) places, stories, and creatures such as monsters and dragons. Fantasy stories may have familiar themes, but they could not really happen. With fantasy, the author—and the reader—must suspend reality. Animals and objects may talk, characters may have magical powers, and the setting can be of any time and any place. Most fantasy stories are filled with adventure. Read this passage from a fantasy story about a young girl's adventure.

From *Alice's Adventures in Wonderland* by Lewis Carroll

Alice opened the door and found that it led into a small **passage,** not much larger than a rat-hole: she knelt down and looked along the passage into the loveliest garden you ever saw. How she **longed** to get out of that dark hall, and wander about among those beds of bright flowers and those cool fountains, but she could not even get her head through the doorway; "and even if my head would go through," thought poor Alice, "it would be of very little use without my shoulders. Oh, how I wish I could shut up like a telescope! I think I could, if I only knew how to begin." For, you see, so many out-of-the-way things had happened lately, that Alice had begun to think that very few things indeed were really impossible.

▶ **Identifying Point of View in Fiction** Every story is told from a particular point of view. This story is told from Alice's point of view, but Alice is not the narrator. Alice is not telling her own story. Someone is telling the story about her.

In this story, we have a third-person limited narrator. The narrator is unseen and shares what one character—Alice—is feeling or thinking. For example, readers feel as if they're seeing and hearing the action through the main character's eyes and ears. In another story, the point of view might let the reader know what every character is thinking or feeling.

To identify point of view when you read, ask yourself whose actions you are following most closely. Whose thoughts do you know?

Which phrase shows the story is told from Alice's point of view?
A.   For, you see, so many out-of-the-way things had happened lately . . .
B.   How she longed to get out of that dark hall . . .

There seemed to be no use in waiting by the little door, so she went back to the table, half hoping she might find another key on it, or at any rate a book of rules for shutting people up like telescopes: this time she found a little bottle on it, ("which certainly was not here before," said Alice,) and round the neck of the bottle was a paper label, with the words "DRINK ME" beautifully printed on it in large letters.

It was all very well to say "Drink me," but the wise little Alice was not going to do that in a hurry. "No, I'll look first," she said, "and see whether it's marked 'poison' or not"; for she had read several nice little histories about children who had got burnt, and eaten up by wild beasts and other unpleasant things, all because they would not remember the simple rules their friends had taught them: such as, that a red-hot poker will burn you if you hold it too long; and that if you cut your finger very deeply with a knife, it usually bleeds; and she had never forgotten that, if you drink much from a bottle marked "poison," it is almost certain to disagree with you, sooner or later.

However, this bottle was not marked "poison," so Alice **ventured** to taste it, and finding it very nice, (it had, in fact, a sort of mixed flavour of cherry-tart, custard, pine-apple, roast turkey, toffee, and hot buttered toast,) she very soon finished it off.

"What a **curious** feeling!" said Alice; "I must be shutting up like a telescope."

And so it was indeed: she was now only ten inches high, and her face brightened up at the thought that she was now the right size for going through the little door into that lovely garden. First, however, she waited for a few minutes to see if she was going to shrink any further: she felt a little nervous about this; "for it might end, you know," said Alice to herself, "in my going out altogether, like a candle. I wonder what I should be like then?"

And she tried to **fancy** what the flame of a candle is like after the candle is blown out, for she could not remember ever having seen such a thing.

▶ **Understanding the Setting** Setting tells where and when the action in a story takes place. This can be especially important in a fantasy story, as it helps the reader better understand what is happening in a story that can be hard to follow because of the fantastical elements. As you read, look for clues about the setting. For example, look for words that tell whether the characters are indoors or outdoors. Look for words that describe the time—past, present, future. Look for words that tell how things around the characters look and sound.

In the passage above, many strange things happen to Alice. Which of the following *best* describes the place?

    A. a beautiful flower garden

    B. a small room inside a house

After a while, finding that nothing more happened, she decided on going into the garden at once; but, alas for poor Alice! when she got to the door, she found she had forgotten the little golden key, and when she went back to the table for it, she found she could not possibly reach it: she could see it quite plainly through the glass, and she tried her best to climb up one of the legs of the table, but it was too slippery; and when she had tired herself out with trying, the poor little thing sat down and cried.

"Come, there's no use in crying like that!" said Alice to herself, rather **sharply**; "I advise you to leave off this minute!" She generally gave herself very good advice, (though she very seldom followed it), and sometimes she scolded herself so severely as to bring tears into her eyes; and once she remembered trying to box her own ears for having cheated herself in a game of croquet she was playing against herself, for this curious child was very fond of pretending to be two people. "But it's no use now," thought poor Alice, "to pretend to be two people! Why, there's hardly enough of me left to make *one* **respectable** person!"

Soon her eye fell on a little glass box that was lying under the table: she opened it, and found in it a very small cake, on which the words "EAT ME" were beautifully marked in currants. "Well, I'll eat it," said Alice, "and if it makes me grow larger, I can reach the key; and if it makes me grow smaller, I can creep under the door; so either way I'll get into the garden, and I don't care which happens!"

She ate a little bit, and said **anxiously** to herself, "Which way? Which way?", holding her hand on the top of her head to feel which way it was growing, and she was quite surprised to find that she remained the same size: to be sure, this generally happens when one eats cake, but Alice had got so much into the way of expecting nothing but out-of-the-way things to happen, that it seemed quite dull and stupid for life to go on in the common way.

▶ Applying Ideas An author gives the reader many ideas about the characters in a story. When you have this information, you can sometimes figure out how a character will act later in the story. You can apply an idea about a character to another situation. Most characters have a particular personality and are likely to react the same way in many situations.

Apply what you know about Alice. If Alice found a sweater that had a note on it that said "PUT ME ON," what would she *most likely* do?

A. She would ignore the sweater and walk away.

B. She would examine the sweater and then put it on if it seemed safe.

Thinking About the Story

Practice Vocabulary

▶ **Complete each sentence by writing the correct word.**

passage	longed	ventured	curious
fancy	anxiously	sharply	respectable

1. Tim hurried down the narrow _____ to the darkened shop.

2. When Sarah saw the chocolate cupcake she _____ for just a bite.

3. Marlon waited _____ to hear how he did on the final exam.

4. Do you ever _____ the thought of taking a trip around the world?

5. Sam _____ only a short way into the icy water of the lake.

6. My dog barked so _____ , it hurt my ears.

7. In a _____ coincidence, the twins gave each other the same present on their birthday.

8. Mr. Estrada was elected mayor because he is a _____ citizen of his community.

Understand What You Read

▶ **Write the answer to each question.**

9. In the beginning of the passage, why couldn't Alice enter the garden?

_____

10. What does Alice mean when she says, "Oh, how I wish I could shut up like a telescope!"?

_____

_____

11. What happens when Alice eats the cake?

_____

Apply Your Skills

▶ **Circle the letter of the best answer for each question.**

12. Imagine that the author wanted to change the story and tell it from another character's point of view. Which of the following sentences would *not* belong in the story with this new point of view?

    A.   I saw Alice put her head through the door.

    B.   Alice was now only ten inches high.

    C.   Alice opened the door and found that it led into a small passage.

    D.   Alice felt a little nervous and wondered what she should do.

13. Which of the following tells the most about the setting?

    A.   . . . she knelt down and looked along the passage into the loveliest garden you ever saw.

    B.   How she longed to get out of that dark hall, and wander about among those beds of bright flowers and those cool fountains . . .

    C.   There seemed to be no use in waiting by the little door . . .

    D.   . . . her face brightened up at the thought that she was now the right size for going through the little door into that lovely garden.

14. Which of the following *best* describes Alice in this passage?

    A.   She gives up on challenges easily.

    B.   She frightens easily.

    C.   She can be very critical and hard on herself.

    D.   She would rather be indoors than outdoors.

Connect with the Story

▶ **Write your answer to each question.**

15. If you were retelling this story, what would you say about Alice and the obstacles she faces?

_____

_____

16. Recall that *Alice's Adventures in Wonderland* is a fantasy, and Alice faces many unusual circumstances. How would you handle living in such an unusual place? Would you handle the obstacles the same way Alice does, or would you do something else? Give reasons for your answer.

_____

_____

LESSON 16

Vocabulary

acute

dissimulation

sufficient

sagacity

stifled

suppositions

enveloped

unperceived

crevice

stealthily

CLASSIC

A classic piece of fiction is a story that has stood the test of time. It is read over and over again, generation after generation. Over time, readers are still able to relate to the story's characters, plot, and theme. A very famous writer who wrote many classics was Edgar Allan Poe (1809–1849). His spine-chilling stories have been made into movies and TV shows.

Most of the passage you are about to read takes place inside a dark bedroom where an old man sleeps. The narrator of the story describes his method for sneaking into that room at night, trying not to awaken the old man. The narrator imagines what the man in the bedroom is feeling after a sound awakens him one night.

From "The Tell-Tale Heart" by Edgar Allan Poe

True!—nervous—very, very dreadfully nervous I had been and am; but why *will* you say that I am mad? The disease had sharpened my senses—not destroyed—not dulled them. Above all was the sense of hearing **acute.** I heard all things in the heaven and in the earth. . . . How, then, am I mad? Hearken! and observe how healthily—how calmly I can tell you the whole story.

It is impossible to say how first the idea entered my brain; but once conceived, it haunted me day and night. Object there was none. Passion there was none. I loved the old man. He had never wronged me. He had never given me insult. For his gold I had no desire. I think it was his eye! Yes, it was this! One of his eyes resembled that of a vulture—a pale blue eye, with a film over it. Whenever it fell upon me, my blood ran cold; and so by degrees—very gradually—I made up my mind to take the life of the old man, and thus rid myself of the eye forever.

▶ **Using Definitions as Context Clues** The context of a word or phrase is the language around it that gives clues to its meaning. Sometimes an author defines an unfamiliar word or phrase for the reader by using context clues. For example, in the passage above, the phrase "sharpened my senses" is used. By stating the opposite, "not destroyed—not dulled them," the author makes the meaning of the phrase clear. Definition clues are usually found after a word and are set off by commas or dashes.

In the second paragraph of the passage above, the author uses the phrase *by degrees.* Based on the context clue, what is the meaning of this phrase?

    A. very gradually

    B. decisively

Now this is the point. You fancy me mad. Madmen know nothing. But you should have seen *me*. You should have seen how wisely I proceeded—with what caution—with what foresight—with what **dissimulation** I went to work! I was never kinder to the old man than during the whole week before I killed him. And every night, about midnight, I turned the latch of his door and opened it—oh, so gently! And then, when I had made an opening **sufficient** for my head, I put in a dark lantern, all closed, closed, so that no light shone out, and then I thrust in my head. Oh, you would have laughed to see how cunningly I thrust it in! I moved it slowly—very, very slowly, so that I might not disturb the old man's sleep. It took me an hour to place my whole head within the opening so far that I could see him as he lay upon his bed. Ha!—would a madman have been so wise as this? And then, when my head was well in the room, I undid the lantern cautiously—oh, so cautiously—cautiously (for the hinges creaked)—I undid it just so much that a single thin ray fell upon the vulture eye.

And this I did for seven long nights—every night just at midnight—but I found the eye always closed; and so it was impossible to do the work; for it was not the old man who vexed me, but his Evil Eye. And every morning, when the day broke, I went boldly into the chamber, and spoke courageously to him, calling him by name in a hearty tone, and inquiring how he had passed the night. So you see he would have been a very profound old man, indeed, to suspect that every night, just at twelve, I looked in upon him while he slept.

Upon the eighth night I was more than usually cautious in opening the door. A watch's minute hand moves more quickly than did mine. Never before that night had I *felt* the extent of my own powers—of my **sagacity.** I could scarcely contain my feelings of triumph. To think that there I was, opening the door, little by little, and he not even to dream of my secret deeds or thoughts. I fairly chuckled at the idea; and perhaps he heard me; for he moved on the bed suddenly, as if startled. Now you may think that I drew back—but no. His room was as black as pitch with the thick darkness (for the shutters were close fastened, through fear of robbers), and so I knew he could not see the opening of the door, and I kept pushing it on steadily, steadily.

I had my head in, and was about to open the lantern, when my thumb slipped upon the tin fastening, and the old man sprang up in the bed, crying out— "Who's there?"

I kept quite still and said nothing. For a whole hour I did not move a muscle, and in the meantime I did not hear him lie down. He was still sitting up in the bed listening;—just as I have done, night after night, hearkening to the death watches in the wall.

Presently I heard a slight groan, and I knew it was the groan of mortal terror. It was not a groan of pain or of grief—oh, no!—it was the low **stifled** sound that arises from the bottom of the soul when overcharged with awe. I knew the sound well. Many a night, just at midnight, when all the world slept, it has welled up from my own bosom, deepening, with its dreadful echo, the terrors that distracted me. I say I knew it well. I knew what the old man felt, and pitied him, although I chuckled at heart. I knew that he had been lying awake ever since the first slight noise, when he had turned in the bed. His fears had been ever since growing upon him. He had been trying to fancy them causeless, but could not. He had been saying to himself—"It is nothing but the wind in the chimney—it is only a mouse crossing the floor," or "it is merely a cricket which has made a single chirp." Yes, he had been trying to comfort himself with these **suppositions;** but he has found all in vain. *All in vain;* because Death, in approaching him, had stalked with his black shadow before him, and **enveloped** the victim. And it was the mournful influence of the **unperceived** shadow that caused him to feel— although he neither saw nor heard—to *feel* the presence of my head within the room.

▶ **Understanding Mood** The mood of a story is like the mood of a person. It can be tense and gloomy, light and joyous, or dark and frightening. An author has many ways of creating mood: telling what the characters are like, describing the setting, and indicating how quickly or slowly events occur.

In this passage, the author creates the mood by introducing a peculiar and nervous character and making him sneak around at night. The language "hinges creaked," "vulture eye," and "stalked with his black shadow" also contributes to the mood.

What is the mood of this passage?
A. light and comical   B. dark and spooky

When I had waited a long time, very patiently, without hearing him lie down, I resolved to open a little—a very, very little **crevice** in the lantern. So I opened it—you cannot imagine how, **stealthily,** stealthily—until, at length, a single dim ray, like the thread of the spider, shot from out the crevice and full upon the vulture eye.

It was open—wide, wide open—and I grew furious as I gazed upon it. I saw it with perfect distinctness—all a dull blue, with a hideous veil over it that chilled the very marrow in my bones; but I could see nothing else of the old man's face or person: for I had directed the ray as if by instinct, precisely upon the . . . spot.

And now have I not told you that what you mistake for madness is but over-acuteness of the senses?—now, I say, there came to my ears a low, dull, quick sound, such as a watch makes when enveloped in cotton. I knew *that* sound well too. It was the beating of the old man's heart. It increased my fury, as the beating of a drum stimulates the soldier into courage.

▶ **Predicting Outcomes** Sometimes an author ends a story without telling what finally happens. The reader must figure out the ending. When you do that, you are predicting the outcome. The outcome you predict must fit the story. It must make sense with what you know about the characters and what has already happened in the story.

In the part of "The Tell-Tale Heart" you have read, you have seen how upset the narrator gets because of the old man's "vulture eye." Now he has finally seen the eye in the middle of the night. What do you think he will do next?
A. He will probably go ahead with his plan to kill the old man.
B. He will probably get control of his feelings and sneak out of the room.

Thinking About the Story

Practice Vocabulary

▶ The words below are in bold type in the passage. Study the way each word is used. Then match each word with its meaning. Write the letter.

_____	**1.**	acute	A.	not seen
_____	**2.**	stealthily	B.	surrounded
_____	**3.**	sufficient	C.	enough
_____	**4.**	enveloped	D.	wisdom
_____	**5.**	sagacity	E.	small crack
_____	**6.**	stifled	F.	the process of disguising one's intentions
_____	**7.**	suppositions	G.	sharp
_____	**8.**	unperceived	H.	ideas assumed to be correct
_____	**9.**	crevice	I.	held in
_____	**10.**	dissimulation	J.	quietly and secretly

Understand What You Read

▶ Write the answer to each question.

11. What about the old man bothered the narrator the most?

_____

_____

12. Why did the narrator enter the man's room for seven nights without carrying out his plan to kill him?

_____

_____

_____

13. According to the narrator, why couldn't the old man comfort himself and go back to sleep on the eighth night?

_____

_____

_____

Apply Your Skills

▶ **Circle the letter of the best answer for each question.**

14. Find the word *conceived* in the second paragraph of the passage (page 61). Using context clues, decide which of the following *best* defines the word.

A. put in words

B. entered the narrator's brain

C. haunted the narrator

D. wronged the old man

15. Which of the following phrases *best* establishes the mood of the story?

A. . . . when the day broke, I went boldly into the chamber.

B. I knew what the old man felt, and pitied him. . . .

C. He had never given me insult.

D. For a whole hour, I did not move a muscle. . . .

16. Based on what you know of the narrator, what do you predict will happen after he kills the old man?

A. The sound of the old man's heartbeat will haunt the narrator.

B. The narrator will become more peaceful and relaxed.

C. The narrator will decide that he is mad after all.

D. The narrator will regret what he has done because the old man had always been kind to him.

Connect with the Story

▶ **Write your answer to each question.**

17. The narrator keeps saying that he is not crazy. Do you believe him? Why or why not?

_____

_____

18. Do you enjoy Poe's style of writing in this story? Explain your answer. Do you agree that this story should be considered a classic? Why or why not?

_____

_____

_____

▶ Read the following passage from *The Adventures of Tom Sawyer* by Mark Twain. Then answer the questions.

All nature was wide awake and stirring, now; long lances of sunlight pierced down through the dense foliage far and near, and a few butterflies came fluttering upon the scene.

Tom stirred up the other pirates and they all clattered away with a shout, and in a minute or two were stripped and chasing after and tumbling over each other in the shallow **limpid** water of the white sandbar. They felt no longing for the little village sleeping in the distance beyond the majestic waste of water. A **vagrant** current or a slight rise in the river had carried off their raft, but this only gratified them, since its going was something like burning the bridge between them and civilization.

They came back to camp wonderfully refreshed, glad-hearted, and **ravenous;** and they soon had the camp-fire blazing up again. Huck found a spring of clear cold water close by, and the boys made cups of broad oak or hickory leaves, and felt that water, sweetened with such a wildwood charm as that, would be a good enough substitute for coffee. While Joe was slicing bacon for breakfast, Tom and Huck asked him to hold on a minute; they stepped to a promising nook in the river-bank and threw in their lines; almost immediately they had reward. Joe had not had time to get impatient before they were back again with some handsome bass, a couple of sun-perch and a small catfish—provisions enough for quite a family. They fried the fish with the bacon, and were astonished; for no fish had ever seemed so delicious before. They did not know that the quicker a fresh-water fish is on the fire after he is caught the better he is; and they reflected little upon what a sauce open-air sleeping, open-air exercise, bathing, and a large ingredient of hunger make, too.

They lay around in the shade, after breakfast, while Huck had a smoke, and then went off through the woods on an exploring expedition. . . . They discovered that the island was about three miles long and a quarter of a mile wide, and that the shore it lay closest to was only separated from it by a narrow channel hardly two hundred yards wide. They took a swim about every hour, so it was close upon the middle of the afternoon when they got back to camp. They were too hungry to stop to fish, but they fared sumptuously upon cold ham, and then threw themselves down in the shade to talk. But the talk soon began to drag, and then died. The stillness, the solemnity that brooded in the woods, and the sense of loneliness, began to tell upon the spirits of the boys. They fell to thinking. A sort of undefined longing crept upon them. This took dim shape, presently—it was budding homesickness. Even Finn the Red-Handed was dreaming of his doorsteps and empty hogsheads. But they were all ashamed of their weakness, and none was brave enough to speak his thought.

▶ **The words below are in bold type in the passage. Study the way each word is used. Then match each word with its meaning. Write the letter.**

_____ **1.** limpid   A. starving

_____ **2.** vagrant   B. wandering

_____ **3.** ravenous   C. clear

▶ **Circle the letter of the best answer for each question.**

4. Which phrase *best* captures the mood at the beginning of the passage?

A. All nature was wide awake and stirring, now . . .

B. . . . a few butterflies came fluttering upon the scene.

C. Joe had not had time to get impatient before they were back again . . .

D. . . . for no fish had ever seemed so delicious before.

5. The characters Tom, Huck, and Joe run away from home and decide to settle on Jackson Island. If you take that information and put it together with information from the passage, which of the following conclusions makes the *most* sense?

A. Tom, Huck, and Joe are happy at home.

B. Tom, Huck, and Joe do not work well together.

C. Tom, Huck, and Joe have experience in the outdoors.

D. Tom, Huck, and Joe are scared to be on the island.

6. Tom, Huck, and Joe lose the raft they use to get to the island. Based on the passage, if the boys want to go home, what would they *most likely* do?

A. get upset and wait to be rescued

B. figure out a way to build a new raft

C. swim all the way back

D. figure out a way to signal for help

▶ **Write your answers to the following questions on the lines provided.**

7. Reread the last sentence of the third paragraph and retell it in your own words.

_____

_____

_____

8. Compare and contrast the mood at the beginning of the passage with the mood at the end of the passage.

_____

_____

_____

MINI-TEST

 This is a 15-minute practice test. After 15 minutes, mark the last number you finished. Then complete the test and check your answers. If most of your answers were correct but you did not finish, try to work faster next time.

▶ **Directions: Choose the <u>one best answer</u> to each question.**

Questions 1 through 7 refer to the following passage.

(1) Mrs. Darling loved to have everything just so, and Mr. Darling had a passion for being exactly like his neighbors; so, of course, they had a nurse. As they were poor, owing to the amount of milk the children drank, this nurse was a prim Newfoundland dog, called Nana, who had belonged to no one in particular until the Darlings engaged her. She had always thought children important, however, and the Darlings had become acquainted with her in Kensington Gardens, where she spent most of her spare time peeping into perambulators, and was much hated by careless nursemaids, whom she followed to their homes and complained of to their mistresses. She proved to be quite a treasure of a nurse. How thorough she was at bath-time; and up at any moment of the night if one of her charges made the slightest cry. Of course her kennel was in the nursery. She had a genius for knowing when a cough is a thing to have no patience with and when it needs stocking round your throat. She believed to her last day in old-fashioned remedies like rhubarb leaf, and made sounds of contempt over all this new-fangled talk about germs, and so on. It was a lesson in propriety to see her escorting the children to school, walking sedately by their side when they were well behaved, and butting them back into line if they strayed. On John's footer days she never once forgot his sweater, and she usually carried an umbrella in her mouth in case of rain. There is a room in the basement of Miss Fulsom's school where the nurses wait. They sat on forms, while Nana lay on the floor, but that was the only difference. They affected to ignore her as of an inferior social status to themselves, and she despised their light talk. She resented visits to the nursery from Mrs. Darling's friends, but if they did come she first whipped off Michael's pinafore and put him into the one with blue braiding, and smoothed out Wendy and made a dash at John's hair. No nursery could possibly have been conducted more correctly, and Mr. Darling knew it, yet he sometimes wondered uneasily whether the neighbors talked.

(2) He had his position in the city to consider.

(3) Nana also troubled him in another way. He had sometimes a feeling that she did not admire him. "I know she admires you tremendously, George," Mrs. Darling would assure him, and then she would sign to the children to be specially nice to father. . . . There never was a simpler happier family until the coming of Peter Pan.

From *Peter and Wendy* by J. M. Barrie

1. Which word from the story *best* completes the following sentence?

   Her grandfather does not like all of

   the _____

   technology because he doesn't know how to use it.

   A. prim

   B. new-fangled

   C. contempt

   D. resented

2. Which of the following clues tells you this passage is a fantasy story?

   A. The main characters' last name is Darling.

   B. The story is set in England.

   C. The Darlings use a nursemaid.

   D. The Darlings' nursemaid is a dog.

3. Why is Nana "much hated by careless nursemaids"?

   A. Nana sleeps on the floor.

   B. Nana tells their mistresses when they are careless.

   C. Nana is of inferior status.

   D. Nana is a better nurse than they are.

4. From whose point of view is this story told?

   A. Nana

   B. Mrs. Darling

   C. Mr. Darling

   D. a third-person narrator

5. Why did the Darlings choose Nana as their nursemaid?

   A. They love dogs.

   B. Nana is a great nurse.

   C. They do not have a lot of money.

   D. The children adore Nana.

6. Reread the first sentence of the passage and then identify the cause-and-effect relationship reflected in the sentence.

   A. Because the neighbors have a nurse, so do the Darlings.

   B. Because the neighbors have a dog for a nurse, so do the Darlings.

   C. Because Mrs. Darling was so precise, Mr. Darling always agreed with her.

   D. Because Mr. Darling was a passionate man, Mrs. Darling always tried to please him.

7. What troubled Mr. Darling about Nana?

   A. That the nursery was not conducted correctly

   B. That she had contempt over the concept of germs

   C. That the neighbors gossiped about the family and its nurse

   D. That she often forgot to carry an umbrella when there was a chance of rain

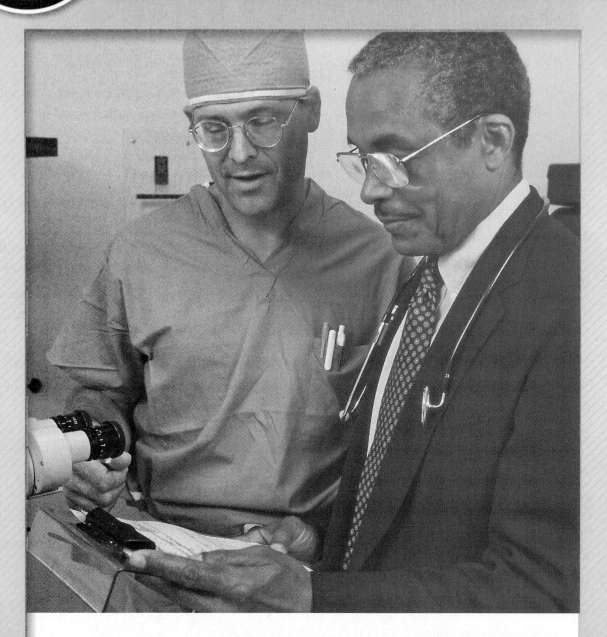

Informational texts are about real people, events, and issues. They can provide important factual information or express someone's point of view on a topic. Some of the most common types of informational texts are brochures, advertisements, legal documents, and other real-life writing. Informational texts also include essays, biographies, and true stories. Informational texts might tell about history, travel, civics, government, geography, or science and often include diagrams and maps.

Thinking About Informational Texts

You may not realize how often you come across informational writing in your daily life. Think about your recent activities.

Check the box for each activity you did.

☐ Did you view an advertisement on the Internet?

☐ Did you read a health brochure that your doctor gave you?

☐ Did you look at a brochure for something you might buy?

☐ Did you read and sign a legal document?

☐ Did you read a biography of a famous American?

☐ Did you read a science article in a magazine?

☐ Did you follow the sequence of events in an article about a historical event?

☐ Did you try to solve a problem by eliminating possible causes?

☐ Did you read the results of a scientific study?

Previewing the Unit

In this unit, you will learn:

● how scientific writing reflects scientific principles and processes

● how to evaluate data and ideas when reading biographies and other social studies material

● how brochures and advertisements try to persuade you to buy

● how to understand forms, manuals, and legal documents

Lesson 17	Informational Science	Lesson 22	Historical Court Cases
Lesson 18	Scientific Research	Lesson 23	Brochures & Advertisements
Lesson 19	Scientific Concepts	Lesson 24	Forms & Documents
Lesson 20	Biographies	Lesson 25	Manuals & Handbooks
Lesson 21	Informational Social Studies	Lesson 26	Legal Documents

INFORMATIONAL SCIENCE

Vocabulary

nutrients

crucial

concentrating

productive

When you read informational science articles, you have to apply your understanding of basic science concepts and use thinking skills to understand and evaluate the author's message. Read the article below, written to help consumers understand the importance of eating fruits and vegetables.

Eat Five to Stay Alive!

Research has shown that it is important for people to eat at least five servings of fruits and vegetables every day. These often-colorful foods offer several significant health advantages. For one, fruits and vegetables are filled with **nutrients** that many people often do not get enough of, including vitamins A and C, potassium, and fiber. All of these nutrients are **crucial** to keeping the body running smoothly. Second, fruits and vegetables have been shown to help reduce the risk of many serious diseases, including diabetes and cancer. And third, fruits and vegetables are relatively low in calories and fat. When you eat more fruits and vegetables, you may eat fewer high-calorie foods that can lead to weight gain. All of this is to say that fruits and vegetables have been shown to help people live healthier lives.

▶ Restating/Summarizing To **restate** information, you repeat it but in a different way, using your own words. When you restate information in a shortened form you are **summarizing**. When you restate or summarize scientific information, ask yourself what subject was investigated and what conclusions the researchers reached.

1. Restate why it is important for people to eat at least five servings of fruit and vegetables every day.

   _____

   _____

2. Summarize the information in the paragraph.

   _____

   _____

To lead a healthy life, you still have to eat a balanced diet, which includes forms of protein, dairy, grains, and oil as well as fruits and vegetables. You also have to be active, drink plenty of water, and get a good night's sleep to stay healthy. But filling your body with good nutrients is an essential part of a healthy lifestyle.

Just imagine what it would be like to fill your car with the worst possible fuel you could find. The car probably wouldn't run that great, would it? The poor fuel may cause the car to have a hard time starting. It would have a difficult time moving properly down the road. Maybe it would chug and sputter at the stoplight and would need to be towed home. Well, the same is true with your body. If you fill your body with fuel (or food) that is low in nutrients and filled with sugars, fats, and other unhealthy ingredients, then it probably won't run too efficiently. As a result, you might have a hard time getting up in the morning. You might have trouble **concentrating** at work or school. You may have a hard time running to catch the bus or walking with your dog. After a long day, your body may be so tired that you do not have the energy to do much of anything.

▶ **Cause and Effect** A **cause** makes something happen. An **effect** is the result of a cause. Cause-and-effect relationships are often signaled by words such as *cause, effect, result, because, as a result, led to,* and *caused by.*

1. What might cause a car not to run properly?

_____

_____

2. What is the effect of filling your body with foods low in healthy nutrients?

_____

_____

_____

So, how can you be sure to get enough fruits and vegetables in your diet every day? One easy way is to include at least one serving of either a fruit or a vegetable at every meal. If you have orange juice for breakfast, for example, you have just had one serving. If you have an apple with lunch, that is another serving. If you have a scoop of carrots or peas with your dinner, then you have just had serving number three. Just think, if you get two more servings for the day, you've reached your goal. How about slicing a banana on your cereal for breakfast and snacking on a handful of raisins or baby carrots when you head out the door to run errands? Or, you could eat a handful of grapes on the train or bus and then eat some celery sticks as a snack after dinner. There are many ways you can easily get in the other two required servings without much effort.

Getting the proper amount of nutrients will help you feel great and live a much healthier and **productive** life! Start today by adding more fruits and vegetables to your diet. You'll feel so great that you'll wish you had started this a long time ago!

▶ Application The GED® test has questions that involve the **application** of ideas. When you apply ideas to a new context, you take information from one situation and use it in another situation.

1. List five ways not listed in the article that you can add a serving of fruits or vegetables to your day.

2. Another part of a healthy lifestyle is drinking plenty of water. List three ways you can drink more water each day.

Thinking About the Text

Practice Vocabulary

▶ The words below are in bold type in the passage. Study the way each word is used. Then match each word with its meaning.

_____ **1.** nutrients   A. focusing attention

_____ **2.** crucial   B. essential

_____ **3.** concentrating   C. vitamins and minerals

_____ **4.** productive   D. yielding results

Understand What You Read

▶ Write the answer to each question.

5. Besides eating proper nutrients, what does the author say people must also do in order to live a healthy life?

_____

_____

6. According to the author, what happens when our bodies do not get the proper nutrients?

_____

_____

7. In the passage, the author compares the body to a car. Summarize in your own words how our bodies are similar to cars.

_____

_____

_____

_____

8. Do you agree or disagree with the author that is it easy to get five servings of fruits and vegetables every day? Explain your answer.

_____

_____

_____

Apply Your Skills

▶ **Circle the letter of the best answer for each question.**

9. Which sentence *best* restates the information in paragraph 4 (on page 74)?

A. Even a car needs to have proper fuel in order to run properly.

B. It is difficult to get up in the morning if you don't get proper nutrition.

C. Scientific research shows that good nutrition equals good health.

D. Adding at least one serving to every meal will help you get the required amount of fruits and vegetables every day.

10. The author gives several suggestions to get more fruits and vegetables every day. Which of these is one of those suggestions?

A. Drink orange juice at breakfast.

B. Eat a salad with dinner every night.

C. Make a smoothie using your favorite fruit.

D. Slice a banana on your peanut butter sandwich.

11. With which of these statements would the author *most likely* agree?

A. Proteins found in meat are the most important food source.

B. Drinking five glasses of fruit juice is the best way to add nutrients to your diet.

C. People tend to feel better when they eat foods with proper nutrients.

D. People should cut out all foods that contain sugars and fats.

12. Which of these is a fact from the passage?

A. "You'll feel so great that you'll wish you had started this a long time ago!"

B. "Research has shown that it is important for people to eat at least five servings of fruits and vegetables every day."

C. "One easy way is to include at least one serving of either a fruit or a vegetable at every meal."

D. "You might have trouble concentrating at work or school."

LESSON

18

SCIENTIFIC RESEARCH

Vocabulary

pathogens

devised

immunity

threat

In informational science texts, the author may present a science-based problem and then explain how researchers worked to develop a solution. Scientists generally do this by asking questions, making observations, testing ideas, and forming conclusions. The information in science texts is often presented as a sequence of events in which the author explains the research process in the order in which it occurred.

The passage on these pages is about fighting germs. One type of germ, called bacteria, is a leading cause of infection and death. Early discoveries about bacteria had a great impact on modern health.

Ways of Fighting Germs

Until the twentieth century, surgery patients often died of bacterial infections. As doctors learned more about disease, it became clear that simple cleanliness could help prevent the spread of some diseases. Today, hospitals and clinics use a variety of technologies to prevent the spread of disease. For example, ultraviolet radiation, boiling water, and chemicals are used in health facilities to kill **pathogens,** or germs.

During the mid-1800s, Louis Pasteur, a French scientist, discovered that tiny germs or microorganisms caused wine to spoil. The uninvited microorganisms were bacteria. Pasteur **devised** a method of using heat to kill most of the bacteria in the wine. This method is called pasteurization, and it is still used today.

▶ Scientific Method The **scientific method** is a series of logical steps that can be used to solve problems. These steps usually include asking questions, making observations, testing ideas, and formulating conclusions. When using the scientific method to approach a problem, try to put the problem in the form of a question.

1. What problem led to the discovery that cleanliness could help prevent the spread of some diseases?

   _____

2. What question may Louis Pasteur have asked?

   _____

Check your answers on page 242.

In the late 1700s, no one knew what a pathogen was. It was during this time that Edward Jenner, a physician, studied a disease called smallpox. He observed that people who had been infected with a similar disease known as cowpox seemed to have protection against smallpox. This protection from or resistance to a disease is called **immunity.** Jenner's work led to the first modern vaccine. A vaccine is a substance that helps your body develop immunity to a disease.

Today, vaccines are used all over the world to prevent many serious diseases. Modern vaccines contain pathogens that are killed or specially treated so that they can't make you very sick. The vaccine is enough like the disease-causing pathogen to allow your body to develop a defense against that disease.

▶ **Sequence of Events** When you **sequence events**, you put them in the order in which they occurred. When you identify the sequence of events, look for clue words to help you determine the order in which things happened. The words *before, after, next, then, first, lastly, later,* and *finally* can help you identify the sequence in a passage. Dates can also help you put events in order.

1. When did Edward Jenner study smallpox?

_____

2. What word in the second paragraph above helps you identify sequence in the passage?
   A. today
   B. modern

3. Restate the sequence of events on this page.

_____

_____

_____

Bacterial infections can be a serious **threat** to your health. Fortunately, doctors can usually treat these kinds of infections with antibiotics. An antibiotic is a substance that can kill or slow the growth of bacteria. Antibiotics may also be used to treat infections caused by other microorganisms, such as fungi. If you take an antibiotic when you are sick, it is important that you take it according to your doctor's instructions to ensure that all the pathogens are killed.

▶ Drawing Conclusions Some questions on the GED® test ask you to draw conclusions based on information in a passage. A **conclusion** is a statement that follows logically from certain facts. Conclusions must be based on facts, which are statements that can be proven true. When you are asked to draw a conclusion, ignore statements that represent opinions.

1. Which conclusion is based on facts from the article?
   A. Antibiotics are the most significant medical discovery in history.
   B. Antibiotics are an important way to help fight infections.

2. Which conclusion can you draw from the passage?
   A. Antibiotics are better than vaccines at fighting bacterial infections.
   B. If you do not take an antibiotic according to your doctor's instructions, it may not work properly.

Thinking About the Text

Practice Vocabulary

▶ **The words below are in bold type in the passage. Study the way each word is used. Then match each word with its meaning.**

_____ **1.** pathogens   A. created

_____ **2.** devised   B. protection

_____ **3.** immunity   C. impending damage

_____ **4.** threat   D. germs

Understand What You Read

▶ **Write the answer to each question.**

5. Show the correct sequence of events by writing a 1, 2, or 3 by each event.

_____ Louis Pasteur discovers tiny germs cause wine to spoil.

_____ Edward Jenner studies a disease called smallpox.

_____ Hospitals and clinics use a variety of technologies to prevent the spread of some diseases.

6. According to the selection, how is pasteurization different from a vaccine in preventing disease?

_____

_____

_____

7. According to the selection, vaccines contain pathogens, so why don't they make people sick?

_____

_____

_____

8. Write a statement to summarize the main idea of the selection.

_____

_____

_____

Apply Your Skills

▶ **Circle the letter of the best answer for each question.**

9. What is the main purpose of this selection?

   A.   to inform readers of the history of immunization

   B.   to persuade readers to update their immunizations

   C.   to inform readers of the history and techniques for fighting bacteria

   D.   to persuade readers to make sure that all milk products they consume are pasteurized

10. According to the selection, which conclusion is *most likely* true?

   A.   Smallpox and cowpox are caused by related pathogens.

   B.   Vaccines can cure bacterial infections.

   C.   No one dies of bacterial infections anymore.

   D.   It is possible to eliminate all bacteria in hospitals and doctors' offices.

11. Based on the selection, what was the *most* significant result from Edward Jenner's discovery of vaccines?

   A.   Edward Jenner became known as the father of vaccination.

   B.   Today, vaccines are used all over the world to prevent serious diseases.

   C.   Vaccines now prevent wine from spoiling all around the world.

   D.   Bacterial infections are no longer a threat to people.

12. Which statement supports the idea that simple cleanliness can help prevent the spread of some diseases?

   A.   A vaccine is a substance that helps your body develop immunity to a disease.

   B.   Boiling water and chemicals are used in health facilities to kill pathogens, or germs.

   C.   Pasteur devised a method of using heat to kill most of the bacteria in wine.

   D.   Doctors can usually treat bacterial infections with antibiotics.

SCIENTIFIC CONCEPTS

Vocabulary

molecules

converted

formation

reactants

Some informational science texts explain major scientific concepts, ideas, and principles. For example, an article might explain how the human body digests food, or another might explain the water cycle. These texts often introduce and explain unfamiliar terms and may present information in tables, graphs, and diagrams. When you come across these texts on the GED® test, you will be challenged to understand terms and their definitions, to use the text and graphics to think about the relationship between concepts and events, and to interpret information and draw conclusions.

Read the following informational science passage about photosynthesis.

Photosynthesis: Making Energy for Life

Almost all the energy used by living organisms, including humans, is originally captured from sunlight. Plants, algae, and some bacteria capture solar energy and use it to make complex **molecules** in a process called photosynthesis. These molecules supply energy, or food, for other organisms.

Photosynthesis occurs in the chloroplasts of plant cells and algae and in the cell membrane of certain prokaryotes. Chloroplasts are organelles, or specialized structures within a cell, that have two membranes and their own DNA. Chloroplasts are green because they contain chlorophyll, a green pigment. Chlorophyll traps the energy of sunlight. This energy is then used to make sugar.

▶ Restate/Summarize To **restate** information, you repeat it in your own words. When you restate information in a shortened form, you are **summarizing**.

1. Restate what happens in photosynthesis.

_____

_____

2. Summarize the role of chlorophyll in photosynthesis.

_____

_____

Stages of Photosynthesis

Photosynthesis has three stages. During stage 1, energy is captured from sunlight. During stage 2, this light energy is **converted** to chemical energy. The chemical energy is temporarily stored in molecules known as ATP and NADPH. During stage 3, the chemical energy stored in ATP and NADPH powers the **formation** of organic compounds using carbon dioxide (CO_2) and water (H_2O).

The most common way this formation of organic compounds happens is called the Calvin cycle. The Calvin cycle uses ATP, NADPH, and a key enzyme to add carbon dioxide molecules to exiting carbon chains, which are used as the building blocks of sugars. The sugars produced during photosynthesis are either used as energy immediately or stored for future use.

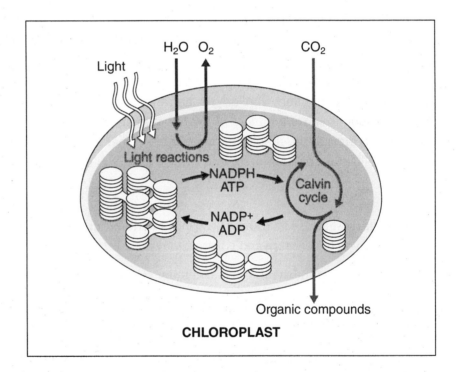

▶ Diagrams Diagrams are drawings of an object, concept, or process. When you see a science diagram, picture the real object or process in your mind.

1. Look at the diagram. Where is this process taking place?
   A. in the chloroplast
   B. in the sun

2. According to the diagram, what substances are needed for photosynthesis?
   A. the Calvin cycle, light, and organic compounds
   B. light, water, and carbon dioxide

Photosynthesis Supplies Energy and Oxygen

Photosynthesis is the process by which cells, such as plant cells, use sunlight, carbon dioxide, and water to make sugar and oxygen. Photosynthesis provides energy for almost all life forms.

Photosynthesis supplies energy and oxygen, which are products of the chemical reactions that take place. Photosynthesis also requires **reactants** for the chemical reactions. These reactants, carbon dioxide and water, are products of a different process known as cellular respiration.

Cellular Respiration

Photosynthesis and cellular respiration are the interrelated processes by which living things capture, transform, and store energy. Photosynthesis is the process by which energy from sunlight is captured and transformed into chemical energy. Cellular respiration is the process cells use to harvest the energy in organic compounds.

Carbon dioxide and water are two reactants of photosynthesis that are products of cellular respiration. Similarly, sugar and oxygen are two **reactants** of cellular respiration that are products of photosynthesis. So, the two processes rely on each other to provide the reactants for each chemical reaction. In this way, photosynthesis and cellular respiration cycle matter and energy in living systems.

▶ Compare and Contrast When you **compare** things, you show how they are alike. When you **contrast** things, you show how they are different. When you come across questions that ask you to compare and contrast, pay close attention to details.

1. How are photosynthesis and cellular respiration alike?

_____

_____

2. How are photosynthesis and cellular respiration different?

_____

_____

Thinking About the Text

Practice Vocabulary

▶ **The words below are in bold type in the passage. Study the way each word is used. Then match each word with its meaning.**

_____ **1.** molecules   A. changed

_____ **2.** converted   B. smallest bit of a substance

_____ **3.** formation   C. substance going into a chemical reaction

_____ **4.** reactants   D. creation

Understand What You Read

▶ **For 5–10, write the answer for each question. For 11, circle the letter of the best answer.**

5. The process of _____ captures energy from the sun and uses it to produce sugar and oxygen from carbon dioxide and water.

6. Photosynthesis occurs in the _____ of plant cells.

7. Chlorophyll is a _____ that captures light.

8. Carbon dioxide and water are _____ in the process of photosynthesis.

9. Photosynthesis and cellular respiration help cycle

_____ and _____ in living systems.

10. Cellular respiration is the process cells use to _____ the energy in organic compounds.

11. Plants use light to make their own food. What happens to the light absorbed by a plant during photosynthesis?

A. It is converted to kinetic energy.

B. It is converted to chemical energy, which the plant stores.

C. It powers a reaction that produces carbon dioxide and water.

D. It powers a reaction that produces oxygen and carbon dioxide.

Apply Your Skills

▷ **Write the answer for each question.**

12. Write a short paragraph about photosynthesis using the terms *plant, chloroplast, chlorophyll, pigment, sugar, oxygen,* and *sunlight.*

_____

_____

_____

13. What substances are needed for photosynthesis, and what substances are produced by photosynthesis?

_____

_____

▷ **Use the following information to answer questions 14 and 15.**
Julia conducted an experimental investigation of the gas production of a water plant. She placed a funnel and test tube upside down over a water plant submerged in water and collected the gas that the water plant produced when kept in sunlight. After several days, a large bubble of gas collected in the upside-down beaker, as shown in the diagram.

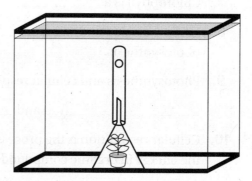

14. Given that the gas came from the water plant, what is the content of the bubble of gas collected in the test tube?

A. oxygen

B. carbon dioxide

C. water vapor

D. hydrogen

15. What process produced this gas?

_____

LESSON 20

Vocabulary

ignorant

divest

supervisor

dynamic

BIOGRAPHIES

Informational social studies texts frequently include biographies, the life stories of real people. Biographies are often filled with dates and significant events told in time order. On the GED® test, you may be asked to follow these events and understand and infer their significance in history and in today's world.

This passage is about Frederick Douglass, a man born into slavery who educated himself and became one of America's greatest speakers and writers. His life was an inspiration to others struggling for civil rights.

Frederick Douglass: Abolitionist Leader

Frederick Douglass's name at birth was Frederick Bailey. As a boy, he wanted to learn to read and write. It was the only way he could hope to escape slavery. He had heard his own master say that a black person with an education could never be kept as a slave. Though he was not yet ten years old, Douglass knew he would use education to free himself.

Douglass was born in Talbot County, Maryland. His mother died when he was young. The boy was treated badly by the slave owner. Then he was shipped off to live with another member of the owner's family in Baltimore.

His new master, Hugh Auld, wanted to make sure Douglass was kept **ignorant.** Auld's wife Sophia was kind, however. She tried to teach him simple spelling and reading. Auld commanded his wife to stop teaching Douglass to read. He said it would make the boy dangerous.

▶ Predict Outcomes On the GED® test, you may be asked to make a prediction about the outcome of an event or sequence of events. A **prediction** is a reasonable guess about what will happen next or sometime in the future. When predicting outcomes, you do not have to know exactly what will happen. You just need to make a guess about what is likely to happen.

1. Predict what might happen to Douglass. Will he use education to free himself?

   _____

   _____

2. Predict what will happen with Sophia. Will she continue to help Douglass?

   _____

   _____

New Name

Even though Douglass knew it would be difficult to learn without a teacher, he was determined. Each time he was left alone, he would look for a book or newspaper. He would do his best to figure out the words and their meanings. If education was the way out of slavery, he knew he didn't have a moment to waste.

*Slavery proved as injurious to her [Sophia] as it did to me. When I went there, she was a pious, warm, and tender-hearted woman. There was no sorrow or suffering for which she had not a tear. She had bread for the hungry, clothes for the naked, and comfort for every mourner that came within her reach. Slavery soon proved its ability to **divest** her of these heavenly qualities. Under its influence, the tender heart became stone, and the lamb-like disposition gave way to one of tiger-like fierceness. The first step in her downward course was her ceasing to instruct me. She now commenced to practise her husband's precepts. She finally became more violent in her opposition than her husband himself.*

—Frederick Douglass, *The Narrative of the Life of Frederick Douglass, An American Slave*

Douglass also began attending Bible classes. After a while, his master became concerned about what he was learning in church. He sent him back to the plantation to work as a field slave. On the plantation, a white **supervisor** beat Douglass to teach him to fear whites. Risking his life, Douglass fought the supervisor. Douglass later said the event was a turning point in his life. He knew he had the courage to be free. Soon Douglass was trying to talk other slaves into running away. When the slave owners in the area learned of the plan, they demanded he be sold or sent elsewhere. He was sent back to Baltimore, where he was put to work on the ship docks.

In 1838, Douglass escaped to New York, where slavery was not permitted. He also changed his last name to escape those who were chasing him. He finally settled on Douglass as his new name. He chose it because Douglass was a character in a popular poem, "The Lady of the Lake" by Sir Walter Scott.

▶ Implication On the GED® test, you will have to identify information that is implied, or not directly stated. Information that is suggested is an **implication**. To understand implications, combine the information given with what you already know.

1. Why did the slave owners want Douglass sold or moved?

_____

_____

2. What does Douglass's choice for a new name tell you about him?

_____

_____

Spokesman and Writer

For three years Frederick Douglass worked at various odd jobs. He was proud to earn money and not have to give it to his master. He also married Anna Murray. It was during this time that he met William Lloyd Garrison, publisher of the antislavery newspaper *The Liberator.*

By 1841, Douglass was not just reading *The Liberator*. He also wrote articles for it. Garrison was very impressed with Douglass. He encouraged him to share his story so the world could hear just how horrible slavery was. His **dynamic** talents proved to the world what black people could accomplish if they were only given the chance.

In 1847, Douglass began his own abolitionist newspaper, *The North Star,* in Rochester, New York. Risking his life, he also helped runaway slaves. However, he was not just interested in helping black people. He became a spokesperson for women's rights as well.

End of Slavery

In 1865, the Civil War was over. Millions of slaves were freed from their masters. Opportunities for blacks slowly increased. In 1877, Douglass was named a United States marshal and in 1881 the recorder of deeds for the city of Washington, D.C. By the end of the decade, he was named ambassador to Haiti.

For the rest of his life, Douglass spoke and wrote about the evils of racism. On February 20, 1895, after attending a rally for women's rights, Douglass returned to his hotel room. While recalling the day's speeches, Douglass suddenly fell to the floor. The great man was dead of natural causes at age 77.

▶ Sequence of Events **Sequence** is the order in which events occur. Questions about sequence often contain time-order words like *when, next, after, before, first,* or *last.* To identify sequence in a passage, look for these words or dates or times.

1. When did Douglass begin his own newspaper?
   A. 1847
   B. 1841

2. Did Douglass die before or after the end of the Civil War?
   A. before
   B. after

Thinking About the Text

Practice Vocabulary

▶ The words below are in bold type in the passage. Study the way each word is used. Then match each word with its meaning.

_____	**1.** ignorant	A.	boss
_____	**2.** divest	B.	energetic
_____	**3.** supervisor	C.	rid, take away
_____	**4.** dynamic	D.	not educated

Understand What You Read

▶ Write the answer to each question.

5. Below are four events from Douglass's life. Put them in time order by placing a 1, 2, 3, or 4 next to each one.

_____ Douglass was sent back to Baltimore.

_____ Douglass started his own newspaper.

_____ Millions of slaves were freed from their masters.

_____ A white supervisor beat Douglass.

6. How did the author organize the details in the passage?

_____

_____

7. List two specific actions that Douglass took that involved him risking his life.

_____

_____

8. Which quote from the passage *best* expresses the author's positive view of Douglass as an important historical figure?

_____

_____

_____

Apply Your Skills

▶ **Circle the letter of the best answer for each question.**

9. The tone of this passage encourages the reader to

    A. be more sympathetic to the views of slave owners.

    B. view slavery as a horrible institution.

    C. question the significance of Frederick Douglass's contribution to civil rights.

    D. comprehend how quickly public opinion about racism changed after the Civil War.

10. Which statement is the main idea of the excerpt from *The Narrative of the Life of Frederick Douglass, An American Slave* (on page 88)?

    A. "When I went there, she was a pious, warm, and tender-hearted woman."

    B. "Slavery proved as injurious to her as it did to me."

    C. "Under its influence, the tender heart became stone, and the lamb-like disposition gave way to one of tiger-like fierceness."

    D. "She now commenced to practise her husband's precepts."

11. Which fact supports the idea that Douglass used his skills to protest slavery?

    A. In 1877, Douglass was named a United States marshal.

    B. In 1865, the Civil War ended.

    C. In 1847, Douglass started his own abolitionist newspaper.

    D. In the 1830s, Douglass worked on a ship dock.

12. Who was William Lloyd Garrison?

    A. the man who first owned Douglass when he was a slave

    B. a poet whom Douglass admired

    C. the publisher of *The Liberator*

    D. Douglass when he was born

Check your answers on pages 243–244.

INFORMATIONAL SOCIAL STUDIES

Vocabulary

ethics

rebellious

brink

heeded

Informational social studies texts are often packed with information in the form of words and images. While telling about the life of one particular person in history, a text may also introduce important events and ideas in history, identify other important historical figures, and explain and show geographical areas with maps. On the GED® test, you may be asked questions that require you to put all of this information together.

Thomas Paine: Bold Voice of Protest

Thomas Paine was born in England in 1737. When Paine was 13 years old, he dropped out of school and worked in his father's shop. Paine used any extra money to buy books about science, religion, and **ethics**— the proper treatment of self and others.

At age 19, Paine left England on a ship called the *Terrible*. A man known as Captain Death headed the crew. Paine's **rebellious** ideas may have begun during this time. While the ship was in port, his father begged him to reconsider life at sea. It was sound advice. Paine left the crew days before the ship was destroyed while attacking a French vessel.

Paine tried other jobs—a grocer, a teacher, and a tax collector. By 1772, his political ideas began to get him into trouble. He wrote a pamphlet urging other tax collectors, known as excise men, to band together and demand higher wages. Because of the pamphlet, Paine was fired as a tax collector. This experience left him with a bitter awareness of unequal and unfair treatment in society.

Paine later met Benjamin Franklin, who was visiting London. Franklin was impressed and called Paine an "ingenious, worthy young man." Franklin convinced Paine to come to America. In 1774, Paine left England.

▶ Cause and Effect On the GED® test, you will answer questions about cause-and-effect relationships. A **cause** is what makes something happen. An **effect** is what happens as the result of a cause. Test questions about causes often begin with *Why* or *What is the reason.* Test questions about effects begin with *What was the result of* or *What happened because of.*

1. What is the reason Paine was fired as a tax collector?

_____

2. What happened as a result of Franklin meeting Paine in England?

_____

Paine arrived in America when the colonists were on the **brink** of revolution. After the battles of Lexington and Concord in 1775, Paine spoke out for another great cause—independence. He declared his opposition to the British monarchy.

In January 1776, Paine published his famous pamphlet *Common Sense*. In less than 50 pages, Paine forcefully spelled out the American cause for liberty. He raised important issues such as: Why should a huge continent be tied to a little island thousands of miles away? Why should American colonists submit to laws that hurt their trade and industry? Why should the colonists show their loyalty to a king who oppresses them? Declaring independence from Great Britain, Paine argued, was the common-sense action to take.

Some writers have so confounded society with government, as to leave little or no distinction between them; whereas they are not only different, but have different origins. Society is produced by our wants, and government by wickedness; the former promotes our happiness positively by uniting our affections, the latter negatively by restraining our vices. The one encourages intercourse, the other creates distinctions. The first is a patron, the last a punisher.

—Thomas Paine, *Common Sense*

In April 1776, George Washington wrote, "I find *Common Sense* is working a powerful change in the minds of many men." Colonial leaders **heeded** the stirring call to break ties with Great Britain. On July 4, 1776, the Second Continental Congress adopted the Declaration of Independence.

▶ Restate/Summarize Remember that to **restate** information means to repeat it in your own words. A **summary** restates information in fewer words, including only the most important points.

1. Summarize in a sentence the most important point in the excerpt from Thomas Paine's *Common Sense*.

2. Restate George Washington's quote about *Common Sense*.

During the Revolutionary War, Paine joined the Continental Army. Between 1776 and 1783, he published 16 pamphlets titled *The American Crisis*. He used the top of a drum as a desk to write. His words lifted the soldiers' spirits.

George Washington ordered that his soldiers at Valley Forge hear Paine's first pamphlet read aloud. Discouraged soldiers felt a new sense of patriotism. John Adams later summed up the power of Paine's writing: "Washington's sword would have been wielded in vain had it not been supported by the pen of Thomas Paine."

Paine's pamphlets were wildly popular. Hundreds of thousands of copies were sold. At the end of the American Revolution, though, Paine was still poor. He had refused to accept any profits so that his works would be available to ordinary people.

Franklin once said, "Where liberty is, there is my country." Paine's version was, "Where liberty is not, there is mine. My country is the world." When the American Revolution was over, Paine looked to other nations to further the cause of liberty.

In 1787, Paine sailed for France and then returned to England. He became drawn into another political struggle—the French Revolution. In 1789, French peasants rebelled. Paine defended the French Revolution and attacked the British monarchy in a two-part book, *The Rights of Man* (1791–1792). As a result, Paine was tried for treason but escaped arrest by fleeing to France.

Thomas Paine's Travels

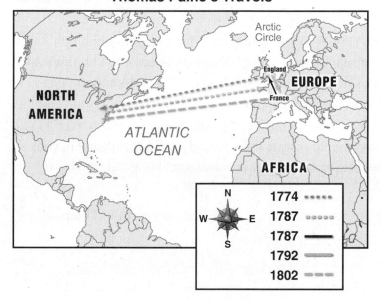

Paine returned to the United States in 1802, but he was no longer welcome there. Before his arrival, he had published two works that angered many Americans. In *The Age of Reason*, Paine expressed his extreme views on religion. This booklet was considered an attack on Christianity. Paine also had written an insulting letter to George Washington. Paine died in 1809 and was buried on his New York farm.

▶ Maps Maps usually show geographical regions. However, maps can also show political boundaries, historical changes in population or ideas, information about climate, routes traveled by people, or the distribution of resources. The GED® test includes questions about interpreting all kinds of maps.

1. What does this map show?

2. Where did Paine travel to and from in 1802?

Thinking About the Text

Practice Vocabulary

▶ **The words below are in bold type in the passage. Study the way each word is used. Then match each word with its meaning.**

_____ **1.** ethics   A.   proper treatment of self and others

_____ **2.** rebellious   B.   paid attention to

_____ **3.** brink   C.   resisting authority

_____ **4.** heeded   D.   edge

Understand What You Read

▶ **Write the answer to each question.**

5. The *Terrible* was a(n) _____ .

6. Why do you think Paine used the top of a drum as a desk during the American Revolutionary War?

_____

_____

7. Review the map on page 94. How many different trips are shown on the map?

_____

8. Summarize Thomas Paine's contribution to America's independence.

_____

_____

_____

Apply Your Skills

▶ **Circle the letter of the best answer for each question.**

9. Which of the following events happened last?

A.   Paine fought in the Revolutionary War.

B.   Paine wrote *The Age of Reason*.

C.   Paine met Benjamin Franklin.

D.   Paine published a pamphlet titled *Common Sense*.

10. Read these sentences from the passage.

> "While the ship was in port, his father begged him to reconsider life at sea. It was sound advice."

In which sentence does the word *sound* have the same meaning that it has in the sentence above?

A. Carlos and Donna heard an unusual sound coming from the gymnasium.

B. Carlos felt that Donna was a sound choice for student body president.

C. Carlos helped Donna guide the tiny rowboat into the calm waters of the sound.

D. Carlos and Donna asked the principal not to sound the alarm for a fire drill.

11. What was the main idea expressed in the pamphlet *Common Sense*?

A. The French people should overthrow their government.

B. Animals should be treated fairly.

C. The American colonies should be independent from Great Britain.

D. Tax collectors should be paid higher wages.

12. John Adams felt that Thomas Paine's writing was

A. inspiring.

B. useless.

C. confusing.

D. scientific.

13. Based on information in the passage, the reader can conclude that

A. few people understood the meaning of *Common Sense*.

B. Paine was famous during his lifetime.

C. nearly all Americans agreed with the views explained in *The Age of Reason*.

D. Paine wanted his native country, England, to win the Revolutionary War.

14. With which of the following statements would the author of this passage *most likely* agree?

A. Paine was eager to share his opinions with the world.

B. Paine was greedy and only cared about making money.

C. Paine was a good writer, but he lacked courage as a soldier.

D. Paine found it difficult to focus on one thing at a time.

HISTORICAL COURT CASES

Informational social studies texts may center on important or significant court cases that changed the law or the U.S. Constitution. When you read these types of social studies texts, you learn about the U.S. government, about how laws are made and changed, and about the people who were involved.

This passage is about a landmark court case that was decided in 1896.

Vocabulary

appealed

spurred

dissented

violation

Plessy v. Ferguson (1896)

In Plessy v. Ferguson, the U.S. Supreme Court ruled on the issue of equal rights for African Americans. In the ruling, the Supreme Court upheld state laws that segregated blacks and whites into separate facilities. The ruling supported discrimination against blacks that continued until the 1950s and 1960s.

The Facts of the Case

In 1890, Louisiana passed a law requiring that railroad passenger cars be segregated. Each train had to have a car for white passengers and a separate car for black ones, or separate sections in the same car.

The law angered African Americans in Louisiana. They decided to break the law deliberately to test its constitutionality in the courts. In 1892, Homer Plessy—who was part African American—entered a Louisiana train and sat in the car reserved for whites.

The conductor asked him to move to the car for blacks. Plessy refused. He was arrested, tried, and found guilty of breaking the state law.

Plessy **appealed** to the state supreme court. His lawyer argued that the state law violated his rights, under the Fourteenth Amendment to the Constitution, to enjoy all the privileges of being a citizen. The state supreme court denied his claim and upheld the trial verdict. Plessy then appealed to the U.S. Supreme Court.

▶ Photographs Think about how the photograph supports the text.

1. What does the photograph that accompanies the passage show?

   _____

2. How does the photograph help you better understand the passage?

   _____

Check your answers on page 244.

Events Surrounding the Case

The case came in the midst of a movement throughout the South to undo the gains that African Americans made after the Civil War. The Thirteenth Amendment, ratified in 1865, had banned slavery. The Fourteenth Amendment, from 1868, had declared that African Americans were citizens. It said that no state could deny any person "the equal protection of the laws."

Soon, though, white Southerners began to pass laws that stripped African Americans of their rights. The U.S. Supreme Court made several decisions in the 1870s and 1880s that supported these Southern laws.

Congress was angered by these decisions. It passed the Civil Rights Act of 1875. This law stated that "all persons within the jurisdiction of the United States shall be entitled to the full and equal enjoyment . . . of inns, public conveyances on land and water," and other public accommodations.

The Supreme Court struck this law down in 1883 as unconstitutional. It said that Congress went beyond the Fourteenth Amendment because the new law would apply to private businesses. The Fourteenth Amendment, the Supreme Court said, was meant to apply only to state actions.

These decisions **spurred** Southern legislatures to further limit African Americans' rights. The 1890 Louisiana law calling for segregated railroad cars was one example of many such laws.

▶ Sequence of Events Recall that **sequence** is the order in which events occur. Sometimes, a text will begin at the occurrence of one event and then go back in time to explain other events that led up to that particular event. It can be a challenge to keep track of the exact sequence. Pay attention to dates and look for time-order words, such as *before, after, next,* or *later.*

1. Was the Fourteenth Amendment passed before or after the Plessy v. Ferguson court case?
   A. before
   B. after

2. Did Louisiana establish a law for segregated railroad cars before or after the Supreme Court struck down the Civil Rights Act of 1875?
   A. before
   B. after

The U.S. Supreme Court's Decision

The U.S. Supreme Court decided, on an eight to one vote, against Plessy. The majority opinion was written by Henry Billings Brown. It agreed that the Fourteenth Amendment was the key to the case. The opinion stated that if the facilities for blacks were inferior to those for whites, then the law would be unconstitutional. But the Supreme Court said this was not the case.

The issue, Brown said, was whether the law was reasonable. He concluded that it was. The opinion went on to say that if the law was seen as a mark of discrimination against blacks, it was only because they felt it that way, not because it was intended to be so. Only one justice **dissented** from the majority view. That was John Marshall Harlan of Kentucky. He had once owned slaves. In the Louisiana law, Harlan saw a clear **violation** of the Fourteenth Amendment. He wrote:

> The fundamental objection . . . to the statute is that it interferes with the personal freedom of citizens. . . . Our constitution is color-blind, and neither knows nor tolerates classes among citizens. In respect of civil rights, all citizens are equal before the law. The humblest is the peer of the most powerful. The law regards man as man, and takes no account of his surroundings, or of his color when his civil rights as guaranteed by the supreme law of the land are involved. . . . The thin disguise of 'equal' accommodations for passengers in railroad coaches will not mislead any one, nor atone for the wrong this day done.

The Impact of the Decision

Harlan's dissent was eloquent but ignored. The case supported states' ability to limit the rights of blacks. States across the country passed "Jim Crow" laws that called for segregated restaurants, hotels, and other public facilities. Not until the mid-1900s, when the National Association for the Advancement of Colored People (NAACP) began to challenge these laws, did the federal courts begin to chip away at segregation.

▶ Cause and Effect On the GED® test you will answer questions about cause-and-effect relationships. Recall that a **cause** is what makes something happen. An **effect** is what happens as the result of a cause. When you read about laws and court cases, there may be many causes and effects.

1. What reason did Brown give for the Supreme Court's ruling in Plessy v. Ferguson?

_____

_____

2. What was an effect of the ruling?

_____

Check your answers on page 245.

Thinking About the Text

Practice Vocabulary

▶ **The words below are in bold type in the passage. Study the way each word is used. Then match each word with its meaning.**

_____ **1.** appealed   A.   disregard

_____ **2.** spurred   B.   disagreed

_____ **3.** dissented   C.   incited action or growth

_____ **4.** violation   D.   to have a case reviewed

Understand What You Read

▶ **Write the answer to each question.**

5. Why did the author include the detail that John Marshall Harlan had once owned slaves?

_____

6. What context clue from the passage tells you the meaning of the word _segregated_?

_____

7. In the passage, what does "public conveyances" refer to?

_____

8. What caused Congress to pass the Civil Rights Act of 1875?

_____

Apply Your Skills

▶ **Circle the letter of the best answer for each question.**

9. Why was the Fourteenth Amendment important to African Americans?

A.   It banned slavery in all the states.

B.   It defined citizenship and protected their rights as citizens.

C.   It upheld that separate but equal accommodations were legal.

D.   It declared that several previous amendments were unconstitutional.

10. Which of the following events happened last?

   A. the arrest of Homer Plessy

   B. the passing of laws in Louisiana requiring railroad cars be segregated

   C. the passing of the Civil Rights Act of 1875

   D. the ratification of the Thirteenth Amendment

11. Read the sentence.

> "The thin disguise of 'equal' accommodations for passengers in railroad coaches will not mislead any one, nor atone for the wrong this day done."

What is another word for *atone*?

   A. hide

   B. follow

   C. make up for

   D. help understand

12. How does the author contrast John Marshall Harlan with the other justices of the Supreme Court?

   A. by describing the things Harlan had in common with Henry Billings Brown

   B. by explaining why Harlan disagreed with the other justices

   C. by showing how Harlan's views were ignored in every case

   D. by illustrating that Harlan was a talented writer

13. What was the main idea of the majority opinion that was written by Henry Billings Brown?

   A. Blacks and whites could be forced to use separate facilities as long as those separate facilities were equal to each other.

   B. A state government did not have the right to pass laws that only applied to citizens living in or passing through that particular state.

   C. Private businesses had to allow blacks and whites to work side by side in jobs that provided goods or services to the general public.

   D. The federal government can determine laws, but it cannot determine the customs, traditions, or social behavior for any group.

BROCHURES & ADVERTISEMENTS

Vocabulary

hypnotized

antibiotics

symptoms

allergic

enhanced

clarity

Brochures & Advertisements are designed to persuade people to accept certain ideas or to buy certain products. Should you believe everything you read in an advertisement or brochure? Certainly not. However, if you read carefully and use common sense, advertisements and brochures can be good sources of information.

A school might provide this brochure to help parents improve their parenting skills. As you read, try to figure out the main idea of the brochure.

Too Much Television and Your Child's Ability to Learn

Television shortens a child's attention span.

Have you watched television with your child recently? If you have, you know that children's television shows are filled with visual images that usually last two or three seconds. Loud music, explosions, and other sound effects grab your child's attention. Many children seem **hypnotized** by the bright colors and quick cuts.

The stories themselves are broken up into short segments separated by commercials. Children who watch a lot of television lose the ability to concentrate for long periods of time. In school, they may have difficulty listening to the teacher read a simple story from start to finish.

Television weakens a child's language skills.

Try this experiment. Spend 15 minutes just listening to the dialogue in a children's television show. What do you hear? When you take out the visual images, sound effects, and music, you will find that the characters speak in short phrases and incomplete sentences. To learn language, children need to hear language with a rich vocabulary and clear sentence structure. They also need to be able to ask and answer questions. Children's television shows usually don't provide these important requirements for learning language.

Television weakens a child's reading skills.

In a way, watching television is the opposite of reading. Reading a good book requires a long attention span, a good vocabulary, and the ability to understand complex sentences. Reading encourages children to ask questions and use their imagination. Television attempts to do all the imagining for the viewer. If children spend too much time watching television, they may lose the ability to make a written story come to life in their minds.

▶ Finding the Main Idea The **main idea** in a brochure is the most important idea. Often the brochure's title and section headings suggest the main idea. Which statement *best* expresses the main idea of the brochure?

    A. Watching too much television may make it difficult for a child to learn.

    B. Watching too much television may cause a child to forget how to read.

Brochures are often used to educate the public. You have probably seen health-care brochures like the one below at a pharmacy or in your doctor's office.

Facts About Antibiotics

Have you ever taken **antibiotics** for an earache? After a few doses, your ear probably stopped hurting. After a few more doses, you may have felt completely cured. Perhaps you stopped taking the medicine, thinking that you could save the rest for another illness. Although this decision seems to make sense, doctors tell us that it could ruin our health.

Antibiotics are prescribed to fight infections. Sore throats, earaches, and other **symptoms** may be caused by the growth of bacteria in your body. As the antibiotics fight to destroy the bacteria, the bacteria struggle to become stronger. When you do not take all your medication, the bacteria may not be completely destroyed. In a short time, the infection may return, much stronger than before.

Always follow your doctor's instructions. Ask your doctor or pharmacist about the purpose of your medication. Find out exactly what you must do for the treatment to work. Antibiotics can help you only when you take them at the right time and in the right amounts.

Follow these tips:

- Take all the prescribed doses even after you begin to feel better.

- Take the medicine at the same time each day. Make a schedule. If you forget a dose, take it as soon as you remember. Then get back on schedule.

- Follow special instructions. Some antibiotics must be taken with food or milk. Others must be taken on an empty stomach.

- Find out what other medications, foods, or drinks to avoid while taking your prescription.

- Some people may be **allergic** to certain antibiotics. Ask your doctor or pharmacist what side effects to look for. Notify your doctor immediately if you get a rash or have difficulty breathing.

▶ Locating Factual Details The details in a brochure support the main idea or purpose of the brochure. Details are facts about the subject. **Factual details** answer questions about who, what, when, where, why, and how. The brochure on this page gives details about why it is important to follow instructions carefully when taking antibiotics.

1. Reread the second paragraph. Why should you take all the medicine your doctor prescribed even after you feel better?
   A. Antibiotics can kill the bacteria that cause sore throats and earaches.
   B. The bacteria may not all be destroyed if you don't take all your medicine.

2. Reread the list of tips. What should you do if you forget to take a dose of medicine?
   A. Take two doses of medicine next time.
   B. Take it as soon as you remember.

Advertisements are everywhere. You see them on billboards, in newspapers, on the Internet, at sports arenas, at bus stops, and even on the buses. You have probably seen advertisements like the one below in magazines. As you read it, think about how the author tries to persuade you to buy the product.

Don't You Deserve the Best Technology Money Can Buy?

Introducing the Award-Winning Enhanced WAVE-AUDIO Player from MicroTech!

It's Unlike Anything You'd Expect From a CD/MP3 Player. It's Exactly What You'd Expect From MicroTech.

It's finally arrived: the new **Enhanced WAVE-AUDIO** Player from MicroTech. When it's high-quality sound that counts, you can count on MicroTech. You told us that you wanted clear high tones and deep, warm bass tones—all in an elegant, slim, space-age design. We took your suggestions to our Sound Laboratory and produced the Enhanced WAVE-AUDIO Player. The compact CD/MP3 player takes up only 18 by 22 inches of table space, yet its sound can fill a concert hall.

With our unique C400 audio engine, you'll never want to listen to music on any other player again. Be the first among your friends to own the player that *Music World* called the "Invention of the Year."

Experience the Enhanced WAVE-AUDIO Player at your local dealer or visit us today at www.microtech.com. We know you'll be delighted with the **clarity** of sound never before possible from a small player.

▶ **Understanding Persuasive Techniques** An advertisement is a type of persuasive writing. In persuasive writing, authors often use **persuasive techniques,** such as strong emotional words, to convince you to accept a certain point of view. Read advertisements carefully to separate facts from emotional claims about the product.

1. Which two phrases try to appeal to the reader's emotions?
   A. Don't you deserve the best?
   B. Be the first among your friends to own one.
   C. Our compact design takes up very little space.

2. Which of these claims is probably true?
   A. Music World called this player the "Invention of the Year."
   B. You'll never want to listen to music on any other player again.

Thinking About the Texts

Practice Vocabulary

▶ The words below are in bold type in the passages. Study the way each word is used. Then complete each sentence by writing the correct word.

hypnotized	antibiotics	symptoms
allergic	enhanced	clarity

1. After sneezing several times, your friend decides that she may be

    _____ to cats.

2. The new, improved laundry detergent has _____ cleaning power.

3. The patient's _____ are a fever and a sore throat.

4. With my new glasses, I could see with greater _____ .

5. The crowd seemed _____ by the flashing lights of the police cars.

6. Medicines that fight infections are called _____ .

Understand What You Read

▶ Write the answer to each question.

7. Look at the brochure on page 102. What are two reasons to limit the amount of time a child watches television?

    _____

8. What will you hear when you listen to the dialogue in a children's television show?

    _____

9. Look at the brochure on page 103. How do antibiotics get rid of some sore throats and earaches?

    _____

10. Look at the advertisement on page 104. What are two claims made about the CD/MP3 player in the advertisement?

    _____

Apply Your Skills

▶ **Circle the letter of the best answer for each question.**

11. Look at the brochure on page 102. Which statement *best* expresses the main idea of the third paragraph?

    A.   Watching television may weaken a child's language skills.

    B.   Children often speak in short phrases and incomplete sentences.

    C.   Television encourages children to use their imaginations.

    D.   Children who watch television usually have long attention spans.

12. Look at the brochure on page 103. Based on the list of tips, which of these statements about antibiotics is true?

    A.   You should never take antibiotics with milk.

    B.   You should stop taking antibiotics once your sore throat is better.

    C.   If you get well quickly, always throw away any pills that are left.

    D.   For antibiotics to work well, you need to take them on a schedule.

13. Look at the advertisement on page 104. Which of these persuasive phrases from the ad includes a fact about the CD/MP3 player?

    A.   Don't you deserve the best technology money can buy?

    B.   It's unlike anything you'd expect from a player.

    C.   When it's high-quality sound that counts, you can count on MicroTech.

    D.   The compact CD/MP3 player takes up only 18 by 22 inches of table space, yet its sound can fill a concert hall.

Connect with the Texts

▶ **Write your answer to each question.**

14. Think of a product such as clothing, shampoo, or car wax that you have bought based on information you read or heard in an advertisement. How did the advertisement convince you to try the product? Do you think the claims made in the advertisement were true? Why or why not?

_____

_____

15. Do you think that watching a lot of television is bad for adults? Why or why not?

_____

_____

LESSON 24

FORMS & DOCUMENTS

Vocabulary

specify

references

authorize

certify

constitute

introductory

Forms provide a way to gather and organize information. You use many different kinds of forms as an employee, a citizen, and a consumer.

Documents are designed to communicate official or legal information. If you read and sign a document, you are agreeing to the terms in the document. Always read documents carefully before you sign them.

When you apply for a job, you usually have to fill out an employment application. Whether you are asked to fill out an online application or a printed application, the information provided on the application makes it easier for people to learn about your skills and make hiring decisions.

Employment Application

Section 1: General Information Use black ink. Be accurate and complete.

Name (First) (Middle) (Last)	Social Security #	Date

Address (Street, City, State, Zip)	Home Telephone #	Cell Phone #

Are you at least 18 years of age? Yes ☐ No ☐ If no, do you have a work permit? Yes ☐ No ☐	Do you have proof of U.S. citizenship or a U.S. permanent resident visa? Yes ☐ No ☐

Position Desired	Check One: Full-time ☐ Part-time ☐ Short term ☐ Other ☐

Available for Work: Any hour ☐ Any day ☐ Other ☐ Please **specify:**

Section 2: Work Experience List your previous employment in order. Start with your most recent employer first. Write additional work experience on a separate page.

Dates From	To	Name and Address of Employer	Job Title	Wage or Salary	Reason for Leaving
		Company: Address: Supervisor:			
		Company: Address: Supervisor:			

Section 3: References List two **references**. Do not include relatives, persons employed by this company, or previous employers.

Name	Telephone #	Occupation
Name	Telephone #	Occupation

▶ **Understanding Organization** To fill out any form, you need to understand its **organization.** Most forms are divided into sections. Each section has its own subject or purpose. Look for headings and instructions. Use the lines or boxes that separate sections to understand how a form is organized.

Read the headings and instructions for Sections 2 and 3. In which section would you list a former teacher?

    A.   Section 2: Work Experience

    B.   Section 3: References

Check your answer on page 246.

If you have health or dental insurance, you may have to fill out claim forms. Your employer often provides these forms to you. Always read insurance forms carefully. Your claim may not be paid if the form is filled out incorrectly.

Group Dental Claim Form

Instructions to the Employee

1. Please type or print clearly using black ink.
2. Please answer questions in boxes 1 through 12 completely.
3. Sign and date the "Authorization to Release Information" on Line 13.
4. If you wish to have your benefits paid directly to the dentist, sign and date Line 14.
5. Sign and date the certification statement on Line 15.
6. Attach this form to your dental bill and mail to Dental Health, Inc.

1. Patient Name	2. Relationship to Employee Self ☐ Spouse ☐ Child ☐ Other ☐	3. Sex M ☐ F ☐	4. Patient Birthdate (m/d/y)
5. Employee Name (First, Middle, Last)		6. Employee Social Security #	7. Employee Birthdate (m/d/y)

8. Employee Address (Street Address, City, State, Zip)

9. Account / Policy #	10. Employer's Name and Address

11. Is patient covered by another dental plan? Yes ☐ No ☐	12. If yes, please indicate: Dental Plan Name: Group #:

13. *Authorization to Release Information* – I hereby **authorize** the release of any information about my dental history or this treatment to the Insurer for the purpose of determining the benefits payable.	Signature of Patient or Parent	Date
14. *Authorization to Pay Benefits to Dentist* – I hereby authorize payment of benefits directly to my dentist.	Signature of Employee	Date
15. *Certification* – I **certify** the information I have provided is true and correct.	Signature of Employee	Date

▶ **Understanding Directions** Always read the **directions** before filling out a form. The directions may be written at the top or the bottom of the form or even on the back of the page. When directions refer to a specific line or box, find that place on the form and think about what information you will put there.

Some directions are contained within the form. Box 5 on this form asks for the employee's name. The instructions in parentheses tell how to write the name. Some instructions use abbreviations. In box 3 the letter *M* stands for *male* and *F* stands for *female*. In box 4 the letters *m/d/y* stand for *month, day,* and *year.*

1. Look at box 4. What date do you write?
  A. today's date   B. the patient's date of birth

2. Review the instructions at the top. Should every patient sign lines 13, 14, and 15?
  A. Yes
  B. No

Credit card companies send all kinds of offers through the mail. Once you accept an offer, the company will send you a legal document that tells exactly what your responsibilities are to the credit card company. Read these documents carefully before you sign them. Make sure that you understand what you are agreeing to do.

CREDIT CARD AGREEMENT: I understand that the use of the enclosed credit card will **constitute** my acceptance of the terms and conditions listed below.
TERMS AND CONDITIONS

A. Annual Percentage Rate

With a balance transfer from another credit card account: I agree to pay a 5.9% **introductory** rate for purchases and balance transfers for the first six months the account is open; after that, a 12.9% rate on purchases and balance transfers applies.

Without an initial balance transfer: I agree to pay a fixed 12.9% rate for purchases and balance transfers; the rate for cash advances is 19.9%.

B. Late Payments

If payment is received late once during the introductory period, the rate will adjust to 12.9% on purchases and balance transfers. If payment is received late twice within any six-month period, a 19.9% annual rate will immediately take effect.

C. Grace Period

Provided your previous balance was paid in full, you have a grace period of 20 to 25 days from the date of the statement to pay any balance arising from purchases. If the payment is made within the grace period, no interest will be charged.

D. Annual Fee

None.

E. Transaction Fee for Cash Advances

If you use your card to borrow cash, you will be charged a fee of 3% of the amount of each cash advance, but not less than $5 or more than $45.

▶ **Using Context Clues to Understand Meaning** Documents often contain unfamiliar terms. When you come across an unfamiliar word, first look at the words and phrases around it. These surrounding words are the **context clues,** and they can help you figure out the meaning of the unfamiliar word.

1. Reread section C. Based on the context clues, what is the meaning of the term *grace period*?
   A. a period of time in which the customer will not be charged interest
   B. a period of time in which the customer will pay a lower rate of interest

2. Reread section A. Based on context clues, what is a "balance transfer"?
   A. switching an amount of money owed to one credit card over to another
   B. changing the amount of interest owed after the introductory period ends

Thinking About the Texts

Practice Vocabulary

▶ The words below are in bold type in the passages. Study the way each word is used. Then complete each sentence by writing the correct word.

authorize	certify	constitute
introductory	references	specify

1. Breaking a rule of the club will _____ an end to your membership.

2. When she applied for the job, Pat listed two friends

   as _____ .

3. A customer complained that there was an incorrect amount on her bill.

   Please ask her to _____ which amount is incorrect.

4. After you receive your new credit card, you will have a three-month

   _____ period when you will not pay any interest.

5. You can _____ a money transfer over the telephone by giving your account number and security code.

6. Maria signed the job application form to _____ that the information in the form was true.

Understand What You Read

▶ Write the answer to each question.

7. Read Section 1 of the Employment Application on page 107. Who would need to answer the question "Do you have a work permit?"

   _____

8. Look at the form on page 108. What is the purpose of box 2?

   _____

9. Why does box 13 in the Group Dental Claim Form require a signature?

   _____

10. Read section B of the Credit Card Agreement on page 109. What will cause the cardholder's interest rate to increase to 19.9%?

    _____

Apply Your Skills

▷ **Circle the letter of the best answer for each question.**

11. Look at the Employment Application form on page 107. Which of the following types of information would you include in Section 2?

    A.   whether you are seeking full- or part-time work

    B.   the occupation of one of your references

    C.   how much money you made at your last job

    D.   whether you have a work permit

12. Look at the Group Dental Claim Form on page 108. According to the instructions, what should an employee do in order to tell the insurance company to send payment directly to the dentist?

    A.   The employee should fill out boxes 1 through 4.

    B.   The employee should sign and date line 14.

    C.   The employee should check "Yes" in box 11.

    D.   The employee should attach the form to the dental bill.

13. Look at section E in the Credit Card Agreement on page 109. Which provides a context clue for the meaning of the term *cash advance*?

    A.   you will be charged a fee

    B.   for the first six months the account is open

    C.   if the payment is made within the grace period

    D.   if you use your card to borrow cash

Connect with the Texts

▷ **Write your answer to each question.**

14. Suppose you have a friend who is beginning a job search. What advice could you give about filling out employment applications?

15. Do you believe that companies should try harder to write documents in everyday language? Explain.

MANUALS & HANDBOOKS

Vocabulary

probationary

reinstated

eligible

malfunction

affix

contaminated

Manuals & Handbooks are usually not read from cover to cover. Instead, they are used to find specific information. To find out your company's dress code, you would look in the employee handbook for that particular topic. To find out how to set the clock on your microwave oven, you would consult the owner's manual for that particular procedure.

Most workplaces have an employee handbook to explain the company's personnel policies. Employees are usually given a copy of the handbook when they begin work.

Personnel Policies

Probationary Period

Your first six months of employment are a **probationary** period. During this time, your supervisor works closely with you to help you learn your duties. After six months, your supervisor will give you a written evaluation. If your work is satisfactory for this six-month period, you become a permanent employee with healthcare and retirement benefits.

Healthcare Benefits

As a permanent employee, you are entitled to sign up for a medical and dental healthcare plan. Your supervisor will give you a booklet explaining the various group insurance plans available to permanent employees. Please select a healthcare plan and go to the Human Resources Office, Room 201, to fill out the necessary paperwork.

Types of Leave

1. Sick Leave: Each full-time permanent employee earns eight hours of sick leave per month. For part-time employees, sick leave is based on the number of regular hours you are assigned to work. You may use sick leave for any illness, for pregnancy, or for visits to a doctor or dentist. You may also use sick leave when there is illness in your immediate family (parent, brother, sister, husband, wife, or child).

2. Maternity Leave: You may be granted maternity leave if you plan to return to work as soon as your doctor permits. By law, if you return to work within four months of the start of your leave, you must be **reinstated** in the position you held before the leave.

3. Family Leave: After one year of employment, you are **eligible** for family leave to handle urgent family matters. Family leave is limited to four months during a twenty-four-month period.

4. Vacation Leave: Full-time employees receive ten hours of vacation leave for each month worked with a maximum of 15 days per year. Part-time vacation leave is based upon the average number of hours worked per month. Vacation leave must be cleared with your supervisor.

▶ Using Heads and Subheads A **head** is the title of a section. It states the main idea of the section. **Subheads** break the main section into smaller parts.

1. Which of these is a kind of leave described in this employee handbook?
   A. Family Leave   B. Unpaid Leave

2. Which heading would you look under to find out more about your dental benefits?
   A. Sick Leave   B. Healthcare Benefits

Most electronic equipment comes with a manual. The manual provides operating instructions and explains safety guidelines.

Manual for Using Your New DVD Player

Thank you for purchasing this PARKER ELECTRONICS product. Please read these directions thoroughly in order to operate your DVD player properly. After you have finished reading the instructions, save them for future reference.

Inserting the Batteries into the Remote Control

While pressing the back cover, pull out in the direction indicated by the arrow and insert PR6 dry cell batteries. Make sure to match the plus (+) and minus (–) signs on the batteries with the plus and minus signs inside the battery compartment.

Handling the Discs

- Never play a scratched or warped disc. This may damage the player or cause it to **malfunction.** Also, do not **affix** paper or seals to the disc.
- Store the discs carefully. If you store discs stacked on top of each other, discs may become warped even when in their cases.
- Fingerprints on the disc may affect picture quality. To remove dirt or fingerprints, wipe gently from the center of the disc toward the outer edges. Never wipe discs with a circular motion.

Operating the DVD Player

Press the START button for the disc table to come out. Then, load the disc with the label side facing up, using the disc table guide to align the disc. Press START again to close the disc table. Play will begin automatically.

▶ Skimming and Scanning to Find Information **Skimming** means to look over the text to determine the main idea. **Scanning** means to look quickly through the text for specific details, such as numbers, dates, amounts, and important words. Manuals & Handbooks are usually divided into sections or chapters. Each of these sections has a title. If you know the information you want to find in a manual or handbook, you can scan it for the title of the section you need.

1. According to this manual, what size batteries are needed for the remote control?
   A. PR6
   B. D-cell

2. According to this manual, what is the proper way to remove fingerprints from a DVD disk?
   A. Wipe the disk with a circular motion.
   B. Wipe the disk from the center to the outer edges.

Every job site, even an office, has safety procedures to help employees handle emergency situations. Safety procedures may be posted on bulletin boards or kept in special notebooks for employee use. The safety procedures below might be found in a handbook of emergency procedures for a healthcare facility, a community center, or a school office.

CLEANUP OF SPILLS RELATED TO ILLNESS AND INJURY

Goal: To prevent the spread of disease in the workplace.

General Information: Special handling and cleanup procedures are required for fluids that may contain blood or blood products. After contact with blood or other dangerous material, trained personnel must clean all equipment and work surfaces.

Use the following cleaning procedures:

Step 1: Put on appropriate protective clothing and equipment, including vinyl gloves, filter mask and/or face shield, and plastic apron or disposable coveralls.

Step 2: Wipe up any fluids with paper towels and dispose of them in a red trash bag with the biohazard warning symbol (shown here to the right).

Step 3: Clean all **contaminated** areas and materials first with soap and water.

Step 4: Follow with a freshly made bleach solution (1 part bleach to 9 parts cold water).

Step 5: Allow the bleach solution to remain on the contaminated surface for 5 to 10 minutes. Then rinse the area thoroughly with water to prevent damage to the surface from the bleach.

Note: If the spill occurs outside, use a hose with the water turned on at full force to wash down the area completely.

Step 6: If mops, brooms, dustpans, or other equipment have been used in the cleanup, rinse these items with the bleach solution.

For more information, call the Environmental Health and Safety Department.

▶ **Follow a Sequence of Steps** A procedure is a way to do something. Most procedures have a series of steps that must be done to reach a desired outcome. Usually, the steps must be done in a specific order, or **sequence**. When you read a procedure, make sure you understand the sequence of steps. Some steps may contain one or more related tasks. As you read, picture yourself performing each action. Try to understand why the sequence is the way it is.

1. Which statement describes the correct sequence of steps for cleaning up a spill related to illness or injury?
   A. After wiping the contaminated surface with paper towels, put on protective clothing.
   B. After putting on protective clothing, wipe the contaminated surface with paper towels.

2. When should you use the bleach solution?
   A. before cleaning the area with soap and water
   B. after cleaning the area with soap and water

Thinking About the Texts

Practice Vocabulary

▶ The words below are in bold type in the passages. Study the way each word is used. Then complete each sentence by writing the correct word.

contaminated	eligible	malfunction
probationary	reinstated	affix

1. When an MP3 player won't charge properly, there is a

   _____ in the battery mechanism.

2. The new employee's work during the _____
   period was good.

3. Before you mail a letter, you must _____ a stamp
   to the envelope or the post office will not deliver it.

4. Bacteria in raw chicken _____ surfaces in
   the kitchen.

5. After two years, you will be _____ for our
   retirement plan.

6. After taking time off to care for his elderly father, Kyle was

   _____ to his former work assignment.

Understand What You Read

▶ Write the answer to each question.

7. Look at the Personnel Policies on page 112. After six months, how will a
   supervisor give a new employee feedback?

   _____

8. According to the Personnel Policies, when can an employee use
   sick leave?

   _____

   _____

9. Look at the DVD manual on page 113. What is the reason given to explain
   why DVD discs should not be stored stacked on top of each other?

   _____

Apply Your Skills

▶ **Circle the letter of the best answer for each question.**

10. Look at the Personnel Policies on page 112. Your friend needs to help her mother move to a nursing home. She wants to find out how much time she can take off work without losing her job. Which heading would you tell your friend to look under to find the information she needs?

    A. Probationary Period

    B. Healthcare Benefits

    C. Maternity Leave

    D. Family Leave

11. Scan the DVD manual on page 113. What is the proper way to insert the batteries into the remote control?

    A. Make sure that both batteries' plus and minus signs face the same direction.

    B. Make sure the batteries' plus signs face in opposite directions.

    C. Line up the plus and minus signs on the batteries and battery compartment.

    D. Make sure the batteries' dry cells face the same direction.

12. Look at the safety procedures on page 114. A young child at a day care center cuts her lip. She gets a small amount of blood on a table. After the day care worker puts on gloves and wipes the table with paper towels, what should he do next?

    A. clean the table with soap and water

    B. take the table outside and wash it with a garden hose

    C. make a fresh bleach solution

    D. dispose of the paper towels in a red trash bag

Connect with the Texts

▶ **Write your answer to each question.**

13. Suppose you are starting a new job. Your supervisor gives you a 100-page employee handbook. Should you read the entire handbook? Explain.

_____

_____

14. If you were writing the perfect instruction manual, what features (such as drawings or steps) would you include?

_____

_____

LEGAL DOCUMENTS

Vocabulary

summoned

exempt

retained

incur

prospective

liability

Legal documents spell out exact agreements between people. They carefully detail what each person, or party, is obligated to do. Because these documents legally require you to do certain things, it is very important that you read them carefully before you sign them. Examples of common legal documents include car loans, bank mortgages, and work contracts.

Many people receive an official document informing them that they must appear for jury service. This document, called a jury summons, usually arrives in the mail to a registered voter.

Jury Summons

You are hereby notified that you have been **summoned** for jury service in the trial courts of Any County, Any State. You must report to the Courthouse in Any Town on October 18, 2014, at 9:00 a.m. *Unless you are notified by the court that you are not required to appear, you are subject to being held in contempt of court and being fined up to five hundred dollars ($500.00) plus court costs if you fail to appear.*

Jury Service Information Sheet

Congratulations on being selected for jury service in Any County! Your service is essential to the administration of justice, and your participation is greatly appreciated by the judges, attorneys, and parties.

Length of Service: Your term is 5 days in length. You will not be required to be at the courthouse each day but will merely call a recording each day at 8:00 a.m. to see if you are needed.

Compensation by Court: Juror will receive $40 for each day's attendance.

Exempt from Service: A juror will only be **exempt** from service if serving will cause an undue or extreme physical or financial hardship. A juror may be excused from jury service if the juror has a mental or physical condition that causes him/her to be incapable of performing jury service, or if the juror would:

(1) be required to abandon a person under such juror's personal care or supervision due to the impossibility of obtaining an appropriate substitute caregiver during the period of participation in the jury pool or on the jury;

(2) **incur** costs that would have a substantial adverse impact on the payment of the juror's necessary daily living expenses or on those for whom such juror provides the principle means of support;

(3) suffer physical hardship that would result in illness or disease; or

(4) be deprived of compensation due to the fact that the prospective juror is employed by an employer who is not required to compensate jurors and declines to do so voluntarily.

▶ Using Context Clues Remember that **context clues** can help you figure out the meaning of unfamiliar words. In the "Exempt from Service" section, which of the following provides a clue to the meaning of the word *exempt*?

    A. hardship

    B. excused from

People who buy new cars often trade in their used cars. Read the following section of a legal document that explains the agreement between the seller (the auto dealer) and the person who trades in a used car (the new car buyer).

New Car Buyer Agreement for Trade-in of Used Car

The value of the trade-in car listed on the first page of this document is based on the National Auto Dealers Association's *Used Car Guide* or any guide approved by the Commissioner of Motor Vehicles. This value may be further adjusted for mileage, improvements, or any major mechanical defects.

I agree to the following terms:

Trade-in Credit May Change. I agree that at the time the trade-in vehicle is delivered to the seller, should the value of my trade-in be diminished as a result of physical damage, alteration, or deterioration in mechanical condition other than normal wear and tear, the seller has the right to reappraise the vehicle. As a result of this reappraisal, I understand that the trade-in amount on my vehicle may be reduced.

Trade-in: Buyer's Obligations. At the time of delivery, I promise to sign a Bill of Sale and a mileage certification statement and to provide proof of ownership. I guarantee that I owe no money for the vehicle or for repairs to the vehicle, that emission control devices have not been altered, and that nothing has been removed, including the seat belts.

Buyer's Refusal to Purchase. I understand that the cash deposit I have given to the seller can be **retained** to offset seller damages if I refuse to complete my purchase. I also understand that I may be responsible for any damages the seller may **incur** if I fail to perform my obligations under the terms of this agreement.

▶ Summarizing To **summarize** means to put information together into one overall idea. To help you understand a legal document, it is often helpful to summarize each paragraph as you read it.

1. Which of the following summarizes the main idea of the first paragraph?
    A. The value of the car is based on the mileage and any defects or improvements.
    B. The value of the car is based on a used car guide and other factors.

2. Which of the following is a summary of the section titled "Trade-in: Buyer's Obligations"?
    A. The buyer promises to provide proof of ownership and to take care of outstanding problems with the car.
    B. The buyer promises to provide proof of ownership and pledges that nothing has been removed or altered.

An apartment lease includes all of the information a renter needs to understand the legal agreement with the landlord. Read the following apartment lease.

Apartment Lease

This lease is in effect for one year from the date indicated on this lease. Tenant is responsible for payment of rent for the entire year and may not sublet. If Tenant must leave prior to the end of the lease period, Landlord must receive two months' notification.

Rent is due the first of every month and no later than the fifth day of the month. If the fifth day is a weekend or holiday, rent is due the following business day. Tenant is responsible for all utility payments including gas, electricity, and phone. Tenant is not responsible for shoveling snow or any work needed on the exterior of the building.

SECURITY DEPOSIT. Tenant shall pay to Landlord a security deposit of one month's rent to be held and disbursed for Tenant damages to the Premises or other defaults under this Agreement (if any) as provided by law. The security deposit will be deposited into an escrow account until the final day of the lease.

ACCESS BY LANDLORD TO PREMISES. Subject to Tenant's consent (which shall not be unreasonably withheld), Landlord has the right to enter the Premises to make inspections, provide necessary services, or show the unit to **prospective** buyers or workers. Landlord does not assume **liability** for the care of the Premises. In the case of an emergency, Landlord may enter without Tenant's consent. During the last three months of this lease, Landlord may show the Premises to prospective tenants but may not make more than three appointments in any twenty-four hour period, or a total of six appointments per week.

▶ Understanding Information Understanding what you read is especially important for legal documents like the lease above. Both the tenant and landlord must understand what a lease means when it is applied in specific situations. Based on your understanding of what the lease means, decide what to do in the following situations.

1. Suppose you are the landlord. The tenant notifies you that she is being transferred and has to move one month before the lease is up. She leaves without paying the last month's rent. What can you do?
   A. Nothing, because the tenant gave you one month's notice.
   B. Keep the tenant's security deposit as payment for the last month's rent.

2. Suppose you are the tenant. You are moving a new couch into the apartment and accidentally scratch the hardwood floor. According to the lease, what can the landlord do?
   A. Nothing, because there is no part of the lease that covers this possibility.
   B. Keep part or all of the security deposit to pay for the damages.

Check your answers on page 248.

Thinking About the Texts

Practice Vocabulary

▶ **The words below are in bold type in the passages. Study the way each word is used. Then complete each sentence by writing the correct word.**

summoned	exempt	retained
incur	prospective	liability

1. She was not _____ from paying taxes on her tips from waiting tables.

2. She returned the video three days late and knew she would

_____ an additional $3.00 charge.

3. Mack had no _____ for the car accident.

4. We _____ a lawyer to represent us.

5. As a _____ student , she hoped Central State College would accept her application for admission.

6. Angelo was _____ to the supervisor's office.

Understand What You Read

▶ **Write the answer to each question.**

7. Look at the Jury Summons on page 117. What are two acceptable reasons for being excused from jury duty?

_____

_____

8. Look at the New Car Buyer Agreement for Trade-in of Used Car on page 118. What reason might the car dealer have for changing his or her mind about the value of a trade-in vehicle?

_____

_____

9. Look at the Apartment Lease on page 119. In what situation could the landlord legally spend the security deposit?

_____

_____

Apply Your Skills

▷ **Circle the letter of the best answer for each question.**

10. Look on page 117 at the section titled "Compensation by Court." Which word or phrase would be a context clue for the word *compensation?*

    A. juror

    B. attendance

    C. receive $40

    D. each day

11. Which of the following statements is the *best* summary of the section titled "Buyer's Refusal to Purchase" on page 118?

    A. The seller keeps the cash deposit if the buyer doesn't buy the new car, but no other charges are allowed for any reason.

    B. The buyer can stop the purchase agreement for any reason, including refusal to stick to the terms of the agreement.

    C. If the buyer doesn't buy the new car, the seller can charge for damages.

    D. If the buyer doesn't buy the new car or doesn't follow the agreement, the seller can keep the deposit and, if necessary, charge the buyer extra money.

12. Based on the Apartment Lease on page 119, what would you expect the landlord to do if he wanted to enter the apartment?

    A. call the tenant for permission to enter

    B. enter the apartment when the tenant is at work

    C. call the tenant's lawyer to set up a time to enter the apartment

    D. enter the apartment only in the evening or on the weekend

Connect with the Texts

▷ **Write your answers to each question.**

13. Have you ever bought or sold a used car? Did you read and understand the entire sales document? Why or why not?

_____

14. Think about a lease that you or someone you know has signed. Was there anything in the lease you thought was unfair? Explain.

_____

> ▶ **Read the application and then answer the questions.**

Dog Adoption Application

Thank you for your interest in adopting a dog. We want to be sure that every adopted animal goes to a loving home. Our application asks a number of detailed questions. Please answer each one thoroughly.

Name of dog you are interested in:

Personal Information

Your name:	Home telephone:	Your Age:

Home address:

City:	State:	Zip:

About Your Home

Please complete this section for the household in which your dog would reside.

1. Type of residence ☐ house ☐ condo ☐ apartment	2. Do you: ☐ own ☐ rent ☐ live with parents	3. If you rent or live in a condo, does your landlord/ association allow dogs? ☐ yes ☐ no ☐	4. Name of landlord or condo association: Phone number:

5. What would you do if you moved to a residence where dogs are not permitted?

About Your Family

1. How many adults live in this household?	How many children live in this household?	Ages of children in this household	2. For whom would you be adopting this dog?
3. Who will be the primary caregiver for this dog?		4. Who will be financially responsible for this dog?	
5. How often do you travel?	How will you care for your dog when you are away from home?	6. In the event of an emergency, who would care for your dog or what arrangements would you make?	

About Your Current Pet(s)

Name	Species/Breed	Age	Gender	Spayed/Neutered

1. If you have a cat, does it get along with dogs?	2. If you have a dog, does it get along with other dogs?	3. What veterinary hospital do your animals go to? Phone number:

References

Name:	Phone:
Name:	Phone:
Name:	Phone:

▷ **Circle the letter of the best answer for each question.**

1. In which section of the application would you list the name of your cat?

   A. About Your Current Pet(s)

   B. References

   C. About Your Family

   D. About Your Home

2. In which section would you list a neighbor who knows you?

   A. About Your Current Pet(s)

   B. References

   C. About Your Family

   D. About Your Home

▷ **Write your answers to the following questions on the lines provided.**

3. Why do you think this application asks questions about children in the household?

   _____

   _____

4. Why do you think this application asks about travel?

   _____

   _____

5. How would you answer the question, "What would you do if you moved to a residence where dogs are not permitted?"

   _____

   _____

6. What kinds of people should you include in the reference section? What should you do before you list someone as a reference on an application?

   _____

   _____

   _____

Check your answers on page 249.

MINI-TEST

This is a 15-minute practice test. After 15 minutes, mark the last number you finished. Then complete the test and check your answers. If most of your answers were correct but you did not finish, try to work faster next time.

▶ **Directions: Choose the one best answer to each question.**

Questions 1 through 3 refer to the following passage.

THE SILK ROAD

(1)   Human beings have always traveled from place to place, trading goods, skills, and ideas with others they met along the way. More recently, the routes people traveled have come to be known as Silk Roads, as silk and other goods and services were traded among travelers and the people who lived along the route.

(2)   One of the more vast and well-known Silk Roads connected China in the East with the Mediterranean Sea in the West. Its use began as early as 200 BC when Chinese adventurers risked their lives to open the route. One part of the route was in what is now western Iran. It divided into branches and circled the northern and southern borders of the Takla Makan Desert. The branches rejoined at the city of Tunhuang in northwest China.

(3)   The Silk Road was a route along which people would trade silk and many other goods. The Silk Road was not only a route for commerce, however, but also a way for people to trade social and cultural ideas as well. For centuries, travelers shared political, social, artistic, and religious customs. As a result, languages, religions, and cultures developed and were influenced by each other along the Silk Road route.

(4)   When a sea passage was opened between Europe and India in the fifteenth century, use of the Silk Road greatly declined.

1. Which of the following *best* summarizes the main idea of the passage?

 A. The Silk Road ran between western Iran and northwest China.

 B. The Silk Road was an ancient trade route that connected China and the West.

 C. The Silk Road was a route for commerce.

 D. Use of the Silk Road began to decline in the fifteenth century.

2. The final sentence implies that in the fifteenth century

 A. many Europeans visited India.

 B. the Silk Road was destroyed.

 C. travelers preferred using sea routes.

 D. China stopped trading with the West.

3. Besides commerce, what else was the Silk Road used for?

 A. tourist travel between the East and West

 B. quick deployment of armies to troubled countries

 C. an alternate route for people who disliked ships

 D. exchange of social and cultural ideas

Questions 4 through 7 refer to the following passage and diagram.

THE PHASES OF THE MOON

From Earth, the moon can look like a shiny disk. However, the moon does not produce light; it reflects the sun's light. Over a period of 29.5 days, the moon's appearance from Earth changes. During some months, there are two full moons. A second full moon in one month is called a blue moon.

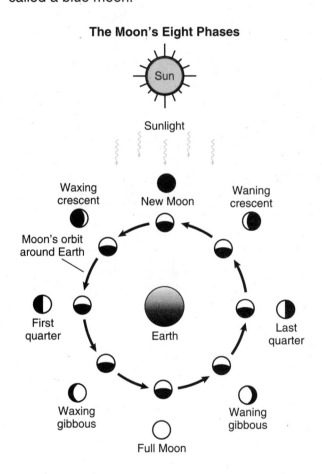

The Moon's Eight Phases

4. Which phase of the moon comes just before a full moon?

   A. waning crescent

   B. waxing crescent

   C. waning gibbous

   D. waxing gibbous

5. Which phase of the moon would appear first in a month with a blue moon?

   A. new moon

   B. full moon

   C. last quarter

   D. waning gibbous

6. Which phase of the moon comes just after a blue moon?

   A. waning crescent

   B. first quarter

   C. last quarter

   D. waning gibbous

7. Why don't we see the moon during a new moon?

   A. the lighted side of the moon is facing the sun

   B. the lighted side of the moon is facing the other side of Earth

   C. the entire moon is dark during a new moon

   D. the sky is always cloudy when there is a new moon

On the writing section of the Reasoning Through Language Arts GED® test, you will be asked to read texts and respond to them in writing. Your response will be scored according to specific criteria, including your ability to write in a logical and organized way. Your writing will also be evaluated for correct spelling and grammar.

How do you feel about your ability to write? How do you feel when you know you have to write?

_____

_____

What areas of your writing do you think need improvement?

_____

_____

Thinking About Writing

You may not realize how familiar you already are with writing and the writing process. Think about what you have written recently, from e-mails or letters to journal entries and essays.

Check the box for each activity you did as part of your writing.

☐ Did you think about what you were going to write before you started to write?

☐ Did you create an outline before you started to write?

☐ Did you create a first or rough draft of your writing?

☐ Did you reread your writing to be sure it was logical and organized?

☐ Did you reread your writing for errors in grammar or spelling?

☐ Did you prepare a final version of your writing, correcting organizational problems and mistakes you found?

Previewing the Unit

In this unit, you will learn:

● how to prepare your ideas before you begin to write.

● how to write a first draft of your writing.

● how to revise and edit your writing.

● how to prepare a final draft of your writing and publish your writing.

● how to write a response to a writing prompt that requires you to analyze other pieces of writing.

Lesson 27	**The Writing Process**
Lesson 28	**Writing Prompt**

THE WRITING PROCESS

Writing does not just happen. Good writing is a process, with steps that should be taken in order. The complete writing process consists of these five steps:

Step 1:   Prewriting
Step 2:   Writing the First Draft
Step 3:   Revising and Editing
Step 4:   Writing the Final Draft
Step 5:   Publishing (Sharing the Final Draft)

Step 1: Prewriting

Prewriting means planning before you begin to write. This first step in the writing process involves defining your topic, generating ideas about it, and organizing those ideas.

Define Your Topic

To define your topic, first define your **purpose** for writing and the **audience** for whom you are writing.

- **Identify Your Purpose** Ask, *Why am I writing?* Possible answers are to tell a story, to describe, to explain, or to persuade.
- **Identify Your Audience** Ask, *Who will read what I am writing?* Possible answers are a friend, a coworker, a teacher, or a potential employer.

EXAMPLE Melissa Sanchez attends a Pre GED® class at a community college. The first night, her instructor asked the students to write an essay. The essay topic was "How Can I Achieve Success in This Class?" Melissa thought about what she might write. First, she defined her purpose and her audience.

Purpose: To explain   **Audience:** My instructor and I

Then she made the following list of possible topics.

1. Everyday math practice
2. Good study habits
3. Improve my reading

Melissa selected "improve my reading" as her topic.

Choose a topic that is neither too general nor too limited. For example, suppose you are asked to write a two-page essay on hobbies. This is a general subject that could fill a book. But some topics that you could cover in a brief essay are "refinishing old furniture" or "getting started in photography."

A topic that is too narrow or limited is also hard to write about because you may run out of things to say. For example, the topic of "wood-refinishing tools" is probably too limited for a two-page essay on hobbies.

Choose a topic that you already know something about or one that you find interesting. This will make your writing task easier.

▶ SKILL PRACTICE

Below each general subject, list two topics that you could write about. The first one has been started for you.

1. Subject: Sports

Purpose: To explain

Audience: A group of children

Topic 1: _How to Play Soccer_

Topic 2: _____

2. Subject: Jobs

Purpose: To describe

Audience: Your friends

Topic 1: _____

Topic 2: _____

3. Subject: Movies

Purpose: To describe

Audience: Your friends

Topic 1: _____

Topic 2: _____

4. Subject: Animals

Purpose: To persuade

Audience: Fellow students

Topic 1: _____

Topic 2: _____

Generate Ideas

After your purpose, audience, and topic are clear in your mind, you are ready to generate ideas about your topic.

- **Explore your thoughts about the topic.** What interests you about the topic? What would interest your readers?
- **Brainstorm ideas.** To brainstorm, let your mind work freely as one thought leads to the next. Write down everything that comes to mind, without making any decisions about which ideas are good or bad. (That will come later.)
- **Ask yourself questions.** Try applying the reporter's basic questions: Who? What? When? Where? Why? How? Write down everything that comes to mind, and keep writing anytime one idea leads to another.
- **Use what you know.** Your own personal observations, knowledge, and experiences are your best sources for ideas. You learn every day just by living, observing people, surfing the Web, and watching TV. What else can you say about this topic?

Organize Your Ideas

While you are generating ideas, write them down. You can refer to them when you begin to write. First, make a list of your ideas. Next, organize the ideas in the order that you want to write about them. Writing an **outline** and drawing an **idea map** are two ways to organize your ideas.

EXAMPLE Melissa thought about different ways she could improve her reading. She listed her ideas. Then she made this outline to organize them.

How I Can Improve My Reading Skills

I. **Read every day**

   A. set aside a time to read each day

   B. read 10 minutes before I get up

   C. read 10 minutes before I go to sleep at night

II. **Read with other people**

   A. join a book club

   B. read to my child

   C. volunteer to read to a blind person

III. **Read lots of different things**

   A. check out books from library

   B. subscribe to a magazine

   C. find interesting Internet sites

   D. read the newspaper

Instead of an outline, Melissa could have created an idea map like this one.

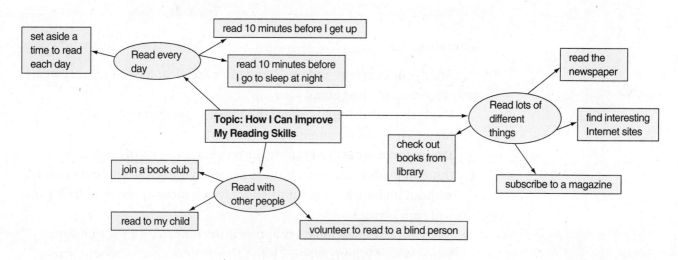

▶ **SKILL PRACTICE** **Brainstorm and list your ideas for this topic: What are the advantages (or disadvantages) of a small (or large) family? Write an outline to organize your ideas. Then make an idea map. Which way of organizing ideas works best for you? Write your response on your own paper.**

Step 2: Writing the First Draft

In Step 1 of the writing process, you created a plan for what you are going to write. In Step 2 you will follow your plan and write the first draft. A **first draft** is the first version of your piece of writing. Sometimes you'll need to write two or three drafts before your piece is final. With each draft you review your writing for problems with content, organization, grammar, usage, and mechanics. You will improve your writing by fixing these types of problems in the revising and editing stage.

When writing the first draft, the main goal is to get your ideas on paper in an organized way. Choose words and develop sentences that express your ideas. Don't worry about perfect word choice, spelling, and punctuation at this stage.

The first draft of the essay will have several paragraphs. Each paragraph will have a topic sentence and supporting details. The **topic sentence** states the main idea that you will develop in the paragraph. The **supporting details** are sentences that relate to the main idea.

Writing an Opening Sentence

An opening sentence tells the **main idea** of your essay. It tells the reader your purpose for writing the essay. If you write a good opening sentence, you can refer back to it as you continue writing to make sure you have not drifted away from your point.

A good opening sentence should be a clearly written summary of the main idea. It should be general enough to introduce the points you will cover in the rest of the piece. Avoid making opening statements that are vague or statements that simply announce the topic.

EXAMPLE   Melissa reviewed her outline. Then she wrote her main idea.

I can achieve success and improve my reading with just a few simple changes.

Melissa wrote three possible opening sentences.

1. This essay is about success in improving my reading.
2. Improving my reading successfully will not be that hard.
3. I can achieve success and improve my reading by making some changes in my daily life.

Sentence 1 just announces what the essay is about in general terms. Sentence 2 states the main idea, but it is vague. Since Melissa's goal was to show that she could make a difference in her reading skills fairly easily, she decided that the third sentence was the best opening statement.

▶ SKILL PRACTICE

Each topic below is followed by three opening statements. Put an X in front of the best statement to introduce each topic.

1. **Topic:** The Case Against Gun Control

_____ A. Owning guns is a constitutional right of all Americans.

_____ B. Some people want gun control, but many others don't.

_____ C. I am going to write about gun control.

2. **Topic:** Every Citizen Should Vote

_____ A. Voting is not a right; it is a duty of every citizen.

_____ B. Voting has been expanded to include almost all adults.

_____ C. Some people don't believe in voting.

3. **Topic:** Avoiding Sun Exposure

_____ A. Many people like to spend hot summer days outside.

_____ B. You don't have to stay inside to avoid getting too much sun.

_____ C. There are all kinds of sunscreens on the market.

Developing Supporting Details

Your outline or idea map will guide you through the main points of the essay. As you get to each main point, begin a new paragraph. Each paragraph in an essay has a topic sentence and other sentences that support the topic sentence. You can write several types of detail sentences to support a topic sentence.

Details may:

- be **facts** or **reasons** that prove or disprove a point
- be **examples** that explain or prove a main idea
- be listed in **time order,** according to the order in which they occur
- be listed in **order of importance,** from the most important to the least important or from the least important to the most important
- show **cause and effect,** how one thing causes another thing to happen
- **compare or contrast** to show how things are alike or different

As you write paragraphs, use several types of details to support your topic sentences.

On page 133 you will find the first two paragraphs of Melissa's first draft. Compare these paragraphs to her outline and idea map. Notice that she wrote a topic sentence for each main point and wrote supporting details to explain those statements. However, she did make some mistakes that we will review in the revising and editing section.

EXAMPLE **Here are Melissa's introductory paragraph and first body paragraph.**

I can acheive success and improve my reading by making some changes in my daily life. Reading is essential to success. At first, I thought it might be hard to get to be a better reader but after careful thought, I realized it doesn't have to be.

My first goal is to make sure I read every day. I can read cereal boxes, junk mail, and coupons. I'll read for 10 minutes before I get ready in the morning. I can put off having to work out that way. I can also read in bed—what could be nicer? I'll read for another 10 minutes before I go to sleep at night. I can learn a lot from reading with other people. I might join a book club at the community center. I can also read to my daughter. Children's books are fun! Finally, if I find the time, and as my skills improve, I might even volunteer to read.

▶ **SKILL PRACTICE** **Place a check mark next to each detail that could be used in a paragraph with this topic sentence: New sports have been catching the interest of Americans everywhere.**

1. Cable sports networks have brought us sports we have never seen before.

2. Football still has its raving fans.

3. Americans are in love with soccer these days.

4. Snowboarding and skateboarding are becoming very popular.

5. We shouldn't leave out an old favorite like baseball.

6. Figure skating now gets the largest TV audiences during the Olympics.

▶ **WRITE** **Write a paragraph about a topic related to sports.**

Prewrite:

A. Jot down a list of possible topics related to sports. Choose one.

B. Make a list of possible supporting details.

- Try to think of examples, facts, and reasons.
- Look for a logical way to include details to compare or contrast.
- See if you can show any cause-and-effect relationships.

Write: Write a topic sentence that states the main idea of your paragraph. Make it specific enough to tell the point you want to make. Then write at least three sentences using details from your list that support your topic sentence.

Review: How did you decide the order for your supporting details? Make sure they are in an order that helps readers understand the paragraph.

Check your answers on page 250. **133**

Organizing Details

When you write supporting details, organize them in the clearest, most logical order. This way, the reader can easily follow your train of thought.

▶ SKILL PRACTICE

A. Each set of sentences below has a topic sentence and supporting details. Find the topic sentence and write *T* by it. Then number the details in the clearest, most logical order. The first paragraph is started for you.

Paragraph 1

_____ First, make sure you have all the ingredients you need.

____T_____ Good cooking habits are worth developing.

_____ As you work, follow each step of the recipe carefully.

_____ Then read through all the directions in the recipe before you begin.

_____ Finally, keep your workspace clear by putting things away as you go.

Paragraph 2

_____ If you don't eat before an interview, you might feel weak and less talkative.

_____ Don't let nervousness spoil your appetite.

_____ Be sure to get a good night's sleep and eat a full meal before a job interview.

_____ Otherwise, you might not be alert during the interview.

_____ Go to bed early the night before.

B. Circle the type(s) of supporting details used in Practice A.

Paragraph 1   examples   time order   cause/effect

Paragraph 2   facts/reasons   compare/contrast   cause/effect

▶ WRITE **On your own paper, write a paragraph about one of the topics below.**

- Morning people and night people are very different.
- Learning to organize your time will change your life.
- Friendship is one of the most important things in life.

Prewrite: List supporting details. Decide how to organize them.

Write: Write the topic sentence and then supporting detail sentences.

Writing the Conclusion

The last paragraph of your essay is the **conclusion.** The topic sentence of the last paragraph should signal that the essay is drawing to a close. The other sentences should highlight what you want the reader to remember.

Certain words and phrases signal a conclusion. The most commonly used are *in conclusion, to conclude, finally, last, as a result, consequently,* and *therefore.* Here are four methods for writing conclusions.

End with a summary and a final thought.

EXAMPLE   As I've shown, I don't think it will be very difficult to improve my reading skills. I can make improvements just by making small changes in my personal habits. I can't wait to get started!

End with a prediction for the future.

EXAMPLE   If I can follow through with my plan, I know I will become a better reader. In fact, I predict that I'll begin to notice my skills improving very soon.

End with a recommendation.

EXAMPLE   Finally, I recommend you consider improving your reading skills too. Think about which ways would work best for you—maybe some of mine, maybe some of your own. Then start building your skills right away.

End with a question.

EXAMPLE   Now that I have a plan for improving my reading skills, I can't wait to get started. What types of new information will I learn as my reading improves?

▶ SKILL PRACTICE   **Choose one of the topics from the Practice exercise on page 134. Then use one of the four methods above to write a concluding paragraph for the topic.**

Step 3: Revising and Editing

The next step of the writing process is to review and evaluate your work. This is your chance to improve your first draft. When you **revise,** you review the **content** of your writing. Does it contain good supporting details? Are they well-organized? Can they be clearer? When you **edit,** you look carefully at the sentences and words. You review word choice, usage, sentence structure, and mechanics—that is, spelling, punctuation, and capitalization.

Editing Marks

You can use editing symbols to mark changes in your writing. These marks help you spot the changes you want to make when you rewrite or retype your final draft. Some basic marks are shown below.

Editing Marks

b B	change to a capital letter
B b	change to a lowercase letter
red, white and blue	insert a comma or period
Will you go?	insert a question mark
and Sue Will you go?	insert word(s)
(sp) (there) car	check spelling
end. ¶We will	insert a paragraph indent
go on away	delete a word or punctuation mark
anda half	add a space between words

Revising

When you revise, you check the content, organization, and clarity of your writing. The Revising Checklist below tells you what to look for when you revise.

Revising Checklist

	YES	NO
Does the content achieve your purpose?	☐	☐
Is the content right for your audience?	☐	☐
Is your main idea stated clearly?	☐	☐
Does each paragraph have a topic sentence?	☐	☐
Are topic sentences supported by details?	☐	☐
Are details written in a logical order?	☐	☐
Is the right amount of information included? (Check for details that are missing or not needed.)	☐	☐
Will the writing hold the reader's interest?	☐	☐
Are thoughts and ideas expressed clearly?	☐	☐

EXAMPLE Here is the first body paragraph from the first draft of Melissa's essay on page 133. You can see how Melissa used the Revising Checklist. She also used editing marks to indicate the revisions to make.

My first goal is to make sure I read every day. I can read ~~signs~~ [add new detail]

cereal boxes, junk mail, and coupons. I'll read for 10 minutes [move this sentence for more logical order]

before I get ready in the morning. I can put off having to work out [delete unnecessary detail]

that way. I can also read in bed—what could be nicer? I'll read for

another 10 minutes before I go to sleep at night. I can learn a lot [begin new paragraph]

from reading with other people. I might join a book club at the [add cause-effect detail] I understand better when I talk about what I've read with other people, and that will help my reading improve.

community center. I can also read to my daughter. Children's

books are fun! Finally, if I find the time, and as my skills improve, I

might even volunteer to read ~~to a blind person~~ . [add new detail]

EXAMPLE Here is the revised version of the paragraphs. Read the new version and compare it with the previous one.

My first goal is to make sure I read every day. I can read signs, cereal boxes, junk mail, and coupons. I can also read in bed—what could be nicer? I'll read for 10 minutes before I get ready in the morning. I'll read for another 10 minutes before I go to sleep at night.

I can learn a lot from reading with other people. I might join a book club at the community center. I understand better when I talk about what I've read with other people, and that will help my reading improve. I can also read to my daughter. Children's books are fun! Finally, if I find the time, and as my skills improve, I might even volunteer to read to a blind person.

▶ SKILL PRACTICE

A. Read the following paragraph. Using the Revising Checklist and editing marks on page 136, make at least three changes to improve the paragraph.

Kingston Heritage Chorus is a great group. The spring retreat is one of the highlights of our year. We go away for a long weekend to a camp in the mountains. We learn a lot of music for our spring program. We always plan our concert outfits earlier in the fall. We also get to know each other better and have a lot of fun. Organizing the retreat is a big job. The committee members make all the arrangements. They arrange transportation, make room assignments, coordinate meals, and plan free-time activities. The Retreat Coordinator needs a committee of at least six people. They also set up our rehearsal room and bring all the supplies and snacks.

B. Now that you have marked the paragraph for revision, write the new version on your own paper.

▶ WRITE Using the Revising Checklist and editing marks on page 136, revise the concluding paragraph you wrote on page 135. Then write your revised paragraph on your own paper.

Editing

When you edit, you smooth out and correct words, sentences, and mechanics. The Editing Checklist below tells you what to look for when you edit.

Editing Checklist	YES	NO
Are any ideas repeated?	☐	☐
Are some words used too many times?	☐	☐
Are precise words and fresh language used?	☐	☐
Are all sentences complete sentences?	☐	☐
Are any sentences too long and hard to understand?	☐	☐
Are any sentences too short and choppy?	☐	☐
Are nouns and pronouns used correctly?	☐	☐
Are verbs used correctly?	☐	☐
Are adjectives and adverbs used correctly?	☐	☐
Are all words spelled correctly?	☐	☐
Is punctuation used correctly?	☐	☐
Are words capitalized correctly?	☐	☐

EXAMPLE Melissa Sanchez is now editing the introductory paragraph of her essay (from page 133). Notice how she has used editing marks to show where she will make changes.

achieve   *easy*
I can ~~acheive~~ success and improve my reading by making some ^

changes in my daily life. Reading is essential to success. At first, I

become
thought it might be hard to get ~~to bc~~ a better reader but after careful

thought, I realized it doesn't have to be.

▶ **SKILL PRACTICE**

A. Write the new version of Melissa's introduction on your own paper. Make the changes she has marked.

B. Edit the concluding paragraph you wrote on page 135. Use the editing marks on page 136.

Step 4: Writing the Final Draft

Your **final draft** will incorporate all the changes you have marked while revising and editing.

After you have finished writing your final draft, it's time to read your essay one last time. When you read, make sure that you really have made all the changes and corrections you marked. Also make sure that you did not make any new errors. If your final version is typed, look for "typos"—reversed letters, missing words, missing spaces, and so on.

Step 5: Publishing (Sharing the Final Draft)

The final step in the writing process is **publishing** or **sharing the final draft.** Before sharing your final draft, read it aloud to yourself. As you read, think about what you enjoyed most about writing it and what you found to be the hardest part. Make notes.

Then read your essay to a partner or have your partner read it. Ask, *Is the writing clear? Is the piece interesting to read? Is the message clear? What parts need improvement?* Make notes. Use the notes to help you improve your writing.

Date your final draft and notes and keep them in a special folder or notebook. Keep an ongoing record of everything you write. Review your work weekly and add the best pieces to your **writing portfolio.**

GED® Extended Response Rubric

On the writing section of the Reasoning Through Language Arts GED® test, you will be required to analyze one or more passages. In some cases, you may be presented with two passages that take either side of a controversial topic, such as whether or not school uniforms should be mandatory in public schools or whether or not video games lead to violence. In other cases, you may be presented with a short excerpt of a primary document and one or two opinion passages related to the document. You will be asked to read and analyze the passages and then determine which position is better supported. You will be expected to use relevant and specific evidence from both passages to support your response. You will be given 45 minutes to plan and write your response.

Your extended response on the GED® test will be evaluated in the following three traits:

- Creation of Arguments and Use of Evidence
- Development of Ideas and Organizational Structure
- Clarity and Command of Standard English Conventions

Creation of Arguments and Use of Evidence

To gain a top score in this area, your response must show that you can do the following:

1) create an argument that addresses the prompt. This means your response should show that you did a close reading and analysis of the passages.

2) use relevant evidence from the text to support the argument. This means your response should use evidence that is closely tied to the passage to support your claims or assertions about the topic.

3) analyze the issue and validity of the information presented in the text. This means your response should focus on how well the authors of the source texts support their arguments.

Development of Ideas and Organizational Structure

To gain a top score in this area, your response must show that you can do the following:

1) construct a logical explanation that is well developed. While the support for your ideas should come from the passages, you need to develop those ideas fully with additional evidence that builds on the central idea.

2) establish an organizational structure that conveys the message and purpose of the response. Your response should contain a sensible progression of ideas with clear connections and transitions between details and main points.

3) maintain a formal style and appropriate tone that demonstrates awareness of the audience and purpose of the task. You should choose specific words to express ideas clearly.

Clarity and Command of Standard English Conventions

To gain a top score in this area, your response must show that you can do the following:

1) demonstrate largely correct sentence structure with a variety of sentence types. This means that your response uses a variety of sentences that clearly show how ideas are related. It also means that your response does not contain wordy or awkward sentences, run-on sentences, or sentence fragments.

2) use transitional words, conjunctive adverbs, and other words that support logic and clarity. This means that your response makes sense and clearly shows the relationship between ideas.

3) demonstrate competent application of conventions. This means your response uses correct subject-verb agreement, pronoun usage, and modifier placement. It also means that your response uses correct spelling, capitalization, and punctuation.

WRITING PROMPT

The following two passages are similar to those that may appear on the writing section of the Reasoning Through Language Arts GED® test. The two passages take sides on a controversial topic. Read the passages and analyze the evidence of each one.

Plastic Bags Should Be Banned

This is a letter to the editor that appeared in a newspaper in a coastal community along the Pacific Ocean.

I believe our community's widespread use of plastic bags is hurting our environment, especially our oceans and the animals that call the water home. The more we harm the ocean, the more we harm ourselves. Therefore, I believe our community, like many other communities around the country, should ban the use of plastic bags.

Our community depends on the ocean. Fishermen need a healthy supply of fish to sell to customers. Businesses that cater to tourists need clean water and beautiful beaches to survive. To sustain our community, we need to attract new people, who are drawn here because of the beauty of the beaches and the water. However, our dreadful plastic-bag habit is threatening all of these things. When I look around, I see plastic bags everywhere—hanging in trees, lying in the grass and sand, and floating in the water. People rarely recycle the bags and are simply irresponsible with their disposal. Plastic bags are an eyesore, for sure, but they are also hazardous to our health and our way of life.

Plastic bags threaten our marine life. The bags that are left on the ground and in the water can easily become choking hazards to marine mammals and seabirds. I have read that more than one million marine animals die each year because of plastic bags.

Plastic bags hurt sea life in other ways, too. They are made of high-density polyethylene and titanium chloride—complete carbons and transitional metals. In the water, the bags break down into tiny pieces. Researchers have studied water samples taken from the Pacific Ocean. They found six times more plastic than plankton in the water—six times more! Health experts already warn us that our seafood may be contaminated with mercury and other pollutants. I think that plastic could do even more damage to our health.

For the reasons I've listed above, I urge our community to ban plastic bags. Breaking this bad habit is not hard to do. There is a great alternative: reusable bags. They are cheap to buy, easy to carry, and much more sturdy than plastic bags. They hold plenty of groceries and are made to hold everything from a gallon of milk to clothing to hammers and nails. What's more, they can be used for many purposes and a variety of daily outings, too. You can carry them to the beach, on the airplane, or to work.

I think banning plastic bags would help ensure our future as a coastal community. I urge you to spread the word and let the city council know that you support the effort to ban plastic bags.

—John Smith

Bag the Ban on Plastic Bags

This letter was published in response to the letter above.

I am writing in response to John Smith, who says the city council should ban plastic bags in our community. I think he is overreacting to what amounts to a minor problem, and his solution is no better than plastic bags. Ultimately, though, if we ban plastic bags, it will be just another example of government telling us what we can and cannot do in our personal lives.

I do not think Mr. Smith backs up his case against plastic bags with solid evidence. I did some research and found a 2011 study that analyzed the impact different types of bags have on various aspects of the environment, including marine life. The study found that paper bags have a worse effect on the environment than plastic bags. What's more, the study concluded that a typical shopper would have to reuse the same cotton bag nearly 100 to 150 times before it would have less impact on the environment than the number of plastic bags needed to carry the same amount of groceries.

The amount of reuse needed to make reusable bags a better environmental choice varies depending on what aspect of the environment you are studying. For example, researchers found that you would have to reuse a cotton bag 350 times before it would cause less toxicity to the water than all of the plastic bags it would replace over the same period. What's more, a reusable cotton bag is only expected to last about 52 reuses. So you would have to replace that bag seven times! Not to mention that reusable cloth bags could harbor bacteria from leaking foods if they are not washed after each use.

Mr. Smith also argues that people rarely recycle their plastic bags. In fact, people reuse a large portion of plastic bags they get from stores to line garbage containers, pick up dog waste, and so on. By reusing these plastic bags, they are not buying and using other plastic bags that may be even more harmful to the environment.

I care about our community, the ocean, and the seafood we eat just as much as Mr. Smith. I believe we need to do everything we can to protect them. However, I think a ban on plastic bags is misguided. It simply will not make the significant difference that Mr. Smith expects. I urge you to tell the city council to trash the ban on plastic bags!

—Sarah Goldberg

Prompt

These two letters to the editor take either side of a debate over a ban on plastic bags in a coastal community. Mr. Smith believes plastic bags should be banned, while Ms. Goldberg disagrees.

In your response, analyze both letters to determine which position is better supported. Use relevant and specific evidence from both letters to support your response.

Writing Responses

You will have 45 minutes to complete your written response on the GED® test. It is important you practice typing a response in that amount of time. Be sure to read through the passage(s) and the prompt carefully. Then think about the message you want to give in your response. This is when you want to recall and use the steps of the writing process that you learned in Lesson 27: Prewriting, Writing the First Draft, Revising and Editing, and Writing the Final Draft.

Of course, in 45 minutes you will need to move through these steps pretty quickly. This is why it is a good idea to practice going through the steps with a timer. With practice, the steps can become second nature.

Before you begin writing, reread the passage(s). Then, think carefully about the argumentation presented in the passage(s). Argumentation refers to the assumptions, claims, support, reasoning, and credibility on which a position is based. Pay close attention to how the author(s) use these strategies to convey his or her position on the topic. Then, begin the writing process.

Prewriting

First, define your purpose and your audience.

Purpose:
To determine which position is better supported and provide evidence from the passage.

Audience:
GED® test scorer

Keep in mind that the better-supported position is not necessarily the position you agree with. Indicate which position you will write about below.

Next, you want to plan your explanation for why the position you chose is the better-supported one—this will be the bulk of your response. Plan to defend your position with at least three pieces of evidence from the passage(s). Be sure to include related details, examples, facts, or reasons why each piece of evidence helped you choose this position as the better-supported one. You can use an idea map like the one below.

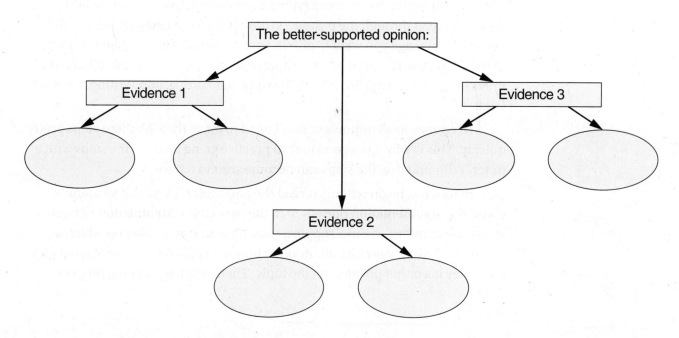

Write the First Draft

After you have established your main points and details in an idea chart, you can begin to write your first draft.

Remember to include an introductory paragraph that identifies your position, body paragraphs that support your position and cite evidence from the texts, and a concluding paragraph that wraps up the points that you made.

Keep the following points in mind as you write:

- build your main points thoroughly
- put your main points in logical order and tie your details to your points
- cite evidence from the texts to support your points
- organize your response carefully and consider your message and purpose
- use transitional words and phrases to connect sentences, paragraphs, and ideas
- choose words carefully to express your ideas clearly
- vary your sentence structure to enhance the flow and clarity of your response
- reread and revise your response to correct any errors in grammar, usage, or punctuation

Revising and Editing

After you write your rough draft, review what you have written. Use the Revising Checklist on page 136 to improve the content of your work. Then use the Editing Checklist on page 138 to polish your writing.

Writing the Final Draft

Once you have incorporated the changes into your final draft, print it out and ask a teacher or classmate to review it and provide feedback, using the rubric on page 140 as a guide.

▶ There are five steps in the writing process. On the lines below, list each step and give a short explanation for each one.

1. Step 1: _____

_____

2. Step 2: _____

_____

3. Step 3: _____

_____

4. Step 4: _____

_____

5. Step 5: _____

_____

▶ Below are general subjects. List two topics that you could write about for each one.

6. Subject: The environment
Purpose: To persuade
Audience: Your friends/family/coworkers

Topic 1: _____

Topic 2: _____

7. Subject: Outer Space
Purpose: To explain
Audience: A group of children

Topic 1: _____

Topic 2: _____

Plan a five-paragraph essay on the following topic. Write an opening sentence or paragraph, outline the body of the essay, and write a conclusion.

8. An old saying is "A bird in the hand is worth two in the bush." It means that it is better to keep what you have than take a risk and try to get something else. Do you agree or disagree with that saying? Give facts, reasons, and examples to support your answer.

Opening _____

_____

_____

_____

I. _____

    A. _____

    B. _____

    C. _____

II. _____

    A. _____

    B. _____

    C. _____

III. _____

    A. _____

    B. _____

    C. _____

Conclusion _____

_____

_____

_____

_____

▶ **Read the following article. Use the editing checklist that follows the article to make at least three changes to improve it. Refer to page 136 for editing marks.**

Most people are familiar with that wide, silver, waterproof tape known as duct tape.

You can buy it at any hardware store you can use it for almost anything. For example, are

you feeling too lazy to do a proper window repair job? If you use a piece of duct tape to

seal your leaky window frame it will probably outlast your house anyway.

It turns out that duct tape is good for warts. In the study, people wore patches of duct

tape over their warts for extended periods. The study did not consider acne or other skin

conditions. The treatment also involved soaking and scraping the warts. The duct tape

treatment was found to be less painful and more effective than freezing.

Editing Checklist	YES	NO
Are any ideas repeated?	☐	☐
Are some words used too many times?	☐	☐
Are precise words and fresh language used?	☐	☐
Are all sentences complete sentences?	☐	☐
Are any sentences too long and hard to understand?	☐	☐
Are any sentences too short and choppy?	☐	☐
Are nouns and pronouns used correctly?	☐	☐
Are verbs used correctly?	☐	☐
Are adjectives and adverbs used correctly?	☐	☐
Are all words spelled correctly?	☐	☐
Is punctuation used correctly?	☐	☐
Are words capitalized correctly?	☐	☐

MINI-TEST

 This is a 45-minute extended response prompt. In your response, analyze both positions presented in the article. Use the 45 minutes, the amount of time you will have on the GED® test, to plan, draft, and edit your response. If you do not finish, try to work faster next time.

▶ **Read this short article. Then complete the writing prompt.**

PROS AND CONS OF CALORIES ON RESTAURANT MENUS

New York City passed a law requiring all chain restaurants with more than ten stores—such as McDonald's and Burger King—to list calorie information on all menu items. More cities and some states are considering following in New York City's footsteps. This may seem like a simple issue, but in fact, it is quite controversial.

Our country has a very serious obesity problem, with a record nearly 40 percent obesity rate. Add to that the fact that more and more people are getting their meals from restaurants, so they often do not really know what they are consuming. It stands to reason that the more information consumers can have about the products they purchase, the better off they are. Armed with facts about the foods they buy in restaurants, for example, they can make better decisions for their health. What's more, the requirement could ultimately encourage restaurants to try harder to make good-tasting foods without relying solely on fat, salt, and sugar to make their foods taste better.

On the other hand, forcing restaurants to publicize calorie counts is not free. They will now be forced to analyze their food products to determine this caloric information. And who pays for these higher costs? Ultimately, it's the consumer, and that's just not fair. Is it the government's place to get between consumers and what they eat in restaurants? If these laws pass universally, what will be next? Government won't allow certain higher-calorie foods on a menu—milkshakes, double cheeseburgers, gravy—because they are deemed not "healthy" for the general public? The line should probably be drawn sooner rather than later.

WRITING PROMPT

This article discusses the pros and cons of requiring restaurants to post the calorie counts of their menu items.

In your response, analyze both positions presented in the article to determine which one is better supported. Use relevant and specific evidence from the article to support your response.

Carefully reread the article and then prepare and write your response on your own paper. Show your prewriting work with an outline or idea web. Next, write a draft, revise and edit the draft, and then prepare a final draft. Set a timer for 45 minutes when you are ready to begin.

5 LANGUAGE SKILLS

Good language skills are essential to your success in writing on the job, in school, or in your personal life. Writing good sentences, spelling correctly, using correct punctuation, and organizing paragraphs effectively are all language skills that help you communicate your ideas. Not only what you write but also how well you write—from work correspondence, to accident reports, to extended responses on the GED® test—will give others an impression of you.

What language skills do you feel confident about when you write?

_____

What language skills do you feel you need help with when you write?

_____

You use language skills every day—sometimes in ways you may not even be aware of. Think about your day-to-day activities.

Check the box for each activity you did.

☐ Did you notice a misspelled word in a magazine or on a sign?

☐ Did you correct something you wrote because it had errors in it?

☐ Did you look up a word in a dictionary to see how it was spelled?

☐ Did you look over a piece of writing for a friend or coworker to see if it had mistakes?

☐ Did you struggle to decide if a sentence you wrote needed a comma?

Write some other activities in which you have used language skills recently.

_____

_____

_____

Previewing the Unit

In this unit, you will learn:

- how to use the basic parts of speech, including pronouns, verbs, and adverbs, to express yourself clearly and correctly.

- how to write varied, interesting, and correct sentences.

- the basic rules for punctuation, spelling, and capitalization.

Lessons 29–37: **Grammar and Usage**

Lessons 38–43: **Conventions**

CONTRACTIONS, HOMONYMS, & CONFUSED WORDS

A **contraction** is a word formed by joining two other words. An apostrophe (') shows where a letter or letters have been left out. Many people use contractions when they speak and write informal letters. Do <u>not</u> use contractions in formal writing such as business letters or an essay.

Contraction	Words It Replaces
I'm	I am
he's, she's, it's	he is, she is, it is; he has, she has, it has
you're, we're, they're	you are, we are, they are
isn't, aren't, wasn't, weren't	is not, are not, was not, were not
he'll, she'll, you'll	he will, she will, you will
I'll, we'll, they'll	I will, we will, they will
won't	will not
doesn't, don't, didn't	does not, do not, did not
I'd	I would, I had
I've, we've, you've, they've	I have, we have, you have, they have
who's	who is, who has
there's	there is, there has
let's	let us
can't	cannot

▶ **SKILL PRACTICE**

Write a contraction to replace the underlined words.

_____ **1.** I know a writer <u>who is</u> writing a book about baseball.

_____ **2.** <u>I have</u> read about the first pro baseball player, Al Reach.

_____ **3.** He <u>was not</u> cheered when he left Brooklyn for the Phillies.

_____ **4.** Fans <u>were not</u> pleased that a player wanted a salary.

_____ **5.** In Reach's time, players <u>did not</u> even get paid.

Write two sentences—one about something you cannot do and one about something you will not do. Change each word to a contraction.

6. (cannot) _____

7. (will not) _____

Check your answers on page 252.   UNIT 5   LANGUAGE SKILLS

Homonyms

Homonyms are words that sound alike but are spelled differently and have different meanings. Study this list of common homonyms to help you use each word correctly.

Word	Meaning
aisle isle	a space between rows an island
brake break	to stop to destroy; a short time off
capital capitol	seat of government building in which a legislative body meets
clothes close	things to wear to shut
fair fare	even, just; a festival money for transportation

Word	Meaning
forth fourth	forward number four in a series
hole whole	opening complete
know no	to understand not at all
lessen lesson	to decrease, make less something that is taught
weak week	not strong seven days

Some words are not exact homonyms, but their sounds and spellings are close enough to cause problems.

I <u>accept</u> your apology.   Do not <u>lose</u> your bus pass.

We're all here <u>except</u> Jim.   Do you have any <u>loose</u> change?

▶ SKILL PRACTICE

Circle the correct word to complete each sentence.

1. Last **(week, weak)** our state passed a new law allowing more dumps.

2. The government thinks the law is **(fair, fare),** but others disagree.

3. Some of us gathered to meet in the **(capital, capitol)** city.

4. The meeting was so crowded that even the **(isles, aisles)** were full.

5. I **(no, know)** we have to work out a way to deal with this problem.

6. We need to **(lessen, lesson)** our need for new dumps.

7. We should be trying to **(clothes, close)** old dumps, not open new ones.

8. We need a **(hole, whole)** new plan for taking care of our environment.

Write a sentence using each word.

9. (accept) _____

10. (brake) _____

Words Often Confused

There are many words that can be confused with similar words, either because they sound the same or have similar shades of meanings. Here are some words that are often confused.

Word	Use/Meaning	Example
few, fewer, many	pieces you can count	I have very few books. I have fewer books than you do. How many books do you have?
little, less, much	amounts you cannot count	I have little patience. I have less patience than you do. How much patience do you have?
good	an adjective; tells about a person, place, or thing	This is a good picture.
well	an adverb; tells about an action	You draw well.
among	three or more	The three fought among themselves.
between	two	The choice was between the two of them.
who, whom	use with people	My children, who are now grown, live close by. He is the one to whom I spoke.
which	use with objects	My car, which was fixed last week, is broken again!
to	toward	We are going to the movies.
too	also	I will be there, too!
two	the number 2	I would like two cups, please.
then	at that time	We will eat and then go home.
than	used in comparisons	I am older than my sister.

▶ SKILL PRACTICE   Circle the correct word to complete each sentence.

1. Michael Cullen, (**who, which**) opened the first "warehouse grocery store," did not know that he was making history.

2. Times were hard (**then, than**), and people were looking for good prices.

3. Almost at once, his store was doing (**good, well**).

4. There was a lot of competition (**among, between**) all the grocery stores.

5. Many people go (**to, too, two**) supermarkets every day.

6. Do you like to shop at supermarkets, (**to, two, too**)?

LESSON 30

SUBJECT-VERB AGREEMENT

In some tenses, subjects and verbs must agree in number. A singular subject must have a singular verb. A plural subject must have a plural verb.

Singular subject and verb: A big ship sails into the harbor.

Plural subject and verb: We are on a big ship.

1. Words between the subject and verb do not affect the agreement.

    The insects on the oak tree are harmful. (The subject is *insects,* not *tree.* The verb is *are.* The phrase *on the oak tree* between the subject and verb does not affect the agreement.)

2. Use a plural verb for subjects joined by *and.*

    The door and window are both stuck.

3. Use a singular verb for singular subjects joined by *or* or *nor.* Use a plural verb for plural subjects joined by *or* or *nor.*

    Each morning Julia or Lucy buys fresh rolls.

    Each morning the sisters or their friends buy fresh rolls.

4. If a singular subject and a plural subject are joined by *or* or *nor,* the verb must agree with the subject that is closer to it.

    Neither the loaf of bread nor the eggs were fresh.

    Neither the eggs nor the loaf of bread was fresh.

▶ SKILL PRACTICE

Circle the correct verb to complete each sentence.

1. The sky **(appears, appear)** blue as we look up from Earth.

2. The moon and the planet Venus **(glow, glows)** at night.

3. Neither Pluto nor Saturn **(is, are)** easy to find, though.

4. Meteors that shoot across the sky **(is, are)** a special treat.

Write a sentence using each word or phrase as the subject of the sentence.

Sample: (Tony or Leo) _Either Tony or Leo is going to help us paint._

5. (cars) _____

6. (buses or the train) _____

_____

Check your answers on page 253.

More on Subject-Verb Agreement

1. Sometimes the subject of a sentence follows the verb. Changing the order of the words in the sentence can help you decide the correct subject-verb agreement.

> On the wall (<u>hangs</u> or <u>hang?</u>) Ray's family portrait.
>
> Ray's family portrait <u>hangs</u> on the wall.

2. In many sentences that begin with *here, there,* or *where,* the subject follows the verb. Be careful not to start a sentence with *here's (here is), there's (there is),* or *where's (where is)* when the subject is plural.

Incorrect:	Here's the paper rolls for the cash register.
Correct:	Here are the paper rolls for the cash register.
Correct:	The paper rolls for the cash register are here.

Incorrect:	There's several items on the agenda for the meeting.
Correct:	There are several items on the agenda for the meeting.
Correct:	Several items are on the agenda for the meeting.

Incorrect:	Where's the screwdriver and the wrench?
Correct:	Where are the screwdriver and the wrench?
Correct:	The screwdriver and the wrench are where?

3. Remember that a collective noun names a group of people, places, or things and is often singular. When the members of the group act as one, use a singular verb.

> The <u>team</u> <u>is running</u> onto the field.

▶ **SKILL PRACTICE**

Circle the correct verb to complete each sentence.

1. Our family **(is, are)** giving a large party.

2. The whole group **(wants, want)** to honor our grandfather, who's 75.

3. Here **(is, are)** the decorations to hang.

4. On top of that shelf **(is, are)** the cups I need.

5. There **(seem, seems)** to be some crumbs on the table.

Complete each sentence. Use correct subject-verb agreement.

6. Here _____

   _____ .

7. The jury _____

   _____ .

Check your answers on page 253.

PRONOUNS

A **pronoun** is a word that takes the place of a noun.

When the Johnsons moved, they hired a moving company to help them. (The pronouns *they* and *them* take the place of the noun *Johnsons.*)

Just like nouns, pronouns can be singular or plural. **First-person pronouns** refer to the speaker or speakers; **second-person pronouns** refer to the person or people being spoken to; **third-person pronouns** refer to the person, people, or things being spoken about.

	Singular	Plural
First-Person:	I, me, my, mine	we, us, our, ours
Second-Person:	you, your, yours	you, your, yours
Third-Person:	he, him, his/she, her, hers/it, its	they, them, their, theirs

These personal pronouns may be divided into three basic types: subject, object, and possessive.

Subject Pronouns

A **subject pronoun** can act as the subject of a sentence. A subject tells who or what the sentence is about. The subject pronouns are *I, you, he, she, it, we,* and *they.*

We are going to get married. (*We* is the subject.)

I need to rent a truck. (*I* is the subject.)

▶ SKILL PRACTICE

Write a subject pronoun to replace the underlined word or words.

_____ **1.** My fiancé and I also have to find a band.

_____ **2.** Mike wants a band to play the hits.

_____ **3.** My mother does not know much about music.

_____ **4.** My parents will pay for part of the wedding.

Write a sentence to go with the one that is given. Use a subject pronoun.

Sample: My neighborhood is very friendly. _It is a good place to live._

5. My neighbors sometimes help me out.

_____

6. My neighbors and I usually get along.

_____

Check your answers on page 253.

Object Pronouns

Object pronouns are pronouns that are used as the object of a verb or preposition. The object pronouns are *me, you, him, her, it, us,* and *them.*

1. An object pronoun can be a **direct object.** A direct object receives the action of the verb in the sentence.

    I met my new boss today, and I like her. (Whom do you like? *Her.*)

    Take the glass, and put it in the sink. (What should you put in the sink? *It.*)

2. An object pronoun can be an **indirect object.** An indirect object tells *to whom* or *for whom* the action of a verb is done.

    My sister sent me a gift for my birthday. (To whom did she send a gift? *Me.*)

3. An object pronoun can be the **object of a preposition.** The object of a preposition is simply the noun or pronoun that follows a preposition. Some common prepositions are *about, above, in, by, to, at, in front of, inside, into,* and *with.*

    I have not spoken to him yet.

    Remember to use an object pronoun correctly even when it is part of a compound object.

    The award for excellent attendance was given to Ricardo and me.

▶ **SKILL PRACTICE**   **Write the correct object pronoun to complete each sentence.**

1. My grandmother told my cousin and _____ **(I, me)** that she once heard Martin Luther King Jr. speak.

2. She heard _____ **(he, him)** when she was a little girl.

3. My brother and I were excited when she told _____ **(we, us)** about how he sounded.

4. At one point, she thought he looked directly at _____ **(she, her).**

5. He was such a good speaker that all the people in the crowd thought he was speaking directly to _____ **(they, them).**

Write a sentence using each object pronoun.

Sample: (him) _____ *I gave the tickets to him.* _____

6. (me) _____

7. (them) _____

8. (us) _____

Possessive Pronouns

Possessive pronouns show ownership.

1. Use the **possessive pronouns** *my, your, his, her, its, our,* and *their* before nouns to show ownership. (These words are sometimes called **possessive adjectives.**)

> Nick left <u>his</u> glove in <u>our</u> car.   <u>Their</u> dog buried <u>its</u> bone.

2. Use the **possessive pronouns** *my, your, his, her, its, our,* and *their* before a gerund. A **gerund,** such as the word *driving,* looks like the *-ing* form of a verb, but it acts as a noun.

> <u>Their</u> driving to Nashville was my idea.
>
> He did not agree with <u>my</u> changing jobs.

3. Use the **possessive pronouns** *mine, yours, his, hers, its, ours,* and *theirs* alone to show ownership.

> Is this coat <u>his</u>?   <u>Mine</u> is in the closet.
>
> Are those papers <u>ours</u>?   No, they are <u>theirs</u>.

4. A possessive pronoun is <u>never</u> written with an apostrophe. Spellings such as *their's, your's,* and *our's* are incorrect.

▶ SKILL PRACTICE

Circle the correct word to complete each sentence.

1. Antonio seemed to have a problem with **(he's, his)** eyes.

2. **(His, Him)** squinting was obvious to everyone.

3. "We are worried about **(you're, your)** vision," I told him.

4. "My eyes are **(my, mine)**, not **(yours, your's)**," he growled.

5. He finally listened to **(our, ours)** concerns and went to an eye doctor.

Read each sentence about a man named Kim. Write two sentences comparing yourself with Kim. Use *mine* in one sentence and *my* in the other.

Sample: Kim's children are young. _____*Mine are grown up.*_____

_____*My children are grown up.*_____

6. Kim's home is very messy. _____

_____

7. Kim's hometown is a big city. _____

_____

Pronoun Antecedents

A pronoun gets its meaning from the noun to which it refers. This noun is called the **antecedent.** Pronouns usually have specific antecedents.

1. An antecedent is the word to which a pronoun refers. The antecedent usually comes before the pronoun.

   Louisa forgot to buy her weekly bus pass. She had to pay cash every day. (*Louisa* is the antecedent for *her* and *She.*)

   Every cat in the shelter received its shots. (*Cat* is the antecedent for *its.*)

   Carolyn and I left our keys on the desk. We didn't realize that until much later. (*Carolyn and I* is the antecedent for *our* and *We.*)

2. Sometimes the antecedent comes after the pronoun.

   Since they moved, Donna and Jim have not called us. (*Donna and Jim* is the antecedent for *they.*)

   Because of its climate, San Diego is my favorite city. (*San Diego* is the antecedent for *its.*)

▶ SKILL PRACTICE

Circle the antecedent for the underlined pronoun in each sentence.

1. Cities that get a lot of snow must keep their snowplows in good condition.

2. When two snowstorms hit town last January, they nearly shut down the city.

3. On its front page, the newspaper had a photo of a snowplow stuck in the snow.

4. The mayor knew she had to act fast to clear the snow.

5. Even though it was his day off, the police chief met with the mayor to make a plan.

6. My brother worked overtime. He was one of fifty city snowplowers.

Write a sentence using each pronoun. Circle its antecedent.

Sample: (it) _____ When the (phone) rang at 7:00 a.m., it surprised me._____

7. (it) _____

8. (he) _____

Pronoun Agreement

Pronouns and antecedents must match, or agree with one another.

1. A pronoun must agree with its antecedent in number, person, and gender. *Number* means that the words are either singular or plural. *Person* refers to first-person, second-person, or third-person. *Gender* refers to whether the words stand for males, females, or things.

   Lucy gave her bill to the clerk. (Both the antecedent *Lucy* and the pronoun *her* are singular, in the third-person, and used for females.)

2. Use a plural pronoun with two or more antecedents joined by *and*.

   My roommate and I disagree about our responsibilities.

3. Use a singular pronoun with singular antecedents joined by *or* or *nor*. Use a plural pronoun with plural antecedents joined by *or* or *nor*.

   Either Steve or Ricardo should give up his seat for the elderly woman.

   Either the brothers or their friends should give up their seats for the elderly couple.

4. Be sure that the pronoun agrees with the antecedent in person.

   Incorrect: If students want to succeed, you must work hard. (The antecedent is third-person, but *you* is second-person.)

   Correct: If students want to succeed, they must work hard. (The antecedent and pronoun are both third-person.)

▶ SKILL PRACTICE **Circle the correct pronoun to complete each sentence.**

1. My sister and I have (**my, our**) own views on women in sports.

2. In my opinion, female athletes don't get the recognition (**you, they**) deserve.

3. If a female athlete is very talented, (**she, they**) can become famous.

4. However, male athletes are more likely to be known for (**his, their**) skills.

5. My uncle or my brother will be happy to give (**his, their**) opinion.

Write a sentence with a pronoun that agrees with each antecedent. Underline the pronoun and its antecedent.

Sample: (man) _____ The man brought his date to the movie._____

6. (actress) _____

7. (beef or chicken) _____

Pronoun and Verb Agreement

A pronoun used as a subject must agree with the verb in number.

1. These pronouns always use singular verbs: *much, neither, no one, nothing, one, other, somebody, someone, something, another, anybody, anyone, anything, each, either, everybody, everyone, everything.*

    Someone has been in the house.

    Everything is fine, thanks.

2. These pronouns always use plural verbs: *both, few, many, others, several.*

    Both of the glasses have been used.

    Several of the glasses are broken.

3. These pronouns use singular or plural verbs, depending on what they refer to: *all, some, most, any, part, none, half.*

    All of the books have been checked out. (*All* refers to *books.*)

    All of the milk was spilled on the floor. (*All* refers to *milk.*)

▶ SKILL PRACTICE   **Circle the correct verb to complete each sentence.**

1. Both of my children (**are, is**) planning to look for famous people in New York.

2. Everyone (**has, have**) told them not to be disappointed if they don't see any.

3. At 11:00 p.m. all of the actors (**take, takes**) their last bow and leave the theater.

4. Each of the actors (**gives, give**) my children a smile and an autograph.

5. Few (**is, are**) this nice.

6. Several (**has, have**) since answered letters from my children.

Complete each sentence. Use *is/are* or *has/have.*

Sample: Several of my friends _____ *have twins* _____ .

7. Everyone in my family _____ .

8. No one in my family _____ .

9. All of my friends _____ .

10. Several of my coworkers _____ .

INFORMAL LANGUAGE

Before you write, you need to think about your audience. If you are writing a text or an e-mail to a friend or family member, it is acceptable to use informal or nonstandard language and style. You might use contractions, slang words, and incomplete sentences. Informal writing is similar to the way you speak when you talk to your friends and family.

When you are writing something more formal, however, including a response to a writing prompt on the GED® test, you should use more formal language and style. In formal writing you want to avoid using contractions, clichés, and slang.

Clichés are overused or overworked words or expressions. They stand out as phrases that do not demonstrate any original thought.

> Studying for the exam was a complete *waste of time.*
>
> I know you are heartbroken now, but *time heals all wounds.*
>
> Mrs. Jones obviously *woke up on the wrong side of the bed* today.

Slang is informal or "trendy" language that changes from year to year and is most often used between friends.

> This new video game is *epic.*
>
> *My bad*—I forgot your birthday.
>
> The special effects in that movie were *sick.*

Whenever you write in a formal situation, you should take the time to reread your writing and look for words or expressions that are not typically acceptable in formal writing situations.

▶ SKILL PRACTICE

Rewrite each informal sentence so that it is more formal.

1. Our city is the most rad city in the whole wide world!

----

2. Our claim to fame is our awesome zoo and gobs of nightlife.

----

3. Our city is on fire with activity 24/7.

----

4. There is no way your city is more happening than ours.

More on Informal Language

Another reason to revise your sentences is to get rid of expressions that are not appropriate to use in formal situations, even though they may be used in informal speech. Here is a list of some words and expressions to avoid.

Avoid: What kind of a movie are you going to see?
Use: What kind of movie are you going to see?

Avoid: Being that I have been here longer, I can help you.
Use: Because I have been here longer, I can help you.

Avoid: We had ought to leave now.
Use: We ought to leave now.

Avoid: My boss, she says I am a good worker.
Use: My boss says I am a good worker.

Avoid: Try and work more.
Use: Try to work more.

Avoid: This here book will help you.
Use: This book will help you.

Avoid: The reason is because the bus was late.
Use: The reason is that the bus was late.

Avoid: Like I told you, he moved to the city.
Use: As I told you, he moved to the city.

Avoid: I saw on TV where a man was hurt.
Use: I saw on TV that a man was hurt.

▶ SKILL PRACTICE

Write C if the sentence is correct. Write I if the sentence contains informal expressions.

_____ **1.** Being that the food is good, the place is always crowded.

_____ **2.** The critics say it is the best restaurant in town.

_____ **3.** You had ought to get there early to get a seat.

_____ **4.** The reason is that all the food is fresh.

_____ **5.** Like I told you, the fish is excellent.

_____ **6.** All the takeout food is listed on this here menu.

_____ **7.** I heard on the radio that they are opening a new place.

_____ **8.** We have to try and get there soon.

MISPLACED & DANGLING MODIFIERS

A **modifier** is a descriptive word or phrase.

1. Place a modifier as close as possible to the word or phrase it describes.

    The woman who delivered the package spoke to the man.

    The batter with the red shirt hit a home run.

2. A **misplaced modifier** is a modifier in the wrong place in a sentence. If the modifier is far from the word it describes, the sentence might change meaning or not make sense.

    Misplaced modifier: The woman spoke to the man who delivered the package. (The sentence now means that the man, not the woman, delivered the package.)

    Misplaced modifier: The batter hit a home run with the red shirt. (The sentence now means that the batter used the red shirt to hit the ball.)

▸ **SKILL PRACTICE**

Write C if the underlined modifier is in the correct place in the sentence. Write M if the modifier is misplaced.

_____ **1.** We saw many smashed houses driving through the storm.

_____ **2.** The storm even wrecked the sidewalks.

_____ **3.** Scarcely people could believe the damage.

_____ **4.** The storm was barely over when people came to help.

_____ **5.** Nearly everyone pitched in.

_____ **6.** First, a list was given to each owner with many items.

_____ **7.** Then Marta picked up the clothes for the children that had been left in the box.

_____ **8.** The house was rebuilt by the owners destroyed by the storm.

On your own paper, describe a bad storm that you experienced. You can make up details if you need to. Use at least three sentences that have correctly placed modifiers.

3. Every modifier must describe a specific word in a sentence.

> Coming up the stairs, he heard the clock strike six. (*Coming up the stairs* describes *he.*)

4. A sentence cannot make sense if the modified word is missing. A **dangling modifier** is a modifier that does not describe anything in the sentence. Watch for dangling modifiers and rewrite them.

Dangling modifier:	Driving down the road, a bad accident happened. (Who was driving down the road?)
Correct:	Driving down the road, they saw a bad accident happen.
Correct:	While they were driving down the road, a bad accident happened.

▶ SKILL PRACTICE

Rewrite each sentence to correct the dangling modifier.

1. While passing a large rock, a clap of thunder made me scream.

2. Sailing up the harbor, the pier was seen.

3. Flying over the town, the cars and houses looked like toys.

4. While putting the chair together, the screw was lost.

5. Opening the jar, the sauce spilled all over the floor.

6. Walking up the steps, the packages fell.

Complete each sentence. Include a word that can be modified by the phrase that is already written.

Sample: Eagerly waiting for news, _I jumped at the ring of the phone_ .

7. Going to my class, _____ .

8. Angry at her husband, _____ .

9. Already hungry, _____ .

10. Without thinking, _____ .

Illogical Order

There are many different ways a writer can misplace modifiers, which can then make a sentence sound awkward or even illogical.

Misplaced **adjectives** are incorrectly separated from the nouns they modify and almost always change the intended meaning of the sentence. Look at these examples of adjectives that are in illogical order.

Illogical order:	I enjoyed a hot bowl of soup for lunch today.
Logical order:	I enjoyed a bowl of hot soup for lunch today.
Illogical order:	The broken child's toy was all over the floor.
Logical order:	The child's broken toy was all over the floor.

Adverbs can also be illogically placed in a sentence, which can lead to confusion.

Illogical order:	We walked to the movie that was playing slowly.
Logical order:	We slowly walked to the movie that was playing.

The placement of adverbs can also change the meaning of a sentence.

Just Clay was chosen to play soccer. (*Just* means only Clay can play.)

Clay was just chosen to play soccer. (*Just* means that Clay was chosen now.)

Clay was chosen to play just soccer. (*Just* means that Clay played only soccer.)

▶ SKILL PRACTICE **Read each sentence. Write _L_ if the sentence is logical. Write _I_ if it is illogical.**

_____ **1.** The blue dog's collar broke when he pulled on it.

_____ **2.** Sam nearly drove the car for two hours a day.

_____ **3.** Joni failed almost every exam she took.

_____ **4.** Only Dad gave me a dollar to rake the lawn.

_____ **5.** Rarely people with cats can walk them on leashes.

COORDINATION & SUBORDINATION

Coordination is a way of combining two complete sentences to create a compound sentence. There are two ways to combine sentences into a single sentence.

1. Join the complete sentences with a comma and a **coordinating conjunction** such as *and, but, or, so, for, nor,* or *yet.*

   > Jill wanted the job, and she knew she had the skills for it.

   > She could accept the job, or she could reject it.

2. Join the complete sentences with a semicolon. Use this method when you do not need a connecting word to show how the thoughts are related.

   > Martin read the book in two hours; he wrote his essay in three.

   > Jess liked the movie; she saw it last Friday.

▶ **SKILL PRACTICE**

Write *CS* if the sentence is a compound sentence. Write *S* if it is not.

_____ **1.** Reality television shows have earned a bad name, but they don't always deserve it.

_____ **2.** Some people watch too much TV; other people take what they watch too seriously.

_____ **3.** This does not make the programs themselves bad.

Add another complete sentence to each complete sentence below to create a compound sentence. Use a coordinating conjunction and a comma.

4. James watches reality TV every day.

_____

_____

5. Some reality TV shows have been on the air for many years.

_____

_____

3. Use a compound sentence to join related ideas. The sentence will not make sense unless the two ideas are related.

   Not related: Computers became popular in the 1970s, for disco music was popular.

   Related: Computers became popular in the 1970s, for they had many different uses.

4. Use a coordinating conjunction that helps show the relationship between the parts of a compound sentence. Each of these connecting words has a certain meaning. Use the word that shows a logical relationship.

Connecting Word	Meaning	Function
and	also	joins ideas
but	on the other hand	contrasts
or	a choice	shows a choice
so	thus	shows a result
for	because	shows a reason
nor	not	joins negative ideas
yet	but	contrasts

▶ SKILL PRACTICE   **Combine the two sentences to create a logical compound sentence.**

1. My first week on the job was a disaster. My boss told me so.

   _____

   _____

2. I was really upset. I knew things had to get better.

   _____

   _____

3. I tried as hard as I could. I really wanted to keep the job.

   _____

   _____

4. My coworker gave me good advice. I felt more confident.

   _____

   _____

5. Next week has to be better. I'll think about quitting!

   _____

   _____

Subordination

1. A **clause** is a group of words with its own subject and verb. A clause that can stand alone as a sentence is called an **independent clause.**

   He woke up at seven o'clock so that he could go fishing.

2. A clause that cannot stand alone as a sentence is a **dependent clause.**

   He woke up at seven o'clock so that he could go fishing.

3. **Subordination** is another way to combine complete sentences. Subordination uses **subordinating conjunctions** to change independent clauses into dependent clauses. Here are some of the most common subordinating conjunctions.

after	although	as	as if	because
before	even though	if	since	so that
though	unless	until	when	while

4. A sentence with both an independent clause and a dependent clause is a **complex sentence.** The dependent clause can come at the beginning or the end of the sentence. Put it where it helps you state your point most clearly. If the dependent clause is at the beginning of the sentence, put a comma after it.

   Even though his alarm didn't go off, he woke up at seven o'clock.

   He woke up at seven o'clock even though his alarm didn't go off.

▶ SKILL PRACTICE

Draw a line under the dependent clause in each complex sentence. This is the clause that cannot stand alone. Then add a comma if needed.

1. Although I have a car I usually take the bus.

2. I prefer the bus because I care about the environment.

3. If we don't help to reduce pollution the problem will only get worse.

4. Let's act before it's too late.

Write directions for walking from one place to another in your neighborhood. Include your favorite shortcuts. Use at least two dependent clauses.

_____

_____

_____

PARALLELISM

Your writing will be clearer if the ideas within each sentence are written in a similar way. Put them all in **parallel,** or similar, form. For example, all verbs should be in the same tense and form. To have **parallelism,** use matching nouns, verbs, adjectives, and adverbs when you write a list.

Not parallel: The store is good for fruit, meat, and to buy cheese.
Parallel: The store is good for fruit, meat, and cheese. (nouns)

Not parallel: Doctors say I should run, swim, and go walking.
Parallel: Doctors say I should run, swim, and walk. (verbs)

Not parallel: The meal was tasty, quick, and the food was good for you.
Parallel: The meal was tasty, quick, and healthful. (adjectives)

Not parallel: In the rain I drive slowly, with care, and defensively.
Parallel: In the rain I drive slowly, carefully, and defensively. (adverbs)

▶ SKILL PRACTICE

Write *P* if the sentence has parallelism. Write *NP* if the sentence does not have parallelism.

_____ **1.** Eating the right foods will help you feel healthier, more attractive, and strongly.

_____ **2.** Fruits, vegetables, and grains are important in a balanced diet.

_____ **3.** They provide vitamins, minerals, and are low in fat.

_____ **4.** Meat, fish, and poultry provide zinc, iron, and B vitamins.

_____ **5.** Fiber, which is good for digestion, is found in plant foods like beans, peas, and whole grain cereals.

_____ **6.** To lose weight, eat smaller portions and limiting second helpings.

_____ **7.** Eat slowly and be careful; be sure to chew your food well.

Complete each sentence. Use parallelism.

Sample: Three important paths to good health are diet, sleep, and _exercise_ .

8. You can buy food at a grocery store, a snack shop, and

_____ .

9. When you are sick, you should stay home, drink fluids, and

_____ .

Check your answers on pages 255–256.

In addition to using parallel words in lists, use parallel phrases in your writing. Write each parallel idea in the same grammatical structure.

Not parallel: The members of the council read the letter, discussed its points, and the decision was to ignore it.

Parallel: The members of the council <u>read</u> the letter, <u>discussed</u> its points, and <u>decided</u> to ignore it.

Not parallel: The council members, the person who wrote the letter, and the audience then got into a shouting match.

Parallel: The <u>council members</u>, the <u>letter writer</u>, and the <u>audience</u> then got into a shouting match.

▶ SKILL PRACTICE

Rewrite each sentence so that it has parallelism.

1. Writing helps people think, speak, and learning.

   _____

   _____

2. Those who can write well will be leaders in the community, state, and nationally in years to come.

   _____

   _____

3. By writing frequently, reading often, and to seek feedback, writers can improve.

   _____

   _____

4. Learning to write clearly, correctly, and be effective is a goal.

   _____

   _____

Answer each question with a complete sentence. Use parallelism.

5. What different things can you write?

   _____

   _____

6. What are three qualities of good writing?

   _____

   _____

36

REVISING SENTENCES

Wordiness

    After you write, revise your sentences to make your meaning as clear as possible. Remove any extra words that make it harder for your reader to grasp your point. If you are saying the same thing twice, you need to cut some words.

Too wordy: Please repeat your comment again.
Revised: Please repeat your comment.

Too wordy: Is that the real truth?
Revised: Is that the truth?

▶ SKILL PRACTICE

Revise each sentence to get rid of the extra words.

1. The baseball game took place at 3 p.m. in the afternoon on Saturday.

   _____

2. When the game started to begin, the players relaxed, and the tension was over with.

   _____

3. The pitcher he did not know where to throw the ball to.

   _____

4. After each inning, they repeated their signals again.

   _____

5. In the last inning, the game ended with a home run with the bases loaded.

   _____

6. Up to this point, no one knows where the next game will be held at.

   _____

On your own paper, describe a sport or game that you know very well. Include details. When you are finished, check your writing for extra words.

Awkward Structure

On the language section of the GED® Reasoning Through Language Arts test, you will need to recognize the best way to rewrite sentences that contain common problems with sentence structure, including incomplete sentences and dangling modifiers. Some questions will present a sentence that must be rewritten by revising the sentence structure. To answer these questions, think through the process of changing a sentence.

1. Identify the main person or thing the sentence is about. Make this the subject of the sentence. Put it first.
2. Identify the main action. Make this the verb. Put it next.
3. Place modifying words and phrases close to the words they modify.
4. Combine related ideas in parallel form.
5. Eliminate unnecessary words.

Unclear sentence: A garage sale can be held by you in order to get rid of things you don't want, and you can also make some money from things you don't want.

Revised sentence: You can hold a garage sale to get rid of things you don't want and to make some money.

The revised sentence has a clear subject: *you.* The verb is in the active voice: *can hold.* Parallel form is used: *to get* and *to make.* The repeated words *things you don't want* are eliminated.

▶ SKILL PRACTICE   **Circle the letter of the best revision of each sentence.**

1. Garage sales have inexpensive things, and some people need to buy these things.
    A. Garage sales have inexpensive things needed by some people, so they buy them.
    B. Some people rely on garage sales to buy the things they need inexpensively.

2. Browsing and haggling are enjoyed by people who go to garage sales.
    A. People enjoy going to garage sales to browse and haggle.
    B. People who enjoy browsing and haggling are others who go to garage sales.

Revise this sentence to make it clear and direct. Keep the same meaning.

3. Things not needed or some things you just don't want anymore can probably be found in your own home.

_____

_____

Repetition

Sometimes closely related sentences repeat words. The repetition does not help make the meaning clear. Instead, it just makes the writing sound wordy. These sentences can be combined by eliminating the repeated words.

Repetition: The newscaster gave her report on the 10 o'clock news. Her report gave unemployment figures for the past year.

Improved: On the 10 o'clock news, the newscaster reported unemployment figures for the past year.

When you combine sentences to eliminate repetition and wordiness, make sure you keep all the important information from the original sentences.

Repetition: Our manager created a plan, and she discussed it with the team. The team is the group that is responsible for writing company policies.

Incomplete: Our manager discussed a plan with the team that is responsible for writing company policies.

Complete: Our manager created a plan and discussed it with the team that is responsible for writing company policies.

▶ SKILL PRACTICE

Circle the letter of the best revision of each pair of sentences.

1.   I make an award-winning bread using a special recipe. It is a recipe for bread that was handed down by my great-grandmother.
    A.   I make an award-winning bread using a special recipe handed down by my great-grandmother.
    B.   I make an award-winning bread using a special recipe, and it was handed down by my great-grandmother.

2.   This request is made by me. I'd like this request to be considered with care, and I'd like what I request to be respected.
    A.   This request is made by me, and it should be considered carefully with respect.
    B.   I'd like my request to be considered with care and respect.

Combine the sentences to eliminate repetition.

3.   The witness said the accident took place last week, and it was on a Sunday. The witness said that the accident involved a red sports car. It also involved a bike.

    ....

    ....

Check your answers on page 256.

TRANSITION WORDS

One way to explain your ideas clearly is to include transition words in your paragraphs. **Transition words** link ideas in specific ways. For example, **time-order transition words** show the order of ideas through time. Common time-order transition words are listed below.

first	next	before	meanwhile
second	then	soon	when
third	last	later	while
fourth	after	during	earlier

No transition words: Go north on Main Street for two miles.
Turn left onto King Street.
Take a left by the park.

Transition words: <u>First</u>, go north on Main Street for two miles.
<u>Next</u>, turn left onto King Street.
<u>Finally</u>, take a left by the park.

▶ **SKILL PRACTICE**

Write time-order transition words to complete the paragraph. Use each word once.

when	second	last	then	first

_____ , go north to the corner. _____ ,

turn right at the food store. Look for the sign for Smith Street.

_____ you see the sign, walk a block more.

_____ turn left. _____ , stop at the dress

shop. Our apartment is on the second floor.

On your own paper, write directions that a friend could use to go from your house or apartment to the nearest grocery store. Be sure to include time-order transition words to make the directions clear. Begin your directions with the word *first*.

Conjunctive Adverbs

Another way to explain your ideas clearly is to include conjunctive adverbs in your writing. Here are some examples of conjunctive adverbs.

also	hence	moreover	similarly
consequently	however	nevertheless	then
finally	indeed	nonetheless	therefore
furthermore	likewise	otherwise	thus

1. Conjunctive adverbs indicate a connection between two independent clauses in one sentence. In this case, the conjunctive adverb should be preceded by a semicolon and followed by a comma.

   I will be renting a small apartment in Brooklyn; hence, I will not have a lot of extra spending money.

2. Conjunctive adverbs link the ideas in two or more sentences. Again, a comma follows the conjunctive adverb.

   The forecast is for 12 inches of snow today. Nonetheless, we will not cancel our field trip.

3. Conjunctive adverbs show a relationship between ideas within an independent clause.

   Roger maintains, however, that he will not pay you back.

▶ SKILL PRACTICE

Complete each sentence with a conjunctive adverb. Use each one only once.

finally   **however**   **furthermore**   **nevertheless**   **thus**

1. Sam waited an hour for help; _____ , someone helped him.

2. I am not very hungry; _____ , I will have lunch with you.

3. There are many reasons to take the job; _____ , I really need the money.

4. I really want to take a vacation; _____ , I will save up my money.

5. Sara really wanted a puppy; _____ , her landlord did not allow pets.

Write a sentence using each conjunctive adverb.

6. (moreover) _____

7. (indeed) _____

8. (consequently) _____

Check your answers on page 257.

Logic/Clarity Words

Using words and phrases that establish clarity and logic helps the reader better understand the relationship between ideas and follow the progression of the discussion. They can be used between sentences or whole paragraphs.

Purpose	Words
to introduce examples	for example, for instance, in fact, in particular, namely, particularly, specifically, such as, that is, to illustrate
to state a purpose	to do this, so that, to this end, for this purpose, for that reason, because of this
to compare objects or ideas	also, by comparison, equally, in the same way, likewise, similarly
to contrast objects or ideas	although, but, however, in contrast, nevertheless, on the contrary, on the other hand, rather, still, though, unlike, whereas, yet
to add thoughts or ideas	and, and then, yet, also, further, moreover, additionally, in addition, besides
to conclude or summarize	in brief, in conclusion, in other words, in short, in summary, to sum up

When deciding which words to use, think about the relationship between your ideas.

Driving to work may be faster, *but* taking the train is much better for the environment.

▶ SKILL PRACTICE   **Use each of the following once to complete the paragraph.**

for example   in addition   in summary   on the other hand   similarly

We should begin a recycling program in the office. There are many ways we could recycle. _____, we could provide a bin for recycled paper near the copier. _____, we could make changes in the cafeteria. We could encourage people to bring their lunches to work in reusable bags. _____, we could encourage recycling by adding bins for people to recycle cans and bottles. _____, we could do nothing and simply contribute to the polluting of Earth.

_____, I care about Earth, and I would like to see us do something about it by starting a recycling program in the office.

CAPITALIZATION

Your writing creates an impression of you in your reader's mind. If you are writing a letter or an e-mail as an employee of a company, it also creates an impression of your company. For anything you write—from a personal e-mail to a formal response to a writing prompt on the GED® test—you want your capitalization to be correct. There are several rules for capitalization.

Capitalize First Word

1. Use a capital letter for the first word of a sentence.

> **D**o I smell something burning? **T**hat paper is on fire! **H**elp!

Capitalize Names of People

1. Capitalize each part of a person's name. Do not capitalize common nouns.

> Louise **C**. **G**uccione
> **S**. **M**. Johnstone
> *No capital:* The man lives next door to me.

2. Capitalize titles and abbreviations that come before and after people's names. Do not capitalize when a title stands alone.

> **M**r. Zell **D**. **M**oore Jr.
> **D**r. Katherine Lord
> *No capital:* The doctor has an office downtown.

3. Capitalize words showing family relationships when they are used as a title or in place of a name. Do not capitalize when the word stands alone.

> **A**unt Jane will not be able to go, but **D**ad will.
> *No capital:* My aunt and my dad will not be able to go.

Capitalize Places

1. Capitalize the names of cities, states, and sections of the country.

> **City and state:** Chicago, Illinois
> **Section:** Midwest

2. Capitalize the names of countries, languages, religions, and regions.

Country: Saudi Arabia **Language:** Arabic
Nationality: Arabian **Religion:** Islam
Region: Middle East

3. Capitalize the names of streets, highways, bodies of water, islands, buildings, monuments, natural landmarks, bridges, and tourist attractions.

Street: Wall Street
Water: Atlantic Ocean
Island: Prince Edward Island
Building: Empire State Building
Highway: New Jersey Turnpike
Monument: Statue of Liberty
Natural landmark: Grand Canyon
Bridge: Golden Gate Bridge
Tourist attractions: Six Flags, Yellowstone National Park

▶ SKILL PRACTICE

Use the editing marks to show where capital letters are needed (a = A) or where letters should be lowercase (A = a).

1. writer ed j. smith reports that people are taking cheaper trips in the Summer.

2. mr. and mrs. mott drove to orlando, florida, and went camping.

3. last year, the Motts went to sea world.

4. this year, dr. ortega and his family went hiking instead of going to mt. rushmore in south dakota.

5. ms. wills visited her friend in Wisconsin rather than flying to the Island of st. kitts.

6. miss e. k. link from newtown, long island, spent two days in maine.

7. she went to lake mead last year.

8. busch gardens in tampa, florida, is still very busy, though.

9. My Doctor wants to go to israel and see the dead sea.

Complete each sentence. Use capital letters correctly.

Sample: My dog is named _____ Fido _____ . (name)

10. My dentist is _____ . (title + name)

11. I would love to go to _____ . (place name)

12. I was born in _____ . (country)

Capitalize Things

1. Capitalize months, days, and holidays. Do not capitalize seasons of the year.

    Month: My birthday is in **N**ovember.
    Day: I love **F**riday afternoons.
    Month and Day: Saturday, **J**uly 9
    Holiday: My favorite holiday is **T**hanksgiving.
    No capital: My birthday is in spring.

2. Capitalize the names of companies and organizations.

    Company: Adams-**C**larke **A**ssociates
    Organization: Veterans **S**ociety

▶ SKILL PRACTICE

Rewrite each sentence using correct capital letters.

1. last year I worked on senator smith's campaign.

    _____

2. the campaign office was on fifth avenue in the chrysler building.

    _____

3. a debate was sponsored by a group called independent voters of america at their building on the hudson river.

    _____

4. laura washington, vice president of the organization, made a speech.

    _____

Use the editing marks to show where capital letters are needed (a = A) or where letters should be lowercase (A = a).

5. This year, monday, january 18, dr. martin luther king jr. day will be a paid holiday.

6. This holiday is in the place of columbus day, which we took as a day off on october 10.

7. The plant will, of course, be closed for the usual Fall and Winter holidays—thanksgiving, christmas, and new year's eve.

8. If any of these holidays fall on a monday or a friday, you will have a long weekend.

9. This year the Company's independence Day picnic will be on sunday, july 7.

10. I will be back at work on Tuesday, september 6, the day after labor day.

11. Some people want to have the party on Flag day, june 14, instead.

12. There has also been talk of a halloween party for october 31, which is a thursday this year.

13. We could hold the party on friday, october 25, if that is a better time.

Answer each question with a complete sentence. Use capital letters correctly.

14. What are your favorite holidays?

_____

15. Which is the best day of the week for you?

_____

16. What is your favorite season of the year?

_____

Use the editing mark to show where capital letters are needed (a = A).

harriet quimby was the first woman to earn a pilot's license. she was a

writer in new york before she flew a plane. she fell in love with airplanes in 1910

when she saw her first flying meet. harriet became a pilot and toured in mexico

with a troupe of pilots. she decided she would be the first woman to cross the

english channel. she took off on april 16, 1912, sitting on a wicker basket in the

cockpit. after a scary flight, she landed on a french beach.

Answer each question with a complete sentence. Use capital letters correctly.

17. What city (or town) and state do you live in?

_____

18. Where do you like to shop? (use names of stores)

_____

Use the editing mark to show where capital letters are needed (a = A).

Bradley Advertising Agency
45 Capital Street
Columbus, OH 43225

may 20, 2014

supreme computer, inc.

958 alexander street

river tower

Columbus, oh 43221

dear mr. Potter:

my supervisor, doris healy, director of sales here at bradley associates, asked me to send you the enclosed brochure detailing the services our company provides to computer stores like yours. If interested, you can take advantage of our free trial offer by calling before may 31. We are closed next Monday because of memorial day.

Sincerely,

James Hobson

james hobson

sales assistant

SENTENCE FRAGMENTS & RUN-ON SENTENCES

A **sentence fragment** is a group of words that does not express a complete thought. Even if a fragment begins with a capital letter and ends with a period, it is not a sentence. Some information is missing from it.

Fragment: Ran away with the bone. (missing a subject)

Correct: A dog ran away with the bone.

Fragment: Helped her get a job as a cashier. (missing a subject)

Correct: Her friend in the diner helped her get a job as a cashier.

Fragment: The rags under the sink. (missing a verb)

Correct: The rags under the sink are dirty.

▶ **SKILL PRACTICE**

Write *C* if the group of words is a complete sentence. Write *F* if it is a fragment.

_____ **1.** "Road rage" is an act of aggression similar to an assault.

_____ **2.** Taking place after two drivers have a disagreement.

_____ **3.** Tailgating, yelling curses, and flashing the headlights.

_____ **4.** Also fall into this category.

_____ **5.** Because driving can be very stressful.

_____ **6.** Some drivers are unable to control themselves.

_____ **7.** Often these drivers are already angry about a problem at home or work.

Change each fragment into a complete sentence.

Sample: One safety rule. ___One safety rule is to use your seat belt.___

8. The minimum driving age.

_____

9. Drive too fast.

_____

There are three ways to test whether a group of words is a fragment. If you answer *no* to one of the following questions, you have a fragment.

1. **Is there a verb?** If there is no verb, the group of words is a fragment. All parts of the verb must be present for a sentence to be complete. To correct this type of fragment, add or complete the verb.

    Fragment: Mark taking a GED® class.

    Correct: Mark is taking a GED® class.

2. **Is there a subject?** To find out if a sentence has a subject, ask <u>who</u> or <u>what</u> is doing the action. If there is no subject, the group of words is a fragment. To correct this type of fragment, add a subject.

    Fragment: Studied hard for the test. (Who studied?)

    Correct: Mark studied hard for the test.

3. **Does the group of words express a complete thought?** Even if the group of words has a subject and a verb, it is not a complete sentence if it does not express a complete thought. To correct this type of fragment, complete the thought.

    Fragment: After we studied a lot. (What is the complete thought?)

    Correct: After we studied a lot, we did well on the test.

▶ SKILL PRACTICE

Explain why each of the following groups of words is a fragment.

1. In the last twenty years, the number of families with adult children living at home.

    This is a fragment because _____ .

2. Increased by 4 percent.

    This is a fragment because _____ .

3. Compared to a generation ago, fewer young adults.

    This is a fragment because _____ .

4. Can afford to set up their own households.

    This is a fragment because _____ .

Change each fragment into a complete sentence.

5. My older sister still living with our parents.

    _____

6. Enjoys spending time with them in the evenings.

    _____

Run-on Sentences

A **run-on** sentence is two or more complete thoughts that are not correctly separated. There are two kinds of run-on sentences.

1. One type is made up of two sentences that are not separated by punctuation.

   Run-on: The storm got worse it turned toward the land.

   Correct: The storm got worse. It turned toward the land.

   Run-on: The Japanese subway is the fastest train it travels over 100 miles per hour.

   Correct: The Japanese subway is the fastest train. It travels over 100 miles per hour.

2. The other type is made up of two sentences joined with a comma when they should be joined with a semicolon or a comma and a coordinating conjunction. This type of run-on is sometimes called a comma splice.

   Run-on: We were not hungry, we had already had lunch.

   Correct: We were not hungry; we had already had lunch.

   Run-on: You can visit the White House, you can tour many rooms.

   Correct: You can visit the White House, and you can tour many rooms.

▶ **SKILL PRACTICE**   Write **RO** if the sentence is a run-on. Write **C** if the sentence is correct.

_____   **1.** Bacteria in food can cause illness you should take care to store food properly.

_____   **2.** Don't keep cooked food that's been standing out for two or more hours, don't even taste it.

_____   **3.** Hamburgers should be eaten well-done, cooking kills bacteria.

_____   **4.** Raw eggs are not safe to eat they may contain salmonella.

_____   **5.** It's a good practice to date your leftovers and throw them out after three to five days.

_____   **6.** Dishes should be washed right away it's better to air-dry them than to use a towel.

_____   **7.** You can use soap to clean the kitchen counter, but bleach is better.

_____   **8.** It's important to store food properly and to keep food preparation areas clean.

How to Correct Run-on Sentences

1. Use an end punctuation mark to separate the two complete thoughts.

   Run-on: Do most people like crowds I don't think so.

   Correct: Do most people like crowds? I don't think so.

2. Use a semicolon to connect two complete thoughts.

   Run-on: I couldn't wait to jump in the water looked so cool.

   Correct: I couldn't wait to jump in; the water looked so cool.

3. Use a comma and a coordinating conjunction—*and, but, or, so, for, nor,* or *yet*—to connect the two complete thoughts.

   Run-on: The sky got dark it started to rain.

   Correct: The sky got dark, and it started to rain.

▶ SKILL PRACTICE

Correct each run-on sentence by using one of the three methods described above.

1. The Special Olympics started in 1968 it is a sports competition for people with disabilities.

   ....

2. More than 7,000 athletes attend they come from 150 nations.

   ....

3. Each nation competes in 19 sporting events athletes do not have to enter every event.

   ....

4. Everyone is a winner each athlete gets a ribbon or medal.

   ....

5. Many people come to watch they are impressed by the athletes.

   ....

Add another complete thought to each complete thought below. Separate the thoughts with correct punctuation and/or a connecting word.

6. I enjoy watching the Olympic Games ....

   ....

7. Winning a gold medal must be a thrill ....

   ....

APOSTROPHES WITH POSSESSIVES

The **possessive** form of a noun shows that something is owned, and it shows who or what the owner is. An **apostrophe** (') shows possession.

1. Use an apostrophe and *s* to form the possessive of singular nouns.

    Troy drove his wife's car to work yesterday.

    I saw him yesterday at Roberto's house.

    The actor's hat fell off his head during the performance.

    That child's toy is about to break.

    Although you do not have to add a second *s* to names ending in *s* or an *s* sound, it is often preferred.

    Kansas's weather can be dicey in the spring.

    We signed for Mr. Mata's package.

    Dr. Hagness's office is closing early today. (Last name is *Hagness.*)

2. To show plural possession, make the noun plural first, then add an apostrophe ('). This holds true for both regular and irregular plural nouns.

    The boys' shirts were on backward. (regular plural)

    The women's book club is closed to new members. (irregular plural)

    I designed the actresses' costumes for the play.

    We are having dinner at the Changs' house tonight.

3. Use an apostrophe where the noun that should follow is implied.

    This was his mother's.

4. Use an apostrophe for possessive nouns only. Do not use an apostrophe with plural nouns that are *not* possessive.

    My sisters and the Matas live near each other.

    The Joneses have two cats and three dogs.

5. To show possession with a compound word, add an apostrophe and *s* to the end of the word.

    The party will be at my father-in-law's house.

    I absolutely loved my sisters-in-law's presents.

6. If two people own the same thing, add an apostrophe and *s* after the second name only. If each person owns something separately, add an apostrophe and *s* after both names.

Mary and Peter's house is on Oak Avenue. (The house belongs to both Mary and Peter.)

Mary's and Peter's houses are on Oak Avenue. (Mary and Peter each own separate houses.)

7. Never use an apostrophe with possessive pronouns, such as *his, hers, its, theirs, ours, yours, whose*. These words already show possession, so they do not need an apostrophe.

▶ SKILL PRACTICE

Circle the correct word to complete the sentence.

1. (**Trans, Tran's**) workday begins very early.

2. He gets up at six o'clock to make his (**childrens', children's**) breakfast.

3. At seven o'clock, he drives by his (**friend's, friends'**) houses to take them to work.

4. By eight o'clock, Tran and his friends are at work on the (**factories, factory's**) main floor.

5. Tran enjoys his work painting car (**body's, bodies**).

Write a sentence with the person and objects below. Use the possessive form.

Sample: (my dogs/game) _My dogs' favorite game is fetch._

6. (Mr. Tillis/sweater) _____

7. (Sarah and Emma/cousin) _____

8. (My boss/desk) _____

9. (My brothers-in-law/tickets) _____

10. (Dr. Reyna/schedule) _____

COMMAS

Commas help to break up sentences to make them easier to read. There are several different uses for commas.

1. Use commas to separate a series of three or more nouns, verbs, or adjectives. So that your sentences are absolutely clear, it is best to put a comma after the word that appears before the word *and* or *or* in the series.

    Nouns Remember, a noun is a person, place, or thing.

    Julio brought Akim, Marcus, and Sammi to his cousin's house.

    My family visited San Francisco, San Diego, and Los Angeles.

    Caitlin, Greg, and Billy all like to eat apples, oranges, and bananas.

    Mom said I could have lasagna, beef stew, or chicken for dinner.

    Verbs Remember, a verb is an action word.

    Abdul likes to play soccer, run track, and wrestle.

    Serena took a shower, brushed her teeth, and got dressed in 10 minutes.

    We need to warm the bread, slice the tomatoes, and wash the lettuce for dinner.

    Adjectives Remember, an adjective is a describing word. There may not always be a combining word such as *and* or *or* in a series of adjectives.

    Alison planted yellow, orange, and red tulips.

    The puppy had a long, narrow, sad face.

    Mom was happy with her shiny, new, expensive sports car.

2. Do not use a comma between the two subjects in a compound subject or the two verbs in a compound predicate.

    Compound subject: Joe and Paul played cards that day.

    Compound predicate: Hector read magazines and sorted his gear.

▶ SKILL PRACTICE   **Add commas where they are needed in each sentence. If the sentence does not need commas, mark it with a C for correct.**

_____ **1.** The picnic was ruined by ants flies and gnats.

_____ **2.** Dogs howl whine or bark when they need to go out.

_____ **3.** My favorite restaurant serves breakfast lunch and dinner.

_____ **4.** Mr. García graded the exams and passed them out.

_____ **5.** Sang Lee has traveled to New York City Boston and Pittsburgh on business.

_____ **6.** Carrie directed acted and sang in the community play.

_____ **7.** I wrote edited proofread and printed my article for the newspaper.

_____ **8.** The bus driver waited for Sara and Meredith to run to the corner.

_____ **9.** Scout likes her tacos hot spicy and crunchy.

_____ **10.** You have to rest eat well and drink plenty of water to get over a cold.

_____ **11.** My new girlfriend is smart, pretty, and creative.

_____ **12.** We gazed in awe at the huge majestic snowy mountain.

_____ **13.** Spot and Tigger play together really well.

Write a sentence with the three words listed, using commas as needed.

14. (the White House, the Capitol, the Washington Monument)

_____

_____

15. (large, comfy, orange) _____

_____

16. (planted, weeded, pruned) _____

_____

17. (ancient, massive, imposing) _____

_____

18. (basil, tomatoes, bay leaves) _____

_____

Appositives

Appositives are words or word groups that rename or provide more information about a noun or pronoun.

Mrs. Johnson, our neighbor, was taken to the hospital. (*Our neighbor* identifies or explains who *Mrs. Johnson* is.)

There are essential and nonessential appositives. An **essential appositive** is necessary to maintain the meaning of a sentence, and you do not use commas to set it off from the rest of the sentence. Often, an essential appositive is a single word closely related to the preceding word.

The baseball player Jackie Robinson really changed the game. (*Jackie Robinson* is essential in this sentence. If you read just, "The baseball player really changed the game," you would not know which baseball player changed the game.)

A **nonessential appositive** may be left out of a sentence without changing the basic meaning of the sentence. Use a comma before and after nonessential appositives.

My uncle, who lives in California, is coming to visit. (The phrase *who lives in California* is not essential to the sentence. You would still know that someone's uncle is coming to visit, whether or not you know where he lives.)

The historic town, which was nestled in the valley, drew many tourists. (The phrase *which was nestled in the valley* is not needed for the sentence to make sense.)

Parenthetical Expressions

Other nonessential elements in a sentence include parenthetical expressions such as *for example, however,* or *of course.* Use commas before and after these words to set them off from the rest of the sentence.

The contract, of course, must be signed in ink.

The average temperature, however, has continued to rise.

In both these examples, the parenthetical expressions could be left out and the sentence would still have the same meaning.

UNIT 5 LANGUAGE SKILLS

▶ SKILL PRACTICE   **Add commas where they are needed in each sentence. If the sentence is correct as is, mark it with a _C_ for correct.**

_____   **1.** We will handle this legally of course by going to the zoning board.

_____   **2.** The ship _Titanic_ sank when it hit an iceberg.

_____   **3.** The woman who interviewed you is my aunt.

_____   **4.** My mom who is eighty years old ran a marathon last year.

_____   **5.** Before you donate Pooky your favorite stuffed animal think about keeping it.

_____   **6.** The kid checking tickets at the door asked for my driver's license.

_____   **7.** The cell phone should be returned to Mr. Brown the owner.

_____   **8.** The plane a Boeing 747 landed safely in Los Angeles.

_____   **9.** The developer however will likely put up a fight.

_____   **10.** I walk my dogs Marley and Bailey around the park every day.

Write a sentence using each group of words as indicated.

11. (_my friend_, appositive) _____

_____

_____

12. (_however_, parenthetical expression) _____

_____

_____

END PUNCTUATION

Punctuation is the set of symbols used in writing to guide the reader. You need to let your readers know when you have finished a complete thought. That is the role of end punctuation. A sentence always ends with a period, a question mark, or an exclamation point. Each type of punctuation signals something different to the reader.

1. Use a **period** to end a statement—a sentence that gives information or states facts. You can also use a period to show the end of a command.

    > I am studying right now.

    > Open your books to page 156.

    > I am not going to ask again. Please clean your room.

2. Use a **question mark** to end a question. Most questions begin with a question word such as *who, what, where, when, why,* and *how.* However, sometimes a question word is not used and the question mark tells readers that the sentence is a question.

    > When are you planning to move?

    > Is heat included in the rent?

    > Would you like cream in your coffee?

    Do not use a question mark at the end of an indirect question. Use a period instead.

    > She wondered when her package would arrive.

    > Suki asked how she could get a better grade on her paper.

3. Use an **exclamation point** to end a sentence that shows strong emotion.

    > That's awesome!

    > Watch out for that truck!

    > Hurrah! Summer is here!

> **TIP**
>
> In more formal writing, such as in a response to a GED® writing prompt, you will want to use a period to end almost all of your sentences. You are usually not asking questions in your response, and exclamation marks are generally not recommended because of the tone they may imply.

Add the correct punctuation to complete each sentence.

1. Would you like to get a dog

2. I love my dog

3. Owning a dog is a big responsibility

4. Puppies are so darn cute

5. But, boy, can they chew

6. If you rent, you have to ask your landlord if it's okay to have a dog

7. To adopt a dog, you have to answer a lot questions

8. Do you have a fenced-in yard

9. Where will the dog stay

10. Owning a dog can be very expensive

11. You will have to ask your vet how much shots cost

12. Do you still want a dog

Write three sentences about dogs. Use correct end punctuation.

13. (statement)

_____

_____

14. (question)

_____

_____

15. (strong emotion)

_____

_____

Check your answers on page 261.

PUNCTUATION IN CLAUSE SEPARATION

A good piece of writing includes a variety of sentences. If all your sentences are short and simple, your writing will also seem simple and uninteresting. If you combine ideas into a variety of sentence structures, your writing will be much more interesting to your readers.

You cannot just throw sentences together, however. There are certain rules of sentence structure and punctuation that you need to learn and follow so that you do not introduce errors into your writing, such as run-on sentences, incomplete sentences, and incorrect use of commas. You can think of writing as representing spoken words. The rules of punctuation are designed to imitate the natural patterns and pauses that we use when we speak.

A **clause** is the basic building block of sentence structure. It includes a subject and predicate, or verb or verb phrase.

> Chaz is happy.
>
> She ate pizza.
>
> He received a package.

An **independent clause** can stand by itself as a complete sentence.

> Four cars crashed into each other.
>
> The farmers' market opens at 8 a.m.
>
> The sun is shining today.

A **dependent clause** cannot stand by itself as a complete sentence.

> while I was eating
>
> because it was a long way
>
> although I felt bad

There are two ways to vary sentence structure by combining ideas, or clauses, into one sentence.

1. Use compound sentences.

2. Use complex sentences.

Punctuation in Compound Sentences

Remember that an independent clause can stand on its own as a complete sentence. A **compound sentence** is made up of *two* independent clauses that are closely related.

The job will be hard, but I can do it.

The complete thoughts in a compound sentence can be joined with a **comma** and a connecting word called a **coordinating conjunction.** The most common coordinating conjunctions are *and, but, or,* and *so.* Make sure you use both a comma and a coordinating conjunction. Otherwise, you will have a **run-on sentence,** which is a mistake in sentence structure.

Simple Sentences:	Rosa takes care of stray animals. Rosa finds new homes for strays.
Compound Sentence:	Rosa takes care of stray animals, or she finds new homes for them.
Simple Sentences:	Rosa's favorite pet is a sad-eyed puppy. Rosa also loves the white alley cat she found.
Compound Sentence:	Rosa's favorite pet is a sad-eyed puppy, but she also loves the white alley cat she found.
Simple Sentences:	The cat roams all over the house. The parakeet has to be kept in its cage.
Compound Sentence:	The cat roams all over the house, so the parakeet has to be kept in its cage.
Simple Sentences:	I help Rosa with the animals. She pays me a small amount for my work.
Compound Sentence:	I help Rosa with the animals, and she pays me a small amount for my work.

▶ SKILL PRACTICE

Combine each pair of independent clauses to make a compound sentence. Use a comma and one of the coordinating conjunctions *and, but, or,* or *so*.

1. The skies opened up. Lightning streaked across the clouds.

   _____

2. Last year we had floods. This year was not as bad.

   _____

3. The storm caused severe damage. Several people were injured.

   _____

4. Windows were shattered by the wind. We went into the basement.

   _____

5. We read books. Sometimes we played cards.

   _____

Complete each sentence below by adding a related second independent clause to make a compound sentence. Use the conjunction listed above the sentence. The first sentence is done for you.

6. **but**
   The steak was tender, *but it was too well-done* _____.

7. **and**
   The street was deserted, _____.

8. **so**
   The couch was new, _____.

9. **but**
   The soldiers marched bravely, _____.

10. **so**
    The sky looked threatening, _____.

11. **so**
    The fruit was ripe, _____.

12. **or**
    I should get gas soon, _____.

13. **or**
    We could see this movie, _____.

Punctuation in Complex Sentences

Another way to vary your writing is to use complex sentences. A **complex sentence** has two parts: one independent clause and one dependent clause. Remember that an independent clause has a subject and predicate and can stand alone as a complete thought. A dependent clause has a subject and verb, but it cannot stand alone because it is not a complete sentence or thought. One way to remember the difference is to think of this: A dependent clause depends on the independent clause to complete the sentence or thought.

A dependent clause may come either before or after an independent clause. If the dependent clause comes first in the sentence, place a comma after it.

<u>Wherever</u> you go, you will see tall buildings.

You will see tall buildings <u>wherever</u> you go.

A dependent clause begins with a connecting word called a **subordinating conjunction.** Here are some common subordinating conjunctions.

after	as soon as	even if	though	when
although	as though	even though	unless	whenever
as	because	if	until	whichever
as if	before	since	whatever	while

Use a conjunction from the box above to combine each pair of clauses to make a complex sentence. Use a comma if the dependent clause is first in the sentence.

1. the weather is still nice/we will take a drive to the mountains

   If the weather is still nice, we will take a drive to the mountains.

2. you drive on the Blue Ridge Parkway/you can stop at many overlooks

   _____

3. most people stop at Mt. Mitchell/that's the most spectacular view of all

   _____

4. you'll want to take pictures/it's hard to get those mountain ranges on film

   _____

5. stay on the parkway/you reach the city of Asheville

   _____

▶ **Write a contraction to replace the underlined words.**

_____ **1.** I <u>am</u> studying to be a teacher.

_____ **2.** The passengers were not happy when the plane <u>did not</u> take off.

_____ **3.** <u>We have</u> not received any compensation from the insurance company.

_____ **4.** <u>She will</u> never be happy.

_____ **5.** Manny <u>will not</u> be able to sleep over at Mac's.

▶ **Write the correct word to complete each sentence.**

6. Those _____ don't fit you properly.
(clothes, close)

7. I weigh less _____ my little sister!
(than, then)

8. Tim's mother is finding it hard to _____ his decision to move away.
(accept, except)

9. That store is open 7 days a _____ , 24 hours a day.
(week, weak)

10. The two sisters battled it out _____ them.
(among, between)

▶ **Write the correct verb to complete each sentence.**

11. Allen and Sheila _____ going to the movie tomorrow.
(is, are)

12. Both of them already _____ how it ends.
(knows, know)

13. The movie is about a boy who _____ his nose in a fight at school.
(breaks, break)

14. Surprisingly, the principal _____ him another chance.
(gives, give)

15. By the end of the movie, everyone in the audience _____ cheering.
(is, are)

▷ **Read each sentence. Then write a follow-up sentence using a correct pronoun to go with the underlined noun or nouns.**

16. <u>Jeff and Melissa</u> decide to buy a new car.

_____

17. Jeff and Melissa go to <u>their bank</u> for a loan.

_____

18. <u>Jeff's dad</u> also offers to lend Jeff and Melissa some money.

_____

19. Jeff's parents rely on <u>Jeff</u> for rides.

_____

▷ **Rewrite each sentence to correct the dangling modifier.**

20. Walking home from school, a bird landed on a white fence.

_____

21. While watching TV, the comedian made me laugh.

_____

22. Making my bed, a mouse ran across the room.

_____

23. While cooking dinner, my dog begged for food.

_____

24. Taking a shower this morning, the water turned freezing cold.

_____

▷ **Use one of the connecting words listed below to create a complex sentence from each group of words.**

after	if	unless
because	since	when
before	so that	whenever

25. Jen walks her dog at night _____.

26. It's also pleasant in the morning _____.

27. _____ she treats her dog like a person.

MINI-TEST

 This is a 15-minute practice test. After 15 minutes, mark the last number you finished. Then complete the test and check your answers. If most of your answers were correct but you did not finish, try to work faster next time.

▶ **Write time-order transition words to complete the paragraph. Use each word once.**

when	second	last	then	first

Finding your way around Chicago is not easy. If you decide to take a train,

_____ you need to decide which train line you need. _____,

you need to find a station along that train line. _____ you need to buy a ticket.

_____ you see a train coming, be ready to get on. _____, get

off the train at the right stop. You can then take the bus or walk to your final destination.

▶ **Rewrite each sentence. Correct any errors in capitalization.**

1. Rob went to new york in September to visit his uncle.

   _____

2. Because it was Autumn, sights like the statue of liberty weren't crowded.

   _____

3. on labor day, rob walked through central park and up fifth avenue.

   _____

4. He ate french food and saw a game at yankee stadium.

   _____

▶ **If the group of words is a sentence, write *S*. If it is a fragment, add words to make it a complete sentence.**

5. The apartment on the fourth floor.

   _____

6. Pedro looked at it last week.

   _____

7. Thinking about it on the way home from work.

   _____

▶ **Correct each run-on sentence by writing it as two complete sentences.**

8. Craig has an unusual job he is a chef.

_____

9. He used to work in a store he was a cashier.

_____

10. Then he went to cooking school for two years, it was a long program.

_____

▶ **Add punctuation marks and correct capitalization where needed in each sentence.**

11. Did you come to our wedding

12. My husband and I were married at a catholic church in Chicago illinois

13. It was the best wedding ever

14. His brothers Ed hal John and joe stood on his side.

15. I on the other hand had only my sister amy stand by me

16. the wedding was beautiful and all the guests had a good time

17. Do you know where we went for our Honeymoon

18. We went to Atlantic city niagara falls and New York city

19. Then we visited Millie my aunt on my mother's side for a few days

20. I was absolutely exhausted

▶ **Circle the word that shows the correct use of an apostrophe in each sentence.**

21. **(Sams', Sam's)** dog got out today.

22. The **(twins', twin's)** bunk bed broke after they jumped on it.

23. **(Mannys', Manny's)** new job does not start till next Monday.

24. **(His, His')** shirt is on backwards.

25. The **(waitresses', waitress's)** tips are not enough for her to feed her kids.

ANSWER SHEET

Posttest Reasoning Through Language Arts

Name: _____ Class: _____ Date: _____

1. (A) (B) (C) (D)

2. (A) (B) (C) (D)

3. **Write response to #3 on your own paper.**

4. (A) (B) (C) (D)

5. (A) (B) (C) (D)

6. **Write response to #6 on your own paper.**

7. (A) (B) (C) (D)

8. (A) (B) (C) (D)

9–13 **Write responses to #9–13 on your own paper.**

14. (A) (B) (C) (D)

15. (A) (B) (C) (D)

16. (A) (B) (C) (D)

17. (A) (B) (C) (D)

18–19 **Write responses to #18–19 on your own paper.**

20. (A) (B) (C) (D)

21. (A) (B) (C) (D)

22. (A) (B) (C) (D)

23. (A) (B) (C) (D)

24. (A) (B) (C) (D)

25. **Write response to #25 on your own paper.**

26. _____

27. _____

28. _____

29. _____

30. _____

31. (A) (B) (C) (D)

32–34 **Write responses to #32–34 on your own paper.**

35. _____ _____

36. _____

37. _____

38. _____ _____

39. **Write response to #39 on your own paper.**

40. (A) (B) (C) (D)

41. (A) (B) (C) (D)

42. (A) (B) (C) (D)

43. (A) (B) (C) (D)

44. (A) (B) (C) (D)

45. **Write response to #45 on your own paper.**

46. (A) (B) (C) (D)

47. _____

48. **Write response to #48 on your own paper.**

49. (A) (B) (C) (D)

50. (A) (B) (C) (D)

51. (A) (B) (C) (D)

52. **Write response to #52 on your own paper.**

53. (A) (B) (C) (D)

54. (A) (B) (C) (D)

55. (A) (B) (C) (D)

56. (A) (B) (C) (D)

57. (A) (B) (C) (D)

58. (A) (B) (C) (D)

59. (A) (B) (C) (D)

60. (A) (B) (C) (D)

61. (A) (B) (C) (D)

62. (A) (B) (C) (D)

63. (A) (B) (C) (D)

64. (A) (B) (C) (D)

65. (A) (B) (C) (D)

66. (A) (B) (C) (D)

67. (A) (B) (C) (D)

68. (A) (B) (C) (D)

69. (A) (B) (C) (D)

70. (A) (B) (C) (D)

71. (A) (B) (C) (D)

72. (A) (B) (C) (D)

73. (A) (B) (C) (D)

74. (A) (B) (C) (D)

75. (A) (B) (C) (D)

76. (A) (B) (C) (D)

77. (A) (B) (C) (D)

78. (A) (B) (C) (D)

Directions

The Pre GED® Reasoning Through Language Arts Posttest consists of three sections: Reading Comprehension, Extended Response, and Language Skills. This is a 150-minute practice test. The Reading Comprehension section should take approximately 60 minutes. The Extended Response section should take approximately 45 minutes. The Language Skills section should take approximately 35 minutes. Time yourself as you work through each section. After the allotted minutes, mark the last number you finished. Complete the test and check your answers. If most of your answers are correct but you did not finish, try to work faster next time.

The Reading Comprehension section consists of fiction and several types of informational selections—social studies, science, and workplace. Each selection is followed by multiple-choice, fill-in-the-blank, and short-answer questions about the reading material. Read each selection and then answer the questions that follow. Refer back to the reading material as often as necessary when answering the questions.

The Extended Response section measures your ability to use clear and effective English in a written response. The extended response requires you to read and analyze two texts. You must use evidence from the text to support your response to the prompt.

The Language Skills section measures your ability to recognize errors in sentence structure, usage, and mechanics. The test will present a number of different skills.

Record your answers on the answer sheet on page 204, which you may photocopy. For multiple-choice items, fill in the lettered circle on the answer sheet that corresponds to the answer you select for each question in the Posttest. For fill-in-the-blank items, write your answers on the line provided. For short-answer and extended-response items, write your answer on your own paper.

EXAMPLE

Sentence 1: **I was excited to receive an invitation to you're party.**

Which correction should be made to sentence 1?

A. change <u>was</u> to <u>is</u>
B. change <u>was</u> to <u>will be</u>
C. change <u>you're</u> to <u>your</u>
D. change <u>receive</u> to <u>recieve</u>

(On Answer Sheet)

Ⓐ Ⓑ ● Ⓓ

The correct answer choice is C.

Reading Comprehension: Fiction Selections

▶ **Read the following selection from *The Adventures of Tom Sawyer* by Mark Twain and then answer questions 1 through 6.**

Will Tom and Becky Find Their Way Home?

(1)   It was but a little while before a certain indecision in his manner revealed another fearful fact to Becky—he could not find his way back!

(2)   "Oh, Tom, you didn't make any marks!"

(3)   "Becky, I was such a fool! Such a fool! I never thought we might want to come back! No—I can't find the way. It's all mixed up."

(4)   "Tom, Tom, we're lost! we're lost! We never can get out of this awful place! Oh, why *did* we ever leave the others!"

(5)   She sank to the ground and burst into such a frenzy of crying that Tom was appalled with the idea that she might die, or lose her reason. He sat down by her and put his arms around her; she buried her face in his bosom, she clung to him, she poured out her terrors, her unavailing regrets, and the far echoes turned them all to jeering laughter. Tom begged her to pluck up hope again, and she said she could not. He fell to blaming and abusing himself for getting her into this miserable situation; this had a better effect. She said she would try to hope again, she would get up and follow wherever he might lead if only he would not talk like that. For he was no more to blame than she, she said.

(6)   So they moved on again—aimlessly—simply at random—all they could do was to move, keep moving. For a little while, hope made a show of reviving—not with any reason to back it, but only because it is its nature to revive when the spring has not been taken out of it by age and familiarity with failure.

(7)   By and by Tom took Becky's candle and blew it out. This economy meant so much! Words were not needed. Becky understood, and her hope died again. She knew that Tom had a whole candle and three or four pieces in his pockets—yet he must economize.

(8)   By and by, fatigue began to assert its claims; the children tried to pay no attention, for it was dreadful to think of sitting down when time was grown to be so precious; moving, in some direction, in any direction, was at least progress and might bear fruit; but to sit down was to invite death and shorten its pursuit.

1. Which statement *best* restates the main idea of paragraph 6?

   A. Hope usually stays only for a brief while.

   B. Hope comes back more easily for the young.

   C. Hope usually has no good reason behind it.

   D. Hope is natural for people, both young and old.

2. What is meant by the phrase "to sit down was to invite death and shorten its pursuit"? (paragraph 8)

   A. They are more likely to die if they don't keep moving.

   B. They are being pursued by someone who wants to kill them.

   C. They will die from exhaustion if they sit down.

   D. They are going to die if they don't admit to being tired and sit down.

3. What would Tom probably do if Becky decisively laid out a plan? Explain your answer. Write your response on your own paper.

4. Based on the information in paragraph 7, which statement would Tom *most likely* make if the paragraph were written from his point of view?

   A. There is no hope! We will die here.

   B. I know we are about to be rescued.

   C. Perhaps the darkness will comfort Becky.

   D. I will save this; we may be here awhile.

5. Mark Twain wrote several novels, including one with a character named Huck Finn. Huck escapes from his father, meets a runaway slave, and journeys down the Mississippi River with him on a raft. Based on this information and the selection, what type of stories did Mark Twain write?

   A. romance

   B. adventure

   C. mystery

   D. biography

6. The title of this selection is "Will Tom and Becky Find Their Way Home?" After reading the selection, what do you think will happen to them? Support your response with your background knowledge of literature and evidence from the selection. Write your response on your own paper.

Reading Comprehension: Fiction Selections

▶ **Read the following selection and then answer questions 7 through 13.**

From *The Open Window* by Saki

(1)   "My aunt will be down presently, Mr. Nuttel," said a very self-possessed young lady of fifteen; "in the meantime you must try and put up with me."

(2)   Framton Nuttel endeavored to say the correct something which should duly flatter the niece of the moment without unduly discounting the aunt that was to come. Privately he doubted more than ever whether these formal visits on a succession of total strangers would do much toward helping the nerve cure which he was supposed to be undergoing.

(3)   "I know how it will be," his sister had said when he was preparing to <u>migrate</u> to this rural retreat; "you will bury yourself down there and not speak to a living soul, and your nerves will be worse than ever from moping. I shall just give you letters of introduction to all the people I know there. Some of them, as far as I can remember, were quite nice."

(4)   Framton wondered whether Mrs. Sappleton, the lady to whom he was presenting one of the letters of introduction, came into the nice division.

(5)   "Do you know many of the people round here?" asked the niece, when she judged that they had had sufficient silent communion.

(6)   "Hardly a soul," said Framton. "My sister was staying here, at the rectory, you know, some four years ago, and she gave me letters of introduction to some of the people here."

(7)   He made the last statement in a tone of distinct regret.

(8)   "Then you know practically nothing about my aunt?" pursued the self-possessed young lady.

(9)   "Only her name and address," admitted the caller. He was wondering whether Mrs. Sappleton was in the married or widowed state. An undefinable something about the room seemed to suggest masculine habitation.

(10)   "Her great tragedy happened just three years ago," said the child; "that would be since your sister's time."

(11)   "Her tragedy?" asked Framton; somehow, in this restful country spot, tragedies seemed out of place.

(12)   "You may wonder why we keep that window wide open on an October afternoon," said the niece, indicating a large French window that opened onto a lawn.

(13)   "It is quite warm for the time of the year," said Framton, "but has that window got anything to do with the tragedy?"

(14)   "Out through that window, three years ago to a day, her husband and her two young brothers went off for their day's shooting. They never came back. In crossing the moor to their favorite snipe-shooting ground, they were all three <u>engulfed</u> in a treacherous piece of bog. It had been that dreadful wet summer, you know, and places that were safe in other years gave way suddenly without warning. The bodies were never recovered. That was the dreadful part of it." Here the child's voice lost its self-possessed note and became falteringly human. "Poor aunt always thinks they will come back someday, they and the little brown spaniel that was lost with them, and walk in at that window just as they used to do. That is why the window is kept open every evening till it is quite dusk. Poor dear aunt, she has often told me how they went out, her husband with his white waterproof coat over his arm, and Ronnie, her youngest brother, singing 'Bertie, why do you bound?' as he always did to tease her. Do you know, sometimes on still, quiet evenings like this, I almost get a creepy feeling that they will all walk through that window—"

(15)   She broke off with a little shudder. It was a relief to Framton when the aunt <u>bustled</u> into the room with a whirl of apologies for being late in making her appearance. . . .

7. What is the main purpose of the flashback in paragraph 3?

    A. to introduce an important character
    B. to explain an important mystery
    C. to introduce a universal theme
    D. to explain the reason for Nuttel's visit

8. Which statement *best* summarizes the theme of this selection?

    A. It is easy to talk to teenagers.
    B. Women are always late when it comes to greeting guests.
    C. The effects of tragedies often linger.
    D. It is difficult to walk abruptly into the lives of others.

9. According to the selection, why is Framton Nuttel visiting Mrs. Sappleton's house? Write your response on your own paper.

10. Based on the context, what does the word *migrate* mean as it is used in the selection? Write your response on your own paper.

11. Based on the context, what does the word *engulfed* mean as it is used in the selection? Write your response on your own paper.

12. Based on the context, what does the word *bustled* mean as it is used in the selection? Write your response on your own paper.

13. According to the niece, what is the terrible tragedy suffered by Mrs. Sappleton? Write your response on your own paper.

Reading Comprehension:
Informational Selections—Social Studies

▶ **Read the following selection and then answer questions 14 through 19.**

First Lady Eleanor Roosevelt met African-American opera singer Marian Anderson in 1935 when Anderson was invited to sing at the White House. Beginning in 1936, the singer performed an annual concert to benefit the Howard University School of Music in Washington, D.C. In January 1939, the university asked the Daughters of the American Revolution (DAR) whether they could use its auditorium, called Constitution Hall, for its annual concert with Anderson. The DAR refused the request because there was an unwritten policy that only whites could perform there. In response, Mrs. Roosevelt wrote this letter to the DAR.

The White House
Washington

February 28, 1939

My dear Mrs. Henry M. Robert Jr.:

(1)   I am afraid that I have never been a very useful member of the Daughters of the American Revolution, so I know it will make very little difference to you whether I resign, or whether I continue to be a member of your organization.

(2)   However, I am in complete disagreement with the attitude taken in refusing Constitution Hall to a great artist. You have set an example which seems to me unfortunate, and I feel obliged to send in to you my resignation. You had an opportunity to lead in an enlightened way and it seems to me that your organization has failed.

(3)   I realize that many people will not agree with me, but feeling as I do this seems to me the only proper procedure to follow.

Very sincerely yours,

Eleanor Roosevelt

Eleanor Roosevelt

14. When Eleanor Roosevelt writes, "I am afraid that I have never been a very useful member," she probably means that

    A. she feels guilty for not having contributed more time and effort to the organization.

    B. she is worried that Mrs. Henry M. Robert Jr. is going to reply angrily to her letter.

    C. she knows that her resignation may not upset the organization very much.

    D. she is willing to resign because she has not been able to lead in an enlightened way.

15. According to Eleanor Roosevelt, what unfortunate example does the organization set?

    A. that discrimination based on race is acceptable

    B. that the members' thoughts and opinions do not matter

    C. that it is a hypocritical organization

    D. that it ignores proper procedures in the treatment of great artists

16. Eleanor Roosevelt's tone could *best* be described as

    A. curious yet polite.

    B. disappointed yet determined.

    C. puzzled yet outraged.

    D. frightened yet amused.

17. In her second paragraph, Eleanor Roosevelt frequently uses the words *you* and *your*. What is the likely intention of such phrasing?

    A. It makes the letter seem more personal, as if she is speaking directly to Mrs. Henry M. Robert Jr.

    B. It emphasizes exactly who is to blame for the failure of the organization.

    C. It makes readers feel more involved by including them in the conversation.

    D. It emphasizes that she is putting distance between herself and this organization from which she is resigning.

18. Summarize what Eleanor Roosevelt means when she says that the DAR "had an opportunity to lead in an enlightened way." Write your response on your own paper.

19. Eleanor Roosevelt says that her decision to resign was " the only proper procedure to follow"—but what other action might she have taken instead? Write your response on your own paper.

Reading Comprehension: Informational Selections—Social Studies

▶ **Read the following selection and then answer questions 20 through 25.**

Settlement in Jamestown

(1)   The members of the London Company knew about the Roanoke colony's failure. They wanted to start a settlement without depending on the wealth of just one person. Instead, investors formed a joint-stock company, which allowed a group to share the cost and risk of founding a colony. Colonies formed in this way were called company colonies. To attract investors and settlers, the London Company printed an advertisement praising Virginia.

(2)   **"The land yields . . . [an] abundance of fish, infinite store [endless supply] of deer, and hares, with many fruits and roots. . . . There are hills and mountains making sensible proffer [offer] of hidden treasure, never yet searched."**

—The Virginia Company of London, quoted in *Ordinary Americans*, edited by Linda R. Monk

(3)   The promise of such wealth attracted adventurers and people who were suffering economic hardship in England.

(4)   On April 26, 1607, the first three ships sent by the London Company arrived off the Virginia coast. The fleet brought 105 male colonists to found a settlement. The ships sailed into Chesapeake Bay and up the James River. About 40 miles upstream the colonists founded their first settlement, named Jamestown, after the English king.

(5)   The men who came to Jamestown were poorly prepared to start a settlement. Most were adventurers interested in making their fortune and returning to England. One of the colonists, Captain John Smith, complained that "ten good workmen would have done more substantial work in a day than ten of these [colonists] in a week." In fact, very few colonists had farming experience or useful skills such as carpentry. Jamestown was also a poor site for a settlement. The settlement was surrounded by marshes full of disease-carrying mosquitoes. In addition, the river water was too salty to drink safely. These conditions proved deadly. By the time winter arrived, two-thirds of the original colonists had died. The few survivors were hungry and sick. The situation temporarily improved after Smith took control of the colony in September 1608. He forced the settlers to work and to build better housing. This reduced the number of deaths from starvation and <u>exposure</u>.

20. Which event happened first?

    A. The London Company began a joint-stock company.

    B. Captain John Smith took over Jamestown.

    C. The Roanoke colony failed.

    D. Three ships sailed to the Virginia coast.

21. Which is the *best* summary of the selection?

    A. A group of investors sent ships to settle the Jamestown colony. The settlement did not do well at first because the settlers lacked the necessary skills and the area itself was not well chosen.

    B. A group of investors decided to travel to Virginia to create a settlement. These investors were not farmers and did not work hard. This became a tremendous problem when the settlers also realized the land was not good for farming.

    C. The Jamestown colony was settled by adventurers who had rich relatives back in England. They did not work hard and were physically weak. Few of them survived the diseases caught from the mosquitoes and the salty water.

    D. King James wanted a colony to replace the lost colony of Roanoke. He started the London Company and sent settlers to Jamestown. The settlement started off poorly but ended up thriving soon after Captain John Smith took over.

22. Reread the last two sentences of the selection. Based on the context, what does *exposure* mean?

    A. not having enough food to eat

    B. a disease caused by sunburn

    C. a disease also known as malnutrition

    D. the lack of proper clothing or shelter

23. This selection includes a quotation from an advertisement printed in the early 1600s. This helps show that the selection is

    A. persuasive.

    B. informative.

    C. narrative.

    D. biased.

24. What is the main effect of the use of the words *fruits, mountains,* and *treasure* in the advertisement included in the selection?

    A. to describe the land as beautiful and wealthy

    B. to appeal to the reader's greed

    C. to appeal to the sense of sight alone

    D. to set the mood of peacefulness

25. List two details that support the main idea that the men who came to Jamestown were poorly prepared to start a settlement. Write your response on your own paper.

Reading Comprehension: Informational Selections—Science

▶ **Read the following selection and then answer questions 26 through 34.**

How Traits Are Inherited

(1)   The cells of all living things contain the molecule deoxyribonucleic acid, or DNA. DNA is the genetic material of living things and carries instructions for the organism's traits. When organisms reproduce, they pass copies of their DNA to their offspring. Passing DNA ensures that the traits of parents are passed to the offspring. This passing of traits is called heredity.

(2)   DNA is a nucleic acid composed of long chains of smaller molecules called nucleotides. A nucleotide has three parts: a sugar, a base, and a phosphate group, which contains phosphorus and oxygen atoms. DNA is a double helix molecule, which means it consists of two strands of nucleotides that spiral around each other. The structure of DNA is shown below.

(3)   Traits are passed from parents to offspring via hereditary units called genes. Genes are sections of DNA that provide instructions for the manufacture of specific proteins. A gene's instructions for making a protein are coded in the sequence of nucleotides in the gene. Therefore, the sequence of nucleotides in DNA is very important. Overall, the traits of an organism are determined by the proteins that an organism produces. All of an organism's genetic material makes up its genome.

(4)   Genes are found at particular locations on chromosomes, which are structures located in the nucleus of cells. Chromosomes are made of protein and DNA. Chromosomes contain long strands of DNA, which store the genetic information of an organism. All members of a species have the same characteristic number of chromosomes in their body cells, much like all atoms of an element have the same characteristic number of protons in their nucleus. For example, all human body cells have 46 chromosomes.

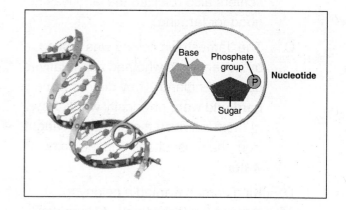

(5)   Chromosomes within an organism can be divided into pairs, called homologous chromosomes. Homologous chromosomes carry alternate versions of a gene at the same location on each chromosome. These alternate versions are called alleles. The different alleles on homologous chromosomes contain genetic information that controls the same trait. However, the genetic information may be different. For example, the gene that controls the color of a flower is located at the same spot on both homologous chromosomes. However, one allele may provide information that results in a red flower, and one allele may provide information that results in a white flower. In organisms that reproduce through sexual reproduction, one set of chromosomes, and therefore one set of alleles, come from one parent. The other set comes from the second parent. The offspring's genome is a combination of the genome of both parents.

214

▶ **Fill in the blanks with the correct word.**

genome	DNA	chromosome
allele	gene	

26. A(n) _____ is a structure that contains DNA and is located in a cell nucleus.

27. All of an organism's genes make up its _____.

28. _____ is nucleic acid composed of long chains of smaller molecules called nucleotides.

29. A(n) _____ provides information for producing proteins.

30. A(n) _____ is an alternate version of a gene.

31. A nucleotide has three parts. What are they?

    A.   a sugar, a base, and a phosphate group

    B.   a sugar, a base, and DNA

    C.   genes, chromosomes, and alleles

    D.   deoxyribonucleic acid, phosphorus, and oxygen

32. What is heredity? Write your response on your own paper.

33. Describe how genes result in the expressed traits of an organism. Write your response on your own paper.

34. What would happen if the nucleotide sequence of a gene got mixed up? Write your response on your own paper.

Reading Comprehension: Informational Selections—Science

▶ **Read the following selection and then answer questions 35 through 41.**

What Is Conservation of Energy?

(1)   Energy has many forms and can be found almost everywhere. The Law of Conservation of Energy states that energy cannot be created or destroyed. In other words, the total amount of energy in the universe never changes, although energy may change from one form to another. The Law of Conservation of Energy is a scientific law because it describes something that always occurs in nature. It is not a theory, however, because it does not explain why energy is conserved.

(2)   Although energy and mass are distinct quantities under normal conditions, nuclear reactions can cause a conversion between energy and mass. A small amount of mass can be converted to a large amount of energy, or a large amount of energy can be converted to a small amount of mass. In these cases, it may appear that the laws of conservation are violated. The total amount of mass and equivalent energy is still conserved, however, even though one is converted into the other.

Energy in Systems

(3)   Accounting for all of the energy in a given case can be complicated. To make studying a case easier, scientists often limit their view to a small area or a small number of objects. These boundaries define a system.

(4)   A system in which energy and matter are exchanged with the surroundings is an open system. If energy but not matter is exchanged, the system is closed. An isolated system is one in which neither energy nor matter is exchanged. Imagine a beaker of water over a burner. If you considered only the flow of energy as the water was heated, it might seem like a closed system. But matter in the form of water vapor leaves the beaker, especially if the water is boiling. Thus, it is an open system. Whenever the total energy in a system increases, the increase must be due to energy that enters the system from an outside source. At the same time, energy is decreased in that source.

Energy Conversions

(5)   According to the Law of Conservation of Energy, energy cannot be created or destroyed. The total amount of energy in a closed system is always the same. Energy can change from one form to another, but all of the different forms of energy in a system always add up to the same total amount.

(6)   An energy conversion is a change from one form of energy to another. Any form of energy can change into any other form of energy. For example, chemical energy in food can be converted into energy that your body can use, and chemical energy in fuels can be converted into thermal energy by burning the fuels.

(7)   For example, gasoline in a lawn mower has stored energy that is released when it is burned. Some of the energy from the gasoline is transferred to the surroundings as heat, which is why the lawn mower gets hot. The total amount of energy released by the gasoline is equal to the energy used to power the lawn mower plus the energy transferred to the surroundings as heat.

▶ **Fill in the blanks with the correct word.**

conversion	created	destroyed
energy	matter	theory

35. Nuclear reactions can cause a conversion between _____

and _____.

36. An energy _____ is a change from one form of energy to another.

37. Conservation of Energy is explained as a scientific law and not a _____
because it describes something that always occurs in nature and does not explain why energy
is conserved.

38. According to the Law of Conservation of Energy, energy cannot be _____

or _____ in ordinary chemical changes.

39. What is the Law of Conservation of Energy? Write your response on your own paper.

40. A system in which energy and matter are exchanged with the surroundings is what kind of
system?

    A.   open

    B.   closed

    C.   isolated

    D.   converted

41. As a roller coaster moves down a hill, potential energy is converted to kinetic energy, thermal
energy, and sound energy. What is true about the total energy of this system?

    A.   Energy is lost as the roller coaster moves.

    B.   Energy is gained as the roller coaster moves.

    C.   Total energy remains the same as the roller coaster moves.

    D.   The total energy constantly changes as the roller coaster moves.

Reading Comprehension:
Informational Selections—Workplace

▶ **Read the following selection and then answer questions 42 through 45.**

Happy Lands Day Care Center Guidelines for Selecting Poems and Stories for Children

At Happy Lands Day Care Center, we believe in building a love of reading and literature in the children in our care. We believe that children of all ages benefit from being read to. We encourage our providers to share a wide variety of stories, songs, and poems with the children.

Keep in mind the following suggestions when selecting your material:

- Select materials with vocabulary that is appropriate for the ages of the children in your class.

- Evaluate the content of the material. Make sure the material will not frighten or confuse the children. Material with adult themes of violence, abuse, and disaster is not appropriate for children.

- Vary the types of material you share with the children. Expose them to different rhythms in songs and poetry and to different kinds of stories.

- Use good judgment. If you have a question about the material, don't use it or ask the Center Director if it is appropriate.

---

42. The guidelines above encourage providers to

    A.   let the children choose which materials should be read aloud.

    B.   let the Center Director select all material for the children.

    C.   expose the children to a wide variety of stories, poems, and songs.

    D.   select materials that appeal to a wide range of ages.

43. Why does the day care center believe providers should read to children?

    A.   It helps keep them quiet and well behaved.

    B.   The center wants children to develop a love of reading and literature.

    C.   Children don't hear stories, poems, and songs anywhere else.

    D.   Providers need activities to fill up the children's time at the center.

44. According to the descriptions, which selection would *not* be appropriate for children at the Happy Lands Day Care Center?

    A.   "Merrily We Roll Along," a happy song with a catchy melody

    B.   "Greedy Dog," a delightful poem about a dog who will eat anything

    C.   "The Old Field," a sad poem about a field abandoned by children and animals

    D.   "The Wild Hog," a poem about a mean hog who kills many men

45. Would your favorite children's story or song be acceptable to the Happy Lands Day Care Center? Why or why not? Write your response on your own paper.

▷ **Read the selection and the bestseller list below. Then answer questions 46 through 48.**

Bookstore clerks should have good personal skills because they have a lot of interaction with customers. They can recommend books by a particular author, time period, or subject area. They must also have good math skills for working with inventory, prices, and discounts. Many bookstore clerks use tools like reference books, computer databases, and bestseller lists.

FICTION Bestsellers Week of April 27			
Rank	Title	Author	Weeks on the Bestseller List
1	**Just Around the Corner**—Super sleuth Shelly Shift chases jewel thief around the globe.	Marcy Boone	3
2	**Fear of the Known**—Supernatural thriller set in 19th century Missouri	Brian Jenkins	7
3	**Windy Days, Sleepless Nights**—Independent young woman climbs Mt. Everest and finds love.	Ellen Stein	2
4	**One More Byte**—Private investigator Ray Fern hunts computer hacker.	Ray Lopez	10
5	**The Sky's the Limit**—Group of friends finds challenges in the Rocky Mountains.	Brett Young	5
6	**Let Me Hear It Again**—Bitter, ailing deaf woman finds hope and romance in the hospital.	Tanisha Jordan	22
7	**Aidan's Image**—Young family moves into haunted house.	Randy Moore	17
8	**Now You See It, Now You Don't**—Shelly Shift uncovers identity of murderous magician.	Marcy Boone	14

46. Choose the *best* reason bookstore clerks use bestseller lists.

   A. to suggest new books for customers to read

   B. to fill up the shelves in the bookstore

   C. to minimize their inventory paperwork

   D. to make the bookstore look attractive

47. Which book has been on the bestseller list the longest? _____

48. What kinds of books do you enjoy reading? Based on the descriptions provided, which book on this bestseller list would you most like to read? Explain why you chose the book you did. Write your response on your own paper.

Reading Comprehension:
Informational Selections—Workplace

▶ **Use the material below to answer questions 49 through 51.**

Creature Comforts
1900 Sleepy Hollow Drive · Wake Forest, NC 27587

Dear Ms. Chambers:

Thank you for ordering our Fit-for-a-King bedroom furniture. I was sorry that some pieces of your furniture arrived damaged and others did not arrive at all. Please be assured that Creature Comforts stands behind every piece of furniture it sells. We want our customers to be totally satisfied with their purchases.

I will send a truck to pick up your damaged dresser. Creature Comforts will cover the cost of this truck. I have also put out a tracer to find the night table you never received. If the table is not found within the next 72 hours, I will order a replacement for you.

If you have any questions or need any further assistance, please contact me at 555-7645.

Sincerely,

Lacey Curtin

Customer Service Representative

49. What is the purpose of the customer service letter?

   A. to tell Ms. Chambers that her furniture was damaged

   B. to deny that there were problems with Ms. Chambers' order

   C. to let Ms. Chambers know that the problems will be fixed

   D. to tell Ms. Chambers to call and give more details about her order

50. Which is a true statement about Ms. Chambers' order?

   A. Nothing that she ordered arrived undamaged.

   B. She ordered the Fit-for-a-King bedroom set.

   C. Her night table was damaged.

   D. It was her first time ordering from Creature Comforts.

51. In her letter, what does the customer service representative tell Ms. Chambers?

   A. She will receive all pieces of furniture within 72 hours.

   B. Creature Comforts will find the missing table within 72 hours.

   C. All the Fit-for-a-King bedroom furniture did not arrive.

   D. Creature Comforts believes in keeping its customers happy.

Extended Response

▶ Read this newspaper article and then respond to the writing prompt. This article presents arguments from both sides about whether social networking sites are good for society.

Are Social Networking Sites Good for Society?

Social networking sites—Twitter, Facebook, LinkedIn, and others—are still relatively new, but they seem poised to stay. They've already had a huge impact on how our society communicates. For example, according to the Pew Research Center, nearly three-quarters of online adults use social networking sites. And they don't use just one. Nearly half of these online adults use many different sites. But are the effects of social media positive or negative for society? It appears there are pros and cons to our growing use of social media.

Benefits of Social Media

Social networking sites started out as a virtual environment where people could connect with each other, even if they lived miles apart. Long-lost high school buddies could find each other. Friends separated by miles could keep up with each other's lives. Business colleagues living in different states could share ideas. Social media has served this purpose well. According to researchers, 70 percent of adult social media users visit sites to connect with friends and family. There's no doubt that online communication can strengthen relationships.

Another reason social networking sites are good for society is that they keep people informed. Information spreads via social media faster than it does by other forms of media. In fact, researchers say that more than 50 percent of people learn about breaking news through social media. In some emergency situations, such as during deadly storms or violent crimes, this speed could mean the difference between life and death. When violence or a storm threatens a college campus, for example, social media sites can give those at risk information and instructions to keep them safe faster than by other means.

Social media also helps students do better in school. According to researchers, 59 percent of students with access to the Internet report that they use social networking sites to discuss educational topics, and 50 percent use the sites to talk about school assignments. One middle school in Portland, Oregon, for example, found that after introducing a social media program for students, grades went up, absenteeism went down, and students did more extra credit assignments, thus helping their grades. College students and professors have also taken advantage of social media, including podcasts, blogs, and Facebook, with great results. In fact, nearly 60 percent of educators believe that the interactive nature of such sites creates a better learning environment for students.

Drawbacks to Social Media

Yes, social networking sites have their benefits, but are they really good for society? There are several reasons to believe these sites may do more harm than good.

More and more people are involved in relationships on social networking sites. This interaction can lead to stress and offline relationship problems. One study found that the more Facebook friends a person has, the more stressful it is for the person because of trying to keep up with Facebook use. And spending time online means people are spending less time in face-to-face interactions, which is a much more healthy way to interact. In one study, one third of the people surveyed admitted they were spending less face-to-face time with family in their homes. What's more, social media only enhances the problem of cyberbullying. According to a 2012 *Consumer Reports* survey, 800,000 minors were harassed or cyberbullied on Facebook.

Yes, news travels fast on social media. However, that news is oftentimes unreliable and false. In a survey, nearly 50 percent of respondents said they have received false news reports by way of social media. And some of the false news is put out there with malice. For example, one Twitter user purposely put out false reports about the New York Stock Exchange flooding during Hurricane Sandy in 2012. More traditional news outlets even picked up the story and also spread it around. This kind of false information causes undue stress and panic.

While some people may say social media helps students, other research has shown that students who are heavy social media users tend to have lower grades. In one study, students who used social media had an average grade point average of 3.06, while nonusers had an average GPA of 3.82. And students who used social networking sites while studying scored 20 percent lower on tests. While educators may see some benefits, a good percentage of them also find that online social media sites can result in more distractions. According to one study, 40 percent of 8- to 18-year-olds spend almost an hour a day on social media sites. And 36 percent of people surveyed said that using social media was their biggest waste of time, surpassing fantasy sports, watching TV, and shopping. In fact, when a person learns about new social networking site activity—such as a new tweet or Facebook message—he or she can take 20 to 25 minutes on average to get back on track with work. For some, it can take two hours to fully return attention to what's really important.

Extended Response Prompt

52. Write a response to the article. In your response, analyze both positions presented in the article and determine which one is better supported. Use relevant and specific evidence from the article to support your response.

Write your response on your own paper. Set a timer for 45 minutes, the amount of time you will have on the GED® test to plan, draft, and edit your response.

Language Skills

▶ **Read the following business memo and then answer questions 53 through 57.**

To: All Employees
From: Ruelle Fox, Benefits Office

(A)

(1) All Cardell Industries employees can now receive free services at Champlin Community Bank (CCB). (2) Free checking has been the most popular service offered at CCB, but there is other nice options as well. (3) I've enclosed a complete brochure of free CCB services. (4) If you have any questions, please stop by the Benefits Office or call me. (5) You can also ask me about the Chamber of Commerce coupon books that are available now!

(B)

(6) Noting one special highlight in the CCB brochure. (7) You'll have easy access to CCB's new branch, located only a block from our main location. (8) Every time you visit this branch, you can enter a drawing to win a gift certificate to a nearby shop restaurant, or movie theater.

53. Which correction should be made to sentence 2?

   A.   remove the comma after CCB

   B.   replace but with since

   C.   replace there with their

   D.   change is to are

54. Which revision would improve the effectiveness of the memo?

   A.   remove sentence 5

   B.   move sentence 5 to the beginning of paragraph B

   C.   move sentence 5 to the end of paragraph B

   D.   No revision is necessary.

55. Sentence 6: **Noting one special highlight in the CCB brochure.**

Which is the *best* way to write the underlined portion of this sentence? If the original is the best way, choose option A.

   A.   Noting one

   B.   Noting, one

   C.   Be sure to note one

   D.   In noting one

56. Which correction should be made to sentence 7?

   A.   change CCB's to CCBs

   B.   change CCB's to CCBs'

   C.   delete the comma after branch

   D.   No correction is necessary.

57. Which correction should be made to sentence 8?

   A.   remove the comma after branch

   B.   insert a comma after shop

   C.   remove the comma after restaurant

   D.   No correction is necessary.

Read the following article and then answer questions 58 through 62.

WHAT IS WORK-LIFE BALANCE?

(A)

(1) Nowadays companies pay more attention to workers' whole lives. (2) This trend was called "work-life balance." (3) However you have your life in balance, you are better able to meet your responsibilities in all areas of your life.

(B)

(4) You may wonder why your Company would want your life balanced. (5) Wouldn't it be better for them if you just worked all the time? (6) Actually, workers perform better when they have more balance in their lives. (7) Their healthier, so they can do more. (8) They worry less about their families, so they can focus better on their work. (9) If you feel that your life is out of balance, visit the Human Resources office at your company. (10) Ask if the staff has any programs on work-life balance. (11) You might get some help!

58. Sentence 2: **This trend <u>was</u> called "work-life balance."**

Which is the *best* way to write the underlined portion of this sentence? If the original is the best way, choose option A.

A. was

B. were

C. will be

D. is

59. Which correction should be made to sentence 3?

A. replace <u>However</u> with <u>When</u>

B. remove the comma after <u>balance</u>

C. replace <u>meet your</u> with <u>meet you're</u>

D. No correction is necessary.

60. Which correction should be made to sentence 4?

A. change <u>may wonder</u> to <u>were wondering</u>

B. change <u>Company</u> to <u>company</u>

C. replace <u>your life</u> with <u>you're life</u>

D. No correction is necessary.

61. Which correction should be made to sentence 7?

A. replace <u>Their</u> with <u>They're</u>

B. remove the comma after <u>healthier</u>

C. replace <u>so</u> with <u>yet</u>

D. No correction is necessary.

62. Which revision would improve the effectiveness of the article?

A. begin a new paragraph with sentence 8

B. remove sentence 8

C. begin a new paragraph with sentence 9

D. No revision is necessary.

Language Skills

▶ **Read the following article and then answer questions 63 through 66.**

HOW TO PREPARE FOR
A JOB INTERVIEW

(A)

(1) Most people dread job interviews, and for good reason. (2) In a job interview, you are not in control of the situation. (3) Someone else chooses the questions you have to answer them.

(B)

(4) No matter how stressed you feel it's better to prepare for the interview in advance. (5) Make a list of the questions the interviewer might ask.

(C)

(6) Then practice answering the questions. (7) Get ready to talk about how you learn from your mistakes, solve problems, and working as part of a team.

63. Sentence 3: **Someone else chooses the questions you have to answer them.**

Which is the *best* way to write the underlined portion of this sentence? If the original is the best way, choose option A.

A. questions you

B. questions, and you

C. questions, you

D. questions and you

64. Which revision would improve the effectiveness of the article?

A. remove sentence 2

B. move sentence 3 to follow sentence 5

C. combine paragraphs A and B

D. combine paragraphs B and C

65. Which correction should be made to sentence 4?

A. insert a comma after feel

B. replace you with they

C. replace it's with its

D. No correction is necessary.

66. Which correction should be made to sentence 7?

A. remove the comma after mistakes

B. change solve to solving

C. insert a comma after and

D. change working to work

Read the following article and then answer questions 67 through 70.

WHAT FACTORS INFLUENCE VOTER TURNOUT?

(A)

(1) Who wins in an election? (2) That depends on which voters show up to cast their votes in november. (3) As a result, many candidates and political organizations pay close attention to voter turnout.

(B)

(4) Some voters feel that their vote does not matter and so they are less likely to vote. (5) On the other hand, when voters feel a personal connection to a candidate, they are likely to vote. (6) Finally, many candidates would like to have more control over the factor of weather! (7) Bad weather tends to keep them away from the polls.

67. Which correction should be made to sentence 2?

  A. change <u>depends</u> to <u>depended</u>

  B. replace <u>their</u> with <u>they're</u>

  C. change <u>november</u> to <u>November</u>

  D. No correction is necessary.

68. Which sentence would be *most* effective if inserted at the beginning of paragraph B?

  A. Voter turnout is influenced by many factors.

  B. Weather most influences voter turnout.

  C. Most people do not care about voting.

  D. Candidates always want voters to turn out, no matter whom they vote for.

69. Sentence 4: **Some voters feel that their vote does not <u>matter and so they are</u> less likely to vote.**

Which is the *best* way to write the underlined portion of this sentence? If the original is the best way, choose option A.

  A. matter and so they

  B. matter, and so they

  C. matter, so they

  D. matter and they

70. Sentence 7: **Bad weather tends to keep <u>them</u> away from the polls.**

Which is the *best* way to write the underlined portion of this sentence? If the original is the best way, choose option A.

  A. them

  B. us

  C. candidates

  D. voters

Language Skills

Read the following memo and then answer questions 71 through 74.

To: Alexa Vargas, Operations Manager
From: Terence Urgan, Security Director
Re: Recommended Action Following Break-in

(A)

(1) The recent break-in at the Water Street warehouse shows our need to improve security. (2) Around a large area, our security guard must walk long distances, leaving the front entrance unattended. (3) The entrance faces a street with very little traffic during the night. (4) The doorway provides a burglar too much cover, and the front of the building was only partly lit.

(B)

(5) We can make the entrance more secure. (6) If we do this, we will not need to hire an additional guard. (7) Instead, I have asked a firm called Secure Construction to renovate the entrance and light the building front. (8) Mr. Torres Martin, an engineer in this firm, will be meeting with you and I next week.

71. Sentence 2: **Around a large area, our security guard must walk long distances, leaving the front entrance unattended.**

    Which is the *best* way to write the underlined portion of this sentence? If the original is the best way, choose option A.

    A. Around a large area, our security guard must walk long distances

    B. Our security guard must walk long distances around a large area

    C. Around a large area, our security guard walking long distances

    D. Around a large area, our security guard walked long distances

72. Which correction should be made to sentence 4?

    A. remove the comma after <u>cover</u>

    B. replace <u>and</u> with <u>or</u>

    C. change <u>was</u> to <u>were</u>

    D. change <u>was</u> to <u>is</u>

73. Which combination of sentences 5 and 6 would be *most* effective?

    A. When we need to hire an additional guard, we can make the entrance more secure.

    B. If we make the entrance more secure, we will not need to hire an additional guard.

    C. Making the entrance more secure is what we will do if we will not need to hire an additional guard.

    D. We will need to hire an additional guard if we can make the entrance more secure.

74. Which correction should be made to sentence 8?

    A. change <u>engineer</u> to <u>Engineer</u>

    B. change <u>firm</u> to <u>Firm</u>

    C. change <u>I</u> to <u>me</u>

    D. No correction is necessary.

Read the following article and then answer questions 75 through 78.

HOW TO WRITE A PERFECT
THANK YOU NOTE

(A)

(1) A thank you note is a simple, polite gesture that is too often forgotten. (2) A perfect thank you note shows that you truly enjoyed you're gift. (3) For example, when ten-year-old Jonah received movie coupons from his aunt, he wrote this charming note:

(B)

Dear Aunt Irene,

(4) Thank you for the movie coupons. (5) I took Jacob to the show last Sunday. (6) Him and I saw *Spiderwoman Lives*. (7) We had a blast, and we even got popcorn.

Love,

Jonah

(C)

(8) Some people are embarrassed to send a thank you note if you feel too much time has slipped by. (9) However, sincere expressions of gratitude is never too late.

75. Which correction should be made to sentence 2?

A. change shows to show

B. replace you with they

C. replace you're with your

D. No correction is necessary.

76. Which correction should be made to sentence 6?

A. change Him to He

B. change Him and I to I and him

C. change saw to seen

D. change saw to sawed

77. Which correction should be made to sentence 8?

A. replace to with too

B. replace you with they

C. replace too with to

D. replace by with bye

78. Sentence 9: **However, sincere expressions of gratitude is never too late.**

Which is the *best* way to write the underlined portion of this sentence? If the original is the best way, choose option A.

A. is

B. are

C. were

D. was

Reasoning Through Language Arts
Posttest Evaluation Chart

The chart below will help you determine your strengths and weaknesses in reading comprehension, writing an extended response, and language skills.

▶ **Directions**

Check your answers on pages 264–267. On the chart below, circle the number of each question you answered correctly on the Posttest. Count the number of questions you answered correctly in each row. Write the number in the Total Correct space in each row. Complete this process for the remaining rows. Then add the four totals to get your Total Correct for Posttest.

Skill Area	Questions	Total Correct	Pages
Reading Comprehension: Fiction	1, 2, 3, 4, 5, 6, 7, 8, 9, 10, 11, 12, 13	_____ out of 13	44–69
Reading Comprehension: Informational	14, 15, 16, 17, 18, 19, 20, 21, 22, 23, 24, 25, 26, 27, 28, 29, 30, 31, 32, 33, 34, 35, 36, 37, 38, 39, 40, 41, 42, 43, 44, 45, 46, 47, 48, 49, 50, 51	_____ out of 38	70–125
Extended Response	52	_____ out of 1	126–149
Language Skills	53, 54, 55, 56, 57, 58, 59, 60, 61, 62, 63, 64, 65, 66, 67, 68, 69, 70, 71, 72, 73, 74, 75, 76, 77, 78	_____ out of 26	150–203

Total Correct for Pretest _____ out of 78

If you answered fewer than 71 questions correctly, look at the skill in the skill areas above. In which areas do you need more practice? Page numbers to review content for each skill area are listed in the right-hand column.

PAGE 3

1. **Silenus is Bacchus's old schoolmaster and foster-father.** *(DOK Level: 1; Content Topic: R.2.2)*

2. **Midas washs his gold-creating power into the river.** *(DOK Level: 1–2; Content Topic: R.3.4)*

3. **Having "the Midas touch" means having the ability to make money easily, no matter what a person does.** *(DOK Level: 1–2; Content Topic: R.3.2)*

4. **D.** *(DOK Level: 2; Content Topic: R.3.2)* Option D is correct because the passage says that Bacchus is "sorry that Midas had not made a better choice." Options A and B are not supported by the passage, and Option C is the opposite of the correct answer.

5. **A.** *(DOK Level: 2; Content Topic: R.3.2)* Midas cares for Silenus for ten days, which shows that he is kind and caring, but his poor choice of a reward shows he is also shallow. Midas does not show wisdom, so Option B is incorrect.

6. **B.** *(DOK Level: 1–2; Content Topic: R.4.1/L.4.1)* Midas is not in conflict (option C), for the passage says "he hated the gift." Nor is he in chaos or constant suffering. Midas is in dismay.

7. **D.** *(DOK Level: 1; Content Topic: R.3.1)* Midas has to recognize Silenus (option D) before he can bring him back to Bacchus (option A). Options B and C occur after Option A.

8. **D.** *(DOK Level: 1–2; Content Topic: R.2.1)* Midas is not happy with the gift of gold, so Options A and B are incorrect. Midas is not being kind to Silenus in order to get a reward, so Option C is incorrect. The reward Midas gets is killing him, so Option D is correct.

PAGE 5

9. **President Madison was with General Winder on the front lines of the war.** *(DOK Level: 2; Content Topic: R.3.2)*

10. **She wants to preserve the President's mansion as part of America's heritage.** *(DOK Level: 2; Content Topic: R.2.8)*

11. **begging** *(DOK Level: 1–2; Content Topic: R.4.1/L.4.1)*

12. **C.** *(DOK Level: 2; Content Topic: R.2.4)* Since Dolley does not want to leave until she sees her husband safe, Options B and D are incorrect. The following sentence refers to their "friends and acquaintances," not to the enemy, making Option A incorrect and Option C correct.

13. **B.** *(DOK Level: 2; Content Topic: R.2.4)* The passage does not say President Madison is injured or nervous, making Options A and C incorrect. The passage does suggest he is in a hurry, making Option B correct.

14. **B.** *(DOK Level: 2; Content Topic: R.2.8)* British forces were underestimated, so Option C is incorrect. President Madison has joined the forces in war, so Option D is incorrect. Since Dolley says she has "no fear but for him" (referring to her husband), she is not angry at him (Option A). This also shows Option B is correct.

PAGE 7

15. **D.** *(DOK Level: 2–3; Content Topic: R.2.7)* The paragraph under the heading Job Sharing does not support Options A, B, or C. It does support Option D.

16. **A.** *(DOK Level: 2–3; Content Topic: R.2.5)* Options C and D are not supported by the handbook. Although Option B is true, it does not support a "family-friendly" workplace. Option A is true and supports a "family-friendly" workplace.

17. **D.** *(DOK Level: 1–3; Content Topic: R.2.8)* The handbook is straightforward and business like, not any of the other options.

18. **A part-time employee is eligible for retirement when he or she has built up enough hours.** *(DOK Level: 1–2; Content Topic: R.2.2)*

19. **Answer should include two of the following benefits: Employees can spend more time with their children, pursue educational opportunities, care for an aging or ill family member, or continue working when illness or physical limitations prevent working full-time.** *(DOK Level: 1–2; Content Topic: R.2.2)*

20. **Answer should include two of the following benefits: Managers can retain highly qualified employees, improve recruitment, increase productivity, and reduce absenteeism.** *(DOK Level: 1–2; Content Topic: R.2.2)*

PAGE 10

21. **Responses will vary. Students should clearly identify which argument is better supported and cite specific evidence from the text. Refer to the Scoring Rubric on page 140.**

PAGE 11

22. **E. Who do you consider to be a hero these days?** *(DOK Level: 1–2; Content Topic: R.2.4)* The sentence is a question and needs a question mark.

23. **E. Many people think of actors, athletes, or singers as heroes.** *(DOK Level: 1–2; Content Topic: R.2.4)* A comma is needed after each item in a series.

24. **E. Some people think football players are heroes, but I think my Aunt Ann is a hero.** *(DOK Level: 1–2; Content Topic: R.2.4)* A comma is needed before the conjunction in a compound sentence.

25. **E. She goes to school during the day and works as a nurse's aide at night.** *(DOK Level: 1–2; Content Topic: R.2.4)* A comma is not needed in a compound predicate.

26. **E. My aunt is a hero to me because she helps people tirelessly.** *(DOK Level: 1–2; Content Topic: R.2.1)* Because the word

aunt is not used as part of a name, it is not capitalized.

27. **parents** *(DOK Level: 1; Content Topic: R.2.3)* The plural noun is needed.

28. **expert's** *(DOK Level: 1; Content Topic: R.2.3)* The article *an* calls for a singular noun.

29. **children** *(DOK Level: 1; Content Topic: R.2.3)* The word *children* is plural, and the possessive is not needed.

30. **know** *(DOK Level: 1; Content Topic: R.2.3)* The context of the sentence requires the word that means "understand."

31. **break** *(DOK Level: 1; Content Topic: R.1.1)* The context of the sentence requires the word that means "split."

32. **hole** *(DOK Level: 1; Content Topic: R.1.1)* The context of the sentence requires the word that means an "opening."

33. **it's** *(DOK Level: 1; Content Topic: R.1.1)* The context of the sentence requires the word that means "it is."

34. **can't** *(DOK Level: 1; Content Topic: R.1.1)* The apostrophe in a contraction belongs where the letter or letters were left out.

35. **through** *(DOK Level: 1; Content Topic: R.1.1)* The context of the sentence requires the word that means "into one side and out the other."

36. **well** *(DOK Level: 1; Content Topic: W.3)* An adverb is needed to complete the sentence, not an adjective.

37. **worse** *(DOK Level: 1; Content Topic: W.3)* The sentence is comparing two groups of people and needs the comparative adjective.

38. **slowly** *(DOK Level: 1; Content Topic: W.3)* An adverb is needed to complete the sentence, not an adjective.

39. **sooner** *(DOK Level: 1; Content Topic: W.3)* The sentence is comparing two groups of people and needs the comparative adverb.

40. **agree** *(DOK Level: 1; Content Topic: L.1.2, L.1.7)* Use the plural verb form to agree with the plural subject *supervisors*.

41. **are** *(DOK Level: 1; Content Topic: L.1.2, L.1.7)* Use the plural verb form to agree with the plural subject *reasons*.

42. **have** *(DOK Level: 1; Content Topic: L.1.2, L.1.7)* Use the plural verb form to agree with the compound subject.

43. **F** *(DOK Level: 1–2; Content Topic: L.2.2)* The verb is missing.

44. **S** *(DOK Level: 1–2; Content Topic: L.2.2)* The thought is complete.

45. **RO** *(DOK Level: 1–2; Content Topic: L.2.2)* Two complete thoughts run together without correct punctuation or a connecting word.

46. **F** *(DOK Level: 1–2; Content Topic: L.2.2)* The thought is incomplete.

47. **The sun dries out your skin, and it affects the growth of skin cells.** *(DOK Level: 1–2; Content Topic: L.1.9)*

48. **The sun feels good, but it's not good for you.** *(DOK Level: 1–2; Content Topic: L.1.9)*

49. **You should see a doctor if a mole changes shape or color.** *(DOK Level: 1–2; Content Topic: L.1.9)*

50. **to understand** *(DOK Level: 1–2; Content Topic: L.1.6)* "To understand" is needed to be parallel with "to cut" and "to have."

51. **you can more easily** *(DOK Level: 1–2; Content Topic: L.1.6)* The subject *you* is modified by "knowing your stressors."

52. **today's world** *(DOK Level: 1–2; Content Topic: L.1.6)* The second option is too wordy.

UNIT 1: READING SKILLS

LESSON 1

1. **It is difficult to preserve photographs from the past.** *(DOK Level: 2; Content Topic: R.2.2)*

2. **B.** *(DOK Level: 1–3; Content Topic: R.2.5)*

3. **B.** *(DOK Level: 2–3; Content Topic: R.2.4)* The main idea is that Max worked very hard; the other options are supporting details.

LESSON 2

Who? Leo Stuart is a detective.	Supporting Details	What? He is digging in the ground.
When? He begins digging at sunrise.	Where? He is on a hillside, east of the bronze marker.	Why or How? He is searching for something.

1. **The second sentence states that he is "ten feet due east of the ancient bronze marker."** *(DOK Level: 1–2; Content Topic: R.2.1)*

2. **His shovel struck something hollow.** *(DOK Level: 1–3; Content Topic: R.2.3)*

3. **C.** *(DOK Level: 1–2; Content Topic: R.2.1)* The third sentence of the paragraph supports Option C. The other descriptions are not supported by the paragraph.

LESSON 3
PAGE 21

Statement ——→	Inference
• His owners begin every meal by giving him a scrap of food from their plates.	• His owners have trained Riley to beg by feeding him at the table.
• He will only stop if they shout, "Lie down!" Then Riley lies down on the floor immediately.	• **Riley responds to direct commands.**
• His owners have tried reasoning with him, but nothing works.	• **The owners do not understand that you cannot reason with a dog.**

1. **For each thing that Riley does wrong, the writer points out that the owners are also doing something wrong. The owners don't realize they are rewarding Riley's bad behavior. Clearly Riley can be trained because he has learned to lie down on command.** *(DOK Level: 2–3; Content Topic: R.2.4)*

2. **A.** *(DOK Level: 2–3; Content Topic: R.2.4)*

3. **C.** *(DOK Level: 2–3; Content Topic: R.2.3)* The second sentence talks about "protecting in-home healthcare workers," which supports Option C.

LESSON 4
PAGE 23

Order of Events		
	1	Andrew wandered to the boathouse.
	2	He entered the building.
	3	He struck a match and saw the lantern.
	4	He lit the lantern.
	5	He heard a voice behind him.

1. **Andrew had intended to walk to the farmhouse. However, he was so lost in thought that he ended up walking to the boathouse instead.** *(DOK Level: 1–2; Content Topic: R.3.1)*

2. **He struck a match from his pocket. He needed a light so he could see in the dark.** *(DOK Level: 1–2; Content Topic: R.3.1)*

3. **B.** *(DOK Level: 1–2; Content Topic: R.3.1)* Since "clapped her hands" is the distraction, Option A is incorrect. The fourth sentence of the paragraph comes just before the distraction, making Option B correct.

LESSON 5
PAGE 25

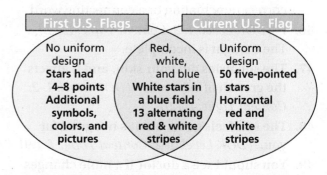

1. **The current flag has fifty stars instead of thirteen.** *(DOK Level: 2–3; Content Topic: R.3.4)*

2. **B.** *(DOK Level: 2–3; Content Topic: R.3.3)*

3. **C.** *(DOK Level: 2–3, 2; Content Topic: R.3.4, R.6.3)* The first two sentences of the paragraph clearly contrast Detroit and Sanibel, making Option C correct.

LESSON 6
PAGE 27

CAUSE	EFFECT
Not all germs are killed when people use antibiotic medicines and cleaners. →	Some strains of bacteria are growing stronger.
Children are exposed to normal amounts of bacteria. →	**Children's ability to fight off disease improves.**

1. **They hope to kill germs so they won't get sick.** *(DOK Level: 2–3; Content Topic: R.3.3)*

2. **The overuse of antibiotics and antibiotic cleaners causes more powerful strains of bacteria to flourish.** *(DOK Level: 2–3; Content Topic: R.3.4)*

3. **C.** *(DOK Level: 2–3; Content Topic: R.3.3)* Option A is incorrect because the second sentence says the economy was slow. Option B is not supported by the passage. Option D is the effect, not the cause. Option C is the cause.

LESSON 7
PAGE 29

CONCLUSION Alan's fear is unreasonable.				
Alan is hugging the cliff wall.	F A C T S	The trail is paved and marked.	F A C T S	His family members are not scared; they are laughing and talking.

1. **They are laughing and talking.** *(DOK Level: 1–2; Content Topic: R.2.5)*

2. **They do not take his fears seriously. They tease him and talk and laugh together, indicating that the situation is not dangerous.** *(DOK Level: 2; Content Topic: R.3.2)*

3. **B.** *(DOK Level: 2–3; Content Topic: R.3.3)* Option A is incorrect because the National Farm Workers Association was founded in 1962. Option B is correct because Chavez founded the association and led it in the strike, which ended in a victory. Options C and D are not supported by the passage.

LESSON 8
PAGE 31

Author's Purpose The author wants to persuade employees to help the company by complying with the new requests.	
Supporting Facts and Opinions	**Key Words and Phrases**
The company must save money to avoid layoffs.	*suffered substantial losses*
Too many absences hurt productivity.	*difficult time*
Employees can help by giving one month's notice of vacation leave and scheduling planned absences.	*hurt our productivity, stretch our budget, your cooperation is critical, severe*

1. **The author wants to persuade employees to help the company avoid budget cuts and layoffs by complying with the new requests.** *(DOK Level: 1–2; Content Topic: R.2.1)*

2. **The author uses words and phrases such as "suffered substantial losses," "difficult time," "stretch our budget," "your cooperation is critical," and "severe" to appeal to readers' emotions.** *(DOK Level: 2–3; Content Topic: R.6.4)*

3. **D.** *(DOK Level: 2–3, 2; Content Topic: R.4.3/L.4.3)* The first three options do not include words that entertain. Option D does include words that would be used in an entertaining story.

LESSON 9
PAGE 33

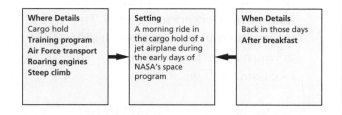

Where Details	Setting	When Details
Cargo hold Training program Air Force transport Roaring engines Steep climb	A morning ride in the cargo hold of a jet airplane during the early days of NASA's space program	Back in those days After breakfast

1. **The author said that the astronauts were the scientists' "lab rats."** *(DOK Level: 2; Content Topic: R.3.2)*

2. **A.** *(DOK Level: 2; Content Topic: R.3.2)*

3. **B.** *(DOK Level: 2; Content Topic: R.3.2)* The second and third sentences state that it is daytime during a workday, making Option B correct.

LESSON 10
PAGE 35

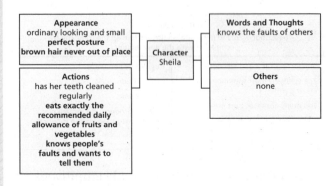

1. **She cannot control her desire to tell people their flaws.** *(DOK Level: 2; Content Topic: R.3.2)*
2. **B.** *(DOK Level: 2; Content Topic: R.3.2)*
3. **C.** *(DOK Level: 2; Content Topic: R.3.2)* Elio does not express admiration, fear, or disgust with new technology, only disapproval.

LESSON 11
PAGE 37

1. **Yes. This is within the scope of the new policies because Walter can do his job full-time during business hours, with no increased costs or problems for his department.** *(DOK Level: 2–3; Content Topic: R.2.7)*
2. **No. If Sue changed her schedule, she would not be available to discuss payroll issues with workers up to 5 P.M. That would violate the rule of keeping each office open during normal business hours.** *(DOK Level: 2–3; Content Topic: R.2.7)*

New Situation	Given Information
Walter	Company Policy
OK	1. 40-hour work week
OK	2. no increased costs
OK	3. office covered
Sue	Company Policy
OK	1. 40-hour work week
OK	2. no increased costs
NO	3. office covered

3. **A.** *(DOK Level: 2–3; Content Topic: R.2.7)* The second sentence says a helmet must "guard against the particular dangers of a sport," making Option A the correct answer.

LESSON 12
PAGE 39

Passage Main Idea	Idea with Question
President Kennedy asked his speechwriter, Ted Sorensen, to write his inaugural address.	Kennedy asked Sorensen to study Lincoln's Gettysburg Address for its "secrets" of success.

Synthesized Idea
Sorensen used Lincoln's speech to help him write Kennedy's speech.

1. **Kennedy knew that Lincoln's speech had been successful and wanted Sorensen to find out what had made it so successful.** *(DOK Level: 2; Content Topic: R.3.2)*
2. **Sorensen used the style of Lincoln's speech as the basis for writing Kennedy's speech.** *(DOK Level: 2–3; Content Topic: R.3.2)*
3. **B.** *(DOK Level: 2; Content Topic: R.3.2)* Since the author has also driven through the night and is proud of the fact, he would describe Russ as determined, not foolish. Options C and D are not supported by the passage.

UNIT 1 REVIEW
PAGE 40

1. **Andy's education, service, and work experience qualify him for the job.** *(DOK Level: 1–2; Content Topic: R.2.1, R.2.2)*
2. **B.** *(DOK Level: 2; Content Topic: R.3.2)* The letter is a polite list of Andy's qualifications for the job, which show he is competent, not playful, demanding, or self-centered.
3. **C.** *(DOK Level: 1; Content Topic: R.3.1)* Andy developed the materials before he graduated from college, so Option C happened first.

PAGE 41

1. **The author wants to inform readers of the new community center in Carverton.** *(DOK Level: 2; Content Topic: R.6.1, R.6.3)*

2. **The evidence that this is the author's purpose includes the words *announced, will have, is a large residential development,* and *consisting.*** *(DOK Level: 2; Content Topic: R.6.1, R.6.3)*

3. **D.** *(DOK Level: 2; Content Topic: R.3.2, R.3.4)* The town of Carverton is building the center, so Option B is incorrect. The property manager would be most interested in how the center will benefit the residents, so Option D is correct. Options A and C are not supported by the passage.

4. **The author included the information because it shows that Spring Meadows has a large number of open places to live, which supports the author's purpose for writing the article: To gain attention and attract residents by informing readers that they are helping to build a recreation center and offering a discount to the center.** *(DOK Level: 3; Content Topic: R.7.2)*

UNIT 1 MINI-TEST

PAGES 42–43

1. **C.** *(DOK Level: 1; Content Topic: R.3.1)* Option C matches the sequence of events from the passage and is correct.

2. **B.** *(DOK Level: 2; Content Topic: R.5.1)* The words *most important* indicate that this sentence is an opinion.

3. **A.** *(DOK Level: 2; Content Topic: R.2.8)* The passage discusses Franklin's success in a variety of activities, so Option A is correct. The passage doe not support the other options.

4. **A.** *(DOK Level: 1–2; Content Topic: R.2.1)* The title and passage support Option A as the main idea. The other options are details.

5. **D.** *(DOK Level: 2; Content Topic: R.2.5)* Option D, the vet may be closed, is the reason why you should know where the nearest emergency hospital is.

6. **B.** *(DOK Level: 2; Content Topic: R.3.2)* A photo would only be necessary if the pet was missing, so Option B is correct. A photo would not help with medications or be a practical ID tag.

7. **D.** *(DOK Level: 2; Content Topic: R.2.2)* Option D expresses the main idea, while the other options express details.

UNIT 2: FICTION

LESSON 13

PAGE 46

A.

PAGE 47

A.

PAGE 48

B.

PAGES 49–50

1. **ceased** *(DOK Level: 1; Content Topic: R.4.1/L.4.1)*

2. **submerged** *(DOK Level: 1; Content Topic: R.4.1/L.4.1)*

3. **propelled** *(DOK Level: 1; Content Topic: R.4.1/L.4.1)*

4. **impede** *(DOK Level: 1; Content Topic: R.4.1/L.4.1)*

5. **veered** *(DOK Level: 1; Content Topic: R.4.1/L.4.1)*

6. **miscalculated** *(DOK Level: 1; Content Topic: R.4.1/L.4.1)*

7. **Hans pulled the rope suddenly.** *(DOK Level: 2–3; Content Topic: R.3.4)*

8. **Thornton ordered Buck to go back to the bank because Buck was struggling in the water.** *(DOK Level: 2; Content Topic: R.3.2)*

9. **to allow Buck time to heal** *(DOK Level: 2; Content Topic: R.3.2)*

10. **D.** *(DOK Level: 2; Content Topic: R.3.2)* Thornton hangs on and eventually makes it to shore in an area of the river where "no swimmer could live;" he holds onto the slippery rock and orders Buck to return to shore because it's too dangerous for the dog to try to save him.

11. **A.** *(DOK Level: 2; Content Topic: R.3.2)* These two men and the dog repeatedly attempt to rescue Thornton.

12. **D.** *(DOK Level: 2; Content Topic: R.3.2)* Thornton is not afraid of difficult situations, and his work on the boat implies that he enjoys the outdoors and working with others rather than working alone.

13. **Responses will vary. Some students may describe similar feats of strength. Others might describe more fearful responses.** *(DOK Level: 2–3; Content Topic: R.2.7)*

14. **Responses will vary. Students should describe what they did and the problem that resulted.** *(DOK Level: 2–3; Content Topic: R.2.7)*

LESSON 14

PAGE 51

1. **Sir Henry is suspicious of Barrymore and is determined to get at the truth.**
2. **Barrymore tells Sir Henry he does not understand why he was asked so many questions and hopes Sir Henry still trusts him.**

PAGE 52

1. **A.**
2. **C.**

PAGE 53

B. and C.

PAGES 54–55

1. **E.** *(DOK Level: 1; Content Topic: R.4.1/L.4.1)*
2. **C.** *(DOK Level: 1; Content Topic: R.4.1/L.4.1)*
3. **A.** *(DOK Level: 1; Content Topic: R.4.1/L.4.1)*
4. **B.** *(DOK Level: 1; Content Topic: R.4.1/L.4.1)*

5. **H.** *(DOK Level: 1; Content Topic: R.4.1/L.4.1)*
6. **D.** *(DOK Level: 1; Content Topic: R.4.1/L.4.1)*
7. **G.** *(DOK Level: 1; Content Topic: R.4.1/L.4.1)*
8. **F.** *(DOK Level: 1; Content Topic: R.4.1/L.4.1)*
9. **B.** *(DOK Level: 2; Content Topic: R.3.2)* The introductory paragraph states that Dr. Watson is writing the letter to Sherlock Holmes.
10. **B.** *(DOK Level: 2; Content Topic: R.2.2)* The last paragraph of the passage on page 51 says that Sir Henry gave Barrymore part of his old wardrobe (clothes) to pacify him.
11. **A.** *(DOK Level: 2; Content Topic: R.2.2)* In the first paragraph on page 52, Dr. Watson states, "on the first night here, I heard her sobbing." It is the next night he hears a key turning in a lock.
12. **The author creates a mood of mystery.** *(DOK Level: 2–3; Content Topic: R.4.3/L.4.3)*
13. **Dr. Watson reports on what he saw to Sir Henry, and they come up with a plan of action.** *(DOK Level: 1–2; Content Topic: R.3.1)*
14. **C.** *(DOK Level: 2–3; Content Topic: R.3.3)* A "guilty and furtive" appearance belongs to a person who is responsible for a reprehensible act and one who is secretive. Students should be able to use their understanding of this phrase to describe the mood.
15. **D.** *(DOK Level: 2–3; Content Topic: R.3.3)* There are many unanswered questions about why Barrymore is sneaking through the house, what he is watching and waiting for, and what door has been opened or locked. All the questions build tension in this mystery.
16. **A.** *(DOK Level: 2–3; Content Topic: R.2.8)* Dr. Watson is an observer of people and their actions. He asks many questions about people's behavior. He is very inquisitive and distrustful.

17. **Responses will vary. Students should give reasons for their response.** *(DOK Level: 2–3; Content Topic: NA)*

18. **Responses will vary. Students should give reasons for their response.** *(DOK Level: 2–3; Content Topic: NA)*

LESSON 15

PAGE 56

B.

PAGE 57

B.

PAGE 58

B.

PAGES 59–60

1. **passage** *(DOK Level: 1; Content Topic: R.4.1/L.4.1)*

2. **longed** *(DOK Level: 1; Content Topic: R.4.1/L.4.1)*

3. **anxiously** *(DOK Level: 1; Content Topic: R.4.1/L.4.1)*

4. **fancy** *(DOK Level: 1; Content Topic: R.4.1/L.4.1)*

5. **ventured** *(DOK Level: 1; Content Topic: R.4.1/L.4.1)*

6. **sharply** *(DOK Level: 1; Content Topic: R.4.1/L.4.1)*

7. **curious** *(DOK Level: 1; Content Topic: R.4.1/L.4.1)*

8. **respectable** *(DOK Level: 1; Content Topic: R.4.1/L.4.1)*

9. **She is too big to fit through the door.** *(DOK Level: 1–2; Content Topic: R.2.1)*

10. **She wishes she could become small temporarily so she can fit through door and then grow big again when she is in the garden.** *(DOK Level: 2–3; Content Topic: R.2.3)*

11. **She stays the same size.** *(DOK Level: 2–3; Content Topic: R.3.4)*

12. **D.** *(DOK Level: 2–3; Content Topic: R.2.7)* Option D is a sentence from Alice's point of view, because it reveals her feelings and thoughts. The question asks about a different character's point of view.

13. **B.** *(DOK Level: 2; Content Topic: R.3.2)* Options C and D are incorrect because they tell very little about the setting. Option A describes the setting Alice would like to get to, but little about the setting in which she is. Option B is correct.

14. **C.** *(DOK Level: 2; Content Topic: R.3.2)* Alice scolds herself which supports Option C as the correct answer. She does not give up or frighten easily, and she would rather be outdoors.

15. **Responses will vary. Students should show an ability to retell the scene described in the passage and make generalizations or draw conclusions about the character and the events in the passage.** *(DOK Level: 2; Content Topic: R.2.8)*

16. **Responses will vary. Students should show an ability to retell the events of the story and discuss different ways that they would handle them.** *(DOK Level: 2–3; Content Topic: R.2.7)*

LESSON 16

PAGE 61

A.

PAGE 63: Understanding Mood

B.

PAGE 63: Predicting Outcomes

A.

PAGES 64–65

1. **G.** *(DOK Level: 1; Content Topic: R.4.1/L.4.1)*

2. **J.** *(DOK Level: 1; Content Topic: R.4.1/L.4.1)*

3. **C.** *(DOK Level: 1; Content Topic: R.4.1/L.4.1)*

4. **B.** *(DOK Level: 1; Content Topic: R.4.1/L.4.1)*

5. **D.** *(DOK Level: 1; Content Topic: R.4.1/L.4.1)*

6. **I.** *(DOK Level: 1; Content Topic: R.4.1/L.4.1)*

7. **H.** *(DOK Level: 1; Content Topic: R.4.1/L.4.1)*

8. **A.** *(DOK Level: 1; Content Topic: R.4.1/L.4.1)*

9. **E.** *(DOK Level: 1; Content Topic: R.4.1/L.4.1)*

10. **F.** *(DOK Level: 1; Content Topic: R.4.1/L.4.1)*

11. **the old man's strange-looking eye** *(DOK Level: 2; Content Topic: R.3.2)*

12. **On the first seven nights, the man's eyes were closed. When the narrator couldn't see the eyes, he didn't feel the need to kill the old man.** *(DOK Level: 2; Content Topic: R.3.2)*

13. **He sensed that the black shadow of death stalked him.** *(DOK Level: 2; Content Topic: R.3.2)*

14. **B.** *(DOK Level: 1–3; Content Topic: R.4.1/L.4.1)* This option is correct because the word *conceived* restates that the idea entered the narrator's brain. The passage does not support options A or D. Option C describes the effect the idea had on the narrator—that it haunted him.

15. **D.** *(DOK Level: 2–3; Content Topic: R.4.3/L.4.3)* This sentence adds to the scary feeling of the passage because it emphasizes how sneaky the narrator is and how slowly the time is passing. Options A and B add little to the mood of fear the author is trying to establish. Option C states a fact.

16. **A.** *(DOK Level: 2–3; Content Topic: R.2.7, R.3.4)* This prediction fits best with the haunted, nervous personality of the narrator, his acute hearing, and the title of the story. Options B and D are extremely unlikely considering the personality of the narrator. Option C cannot be correct because, as he is telling the story, he keeps insisting that he isn't mad.

17. **Responses will vary. Most students will respond that the narrator is crazy. His reason for killing the old man is not the thinking of a sane man.** *(DOK Level: 2–3; Content Topic: R.2.7)*

18. **Responses will vary. Students who like suspense will enjoy many of Poe's stories, and they may be more likely to think the story should be considered a classic. Students who like more cheerful fiction will probably choose to read other authors** and may not agree that this story should be considered a classic. *(DOK Level: 2–3; Content Topic: R.2.7)*

UNIT 2 REVIEW
PAGE 67

1. **C.** *(DOK Level: 1; Content Topic: R.4.1/L.4.1)*
2. **B.** *(DOK Level: 1; Content Topic: R.4.1/L.4.1)*
3. **A.** *(DOK Level: 1; Content Topic: R.4.1/L.4.1)*
4. **A.** *(DOK Level: 1–3; Content Topic: R.4.3/L.4.3)* This phrase helps the reader visualize the mood at the beginning of the passage because the boys are active.
5. **C.** *(DOK Level: 2–3; Content Topic: R.2.8)* Knowing that the boys ran away from home and then head to an outdoor environment and do so well there, the reader can conclude that they have some experience surviving in the outdoors.
6. **B.** *(DOK Level: 2–3; Content Topic: R.2.7)* The boys seem to know what they are doing outdoors and would not just wait for something to happen if they wanted to get across the water. It makes more sense that they would find the materials and build a new raft.
7. **Sample response: The fish probably did taste good, but it tasted even better because the boys were outdoors, had gotten a lot of exercise, and were very hungry, all of which would make the fish taste that much better.** *(DOK Level: 1–3; Content Topic: R.2.2)*
8. **Sample response: At the beginning of the passage the mood is one of excitement because the boys are happy to have made it to the island and to be away from home. The mood at the end of the passage is quite different, as the boys have become bored and are feeling a bit homesick.** *(DOK Level: 2–3; Content Topic: R.9.2)*

UNIT 2 MINI-TEST

1. **B.** *(DOK Level: 1; Content Topic: R.4.1/L.4.1)* The context of the sentence requires an adjective, and new-fangled is the only adjective that fits the context.

2. **D.** *(DOK Level: 2–3; Content Topic: R.5.4)* In fantasy stories, things happen that could not happen in real-life. A dog could not really be a nursemaid, so this tells the reader this passage is a fantasy story. The other things really could happen.

3. **B.** *(DOK Level: 1–2; Content Topic: R.2.1)* The passage says she follows the nursemaids home to tell their mistresses what they do wrong.

4. **D.** *(DOK Level: 1–2; Content Topic: R.2.1)* The passage is told from a third party's point of view. The reader does not get information about how characters feel or what they see from their own personal point of view.

5. **C.** *(DOK Level: 2; Content Topic: R.2.2)* All of the answers are true, but the reason they chose a dog to be their nursemaid was because of a lack of money.

6. **A.** *(DOK Level: 2–3; Content Topic: R.3.4)* Mrs. Darling loves to have things just so, which means she likes things to be done and she likes them to be done right. (cause) A nurse would help her to be sure this would happen. (effect) Mr. Darling likes to be like his neighbors. (cause) His neighbors have a nurse, so he needs to have a nurse too. (effect)

7. **C.** *(DOK Level: 2–3; Content Topic: R.3.4)* The last sentence of paragraph 1 says that Mr. Darling "wondered uneasily whether the neighbors talked" about the nursery, which suggests he worries whether the neighbors gossiped about Nana.

UNIT 3: INFORMATIONAL TEXTS

LESSON 17

1. Fruits and vegetables are filled with nutrients that people need to live healthier lives.

2. Eating at least five servings of fruits and vegetables every day will keep your body running smoothly.

1. Putting bad fuel in a car might cause it to run poorly.

2. Your body will not run too efficiently. You might have a hard time getting up in the morning. You might have trouble concentrating at work or school.

1. Sample response: Drink grapefruit juice at your desk midmorning; eat a salad for lunch; add zucchini or other vegetables to your spaghetti sauce; eat cucumbers with hummus for an appetizer; eat chunks of watermelon as a refreshing afternoon snack at the pool.

2. Sample response: Drink a glass of water with lemon when you wake up; carry a water bottle with you in the car; drink a glass of water right before dinner.

1. **C.** *(DOK Level: 1; Content Topic: R.4.1/L.4.1)*
2. **B.** *(DOK Level: 1; Content Topic: R.4.1/L.4.1)*
3. **A.** *(DOK Level: 1; Content Topic: R.4.1/L.4.1)*
4. **D.** *(DOK Level: 1; Content Topic: R.4.1/L.4.1)*
5. Get plenty of rest, be active, and drink water. *(DOK Level: 1; Content Topic: R.2.2)*
6. Sample response: We do not have a lot of energy, and we may have trouble concentrating. *(DOK Level: 2; Content Topic: R.2.2)*
7. Sample response: If you put bad fuel into a car it will not run very well. The same is true for your body. If you put bad food, such as high-fat or high-sugar foods, into your body, your body will not run well either. *(DOK Level: 2; Content Topic: R.5.1)*

8. Responses will vary. Students should show some understanding of the author's message and should supply a good argument for either agreeing or disagreeing, citing evidence from the text or personal experience. *(DOK Level: 3; Content Topic: R.2.7)*

9. **D.** *(DOK Level: 2; Content Topic: R.5.1)* Paragraph 4 focuses on how to add more fruits and vegetables to your diet, making Option D correct.

10. **A.** *(DOK Level: 2; Content Topic: R.2.2)* Option A is the only suggestion listed that is included in the passage.

11. **C.** *(DOK Level: 3; Content Topic: R.6.1)* The author focuses on practical ways to eat food with better nutrients, making Option C correct. Option A focuses on proteins, which are not discussed in the passage, and Options B and D are impractical.

12. **B.** *(DOK Level: 3; Content Topic: R.6.3)* Option B is a fact. The other options are opinions or possibilities.

LESSON 18

PAGE 77

1. **Surgical patients were dying of bacterial infections.**

2. **What causes wine to spoil?**

PAGE 78

1. **in the late 1700s**

2. **A.**

3. **Responses will vary. Students should include Jenner's studies of smallpox in the late 1700s, his work to develop a vaccine, and today's modern vaccines.**

PAGE 79

1. **B.**

2. **B.**

PAGES 80–81

1. **D.** *(DOK Level: 1; Content Topic: R.4.1/L.4.1)*

2. **A.** *(DOK Level: 1; Content Topic: R.4.1/L.4.1)*

3. **B.** *(DOK Level: 1; Content Topic: R.4.1/L.4.1)*

4. **C.** *(DOK Level: 1; Content Topic: R.4.1/L.4.1)*

5. **2, 1, 3** *(DOK Level: 2; Content Topic: R.3.1)*

6. **Pasteurization uses heat to kill germs, and a vaccine increases immunity against germs.** *(DOK Level: 2; Content Topic: R.2.2)*

7. **They don't make people sick because they have been killed or weakened before being injected into people.** *(DOK Level: 3; Content Topic: R.2.2)*

8. **Sample response: Pasteurization, vaccines, and antibiotics fight bacteria and infection.** *(DOK Level: 2; Content Topic: R.2.1)*

9. **C.** *(DOK Level: 2; Content Topic: R.6.1)* Since the selection covers more ways to fight germs than just immunizations, Options A and B are incorrect. Option D is also too narrow. Option C is the main purpose of the selection, as the title suggests.

10. **A.** *(DOK Level: 2; Content Topic: R.2.8)* Option A is the only valid conclusion. Vaccines prevent infections; they do not cure them. People do die of infections, and it is not possible to eliminate all bacteria.

11. **B.** *(DOK Level: 3; Content Topic: R.2.8)* The most significant result is that vaccines are used worldwide to prevent diseases. The other options are minor or not true.

12. **B.** *(DOK Level: 3; Content Topic: R.2.5)* Option B describes simple cleanliness, whereas the other options do not.

LESSON 19

PAGE 82

1. **In photosynthesis, plants and other organisms capture sunlight and change it into molecules that serve as food for other organisms.**

2. **Chlorophyll traps the energy of sunlight.**

PAGE 83

1. **A.**

2. **B.**

PAGE 84

1. They are both part of the process by which living things capture, transform, and store energy.

2. Photosynthesis is the process by which energy from sunlight is captured and transformed into chemical energy. Cellular respiration is the process cells use to harvest the energy in organic compounds.

PAGES 85–86

1. **B.** *(DOK Level: 1; Content Topic: R.4.1/L.4.1)*

2. **A.** *(DOK Level: 1; Content Topic: R.4.1/L.4.1)*

3. **D.** *(DOK Level: 1; Content Topic: R.4.1/L.4.1)*

4. **C.** *(DOK Level: 1; Content Topic: R.4.1/L.4.1)*

5. **photosynthesis** *(DOK Level: 2; Content Topic: R.3.5)*

6. **chloroplasts** *(DOK Level: 2; Content Topic: R.3.5)*

7. **pigment** *(DOK Level: 2; Content Topic: R.3.5)*

8. **reactants** *(DOK Level: 2; Content Topic: R.3.5)*

9. **matter, energy** *(DOK Level: 2; Content Topic: R.3.5)*

10. **harvest** *(DOK Level: 2; Content Topic: R.3.5)*

11. **B.** *(DOK Level: 2; Content Topic: R.3.2)* Photosynthesis converts sunlight to chemical energy. It also powers a reaction that produces oxygen, but not carbon dioxide; therefore, Options C and D are incorrect.

12. Sample response: Plants are some of the organisms that conduct photosynthesis. During photosynthesis, the pigment chlorophyll in the chloroplasts of plants captures energy from sunlight to form sugar and oxygen from carbon dioxide and water. *(DOK Level: 3; Content Topic: R.3.5, R.3.1)*

13. The substances that are needed for photosynthesis are carbon dioxide and water. The substances that are produced by photosynthesis are sugars and oxygen. *(DOK Level: 2; Content Topic: R.2.1)*

14. **A.** *(DOK Level: 3; Content Topic: R.2.7)* Photosynthesis produces oxygen.

15. The process of photosynthesis produced the gas. *(DOK Level: 3; Content Topic: R.3.2)*

LESSON 20

PAGE 87

1. Sample response: Yes, Douglass will free himself with education because he seems to be a determined person.

2. Sample response: Yes, Sophia will continue to help Douglass learn to read even though her husband tells her not to.

PAGE 88

1. Sample response: They were afraid Douglass was trouble and would cause the other slaves to want to escape.

2. Sample response: The fact that he got his new name from a poem tells me that he enjoys reading all kinds of materials.

PAGE 89

1. **A.**

2. **B.**

PAGES 90–91

1. **D.** *(DOK Level: 1; Content Topic: R.4.1/L.4.1)*

2. **C.** *(DOK Level: 1; Content Topic: R.4.1/L.4.1)*

3. **A.** *(DOK Level: 1; Content Topic: R.4.1/L.4.1)*

4. **B.** *(DOK Level: 1; Content Topic: R.4.1/L.4.1)*

5. **2, 3, 4, 1** *(DOK Level: 2; Content Topic: R.3.1)*

6. The author recounted the events of Frederick Douglass's life in chronological order. *(DOK Level: 2; Content Topic: R.3.2)*

7. He fought a white supervisor, and he helped runaway slaves. *(DOK Level: 2; Content Topic: R.2.2)*

8. "His dynamic talents proved to the world what black people could accomplish if they were only given the chance." *(DOK Level: 2; Content Topic: R.6.1)*

9. **B.** *(DOK Level: 2; Content Topic: R.6.3)* The passage is critical of slavery and slave owners, and complimentary of Frederick Douglass, making Option B the correct answer.

10. **B.** *(DOK Level: 2; Content Topic: R.2.1)* The excerpt describes the negative effect slavery had on Sophia.

11. **C.** *(DOK Level: 2; Content Topic: R.2.5)* An abolitionist protested slavery. Only Option C mentions how Douglass used his skills to protest slavery.

12. **C.** *(DOK Level: 1; Content Topic: R.2.2)* The first paragraph on page 89 identifies William Lloyd Garrison as the publisher of *The Liberator*.

LESSON 21
PAGE 92

1. Paine was fired because he wrote a pamphlet urging other tax collectors to band together and demand higher wages.

2. Because of Benjamin Franklin's encouragement, Paine moved to America.

PAGE 93

1. Sample response: Society is everything good that people can accomplish together, and government is just there to protect people from themselves.

2. Sample response: *Common Sense* is changing people's minds about wanting independence from Britain.

PAGE 94

1. The map shows when and where Thomas Paine traveled.

2. He traveled from France to America.

PAGES 95–96

1. **A.** *(DOK Level: 1; Content Topic: R.4.1/L.4.1)*
2. **C.** *(DOK Level: 1; Content Topic: R.4.1/L.4.1)*
3. **D.** *(DOK Level: 1; Content Topic: R.4.1/L.4.1)*
4. **B.** *(DOK Level: 1; Content Topic: R.4.1/L.4.1)*
5. The *Terrible* was a ship. *(DOK Level: 1; Content Topic: R.2.1)*
6. Paine was a soldier and this was the only writing surface he had. *(DOK Level: 3; Content Topic: R.2.7)*
7. Five different trips are shown on the map. *(DOK Level: 1; Content Topic: R.7.2)*

8. Sample response: Thomas Paine inspired colonists to seek independence from Britain. His words helped motivate them to fight for and ultimately win that independence. *(DOK Level: 3; Content Topic: R.2.2)*

9. **B.** *(DOK Level: 2; Content Topic: R.3.1)* Paine met Franklin in 1774. He published *Common Sense* in 1776. He fought in the Revolutionary War between 1776 and 1783. He wrote *The Age of Reason* in the early 1800s.

10. **B.** *(DOK Level: 2; Content Topic: R.4.1/L.4.1)* The word *sound* in the example sentence is an adjective meaning "valid," which matches Option B.

11. **C.** *(DOK Level: 2; Content Topic: R.2.4)* The selection says in the pamphlet *Common Sense*, "Paine forcefully spelled out the American cause for liberty" from Great Britain.

12. **A.** *(DOK Level: 2; Content Topic: R.2.7)* The quote from John Adams on page 94 supports Option A.

13. **B.** *(DOK Level: 2; Content Topic: R.2.8)* The selection says, "Paine's pamphlets were wildly popular," which supports Option B.

14. **A.** *(DOK Level: 3; Content Topic: R.6.3)* According to the selection, Paine expressed his opinions in many published works, which supports Option A.

LESSON 22
PAGE 97

1. The photograph shows that the waiting rooms at a train or bus station were segregated.

2. Sample response: The photograph shows evidence that what the text says really did happen. This helps me better understand the text because it is hard to believe that African Americans were ever treated this way.

PAGE 98

1. A.
2. B.

PAGE 99

1. Brown said that the facilities for blacks were not inferior to those for whites, so the laws were fair.
2. The ruling led to Jim Crow laws in states across the country.

PAGES 100–101

1. D. *(DOK Level: 1; Content Topic: R.4.1/L.4.1)*
2. C. *(DOK Level: 1; Content Topic: R.4.1/L.4.1)*
3. B. *(DOK Level: 1; Content Topic: R.4.1/L.4.1)*
4. A. *(DOK Level: 1; Content Topic: R.4.1/L.4.1)*
5. The author included this detail to describe a key fact about Harlan's background. *(DOK Level: 3; Content Topic: R.6.3)*
6. Each train had to have a car for white passengers and a separate car for black ones, or separate sections in the same car. *(DOK Level: 2; Content Topic: R.4.1/L.4.1)*
7. The term refers to various means of transportation. *(DOK Level: 3; Content Topic: R.4.1/L.4.1)*
8. The Supreme Court made decisions that supported southern laws that were stripping African Americans of their rights. *(DOK Level: 3; Content Topic: R.3.3)*
9. B. *(DOK Level: 2; Content Topic: R.2.4)* The first paragraph on page 98 says that the Thirteenth Amendment banned slavery and the Fourteenth Amendment declared African Americans as citizens and protected their rights as citizens.
10. A. *(DOK Level: 2; Content Topic: R.3.1)* The Thirteenth Amendment was ratified in 1865. The Civil Rights Act passed in 1875. Louisiana passed a law segregating railroad cars in 1890. Plessy was arrested in 1892.

11. C. *(DOK Level: 2; Content Topic: R.4.1/L.4.1)* The context of the sentence supports the meaning "make up for."
12. B. *(DOK Level: 3; Content Topic: R.3.4)* The author states that Harlan was the only justice that dissented, or disagreed, with the others, which supports option B.
13. A. *(DOK Level: 2; Content Topic: R.2.4)* Brown wrote that separate but equal facilities were constitutional, which supports Option A.

LESSON 23

PAGE 102

A.

PAGE 103

1. B.
2. B.

PAGE 104

1. A. and B.
2. A.

PAGES 105–106

1. allergic *(DOK Level: 1–2; Content Topic: R.4.3/L.4.3)*
2. enhanced *(DOK Level: 1–2; Content Topic: R.4.3/L.4.3)*
3. symptoms *(DOK Level: 1–2; Content Topic: R.4.3/L.4.3)*
4. clarity *(DOK Level: 1–2; Content Topic: R.4.3/L.4.3)*
5. hypnotized *(DOK Level: 1–2; Content Topic: R.4.3/L.4.3)*
6. antibiotics *(DOK Level: 1–2; Content Topic: R.4.3/L.4.3)*
7. Answers should include two of the following: Television can shorten a child's attention span, weaken a child's language skills, and weaken a child's reading skills. *(DOK Level: 1–3; Content Topic: R.8.2)*

8. When sound effects and music are ignored, it becomes apparent that characters speak in short phrases and incomplete sentences. *(DOK Level: 1–3; Content Topic: R.8.2)*

9. Antibiotics fight to kill bacteria that can cause some sore throats and earaches. *(DOK Level: 2; Content Topic: R.6.3)*

10. Answers should include two of the claims made about the CD/MP3 player: Its sound is of high quality and can fill a concert hall; the sound has a clarity never before possible from a small CD/MP3 player; and you'll never want to listen to music on any other CD/MP3 player again. *(DOK Level: 2–3; Content Topic: R.8.4)*

11. A. *(DOK Level: 1–2; Content Topic: R.2.1)* The third paragraph states that children's television shows don't provide important requirements for learning language, which supports Option A.

12. D. *(DOK Level: 2–3; Content Topic: R.8.3)* The tips support Option D. The opposite is true for Options A–C.

13. D. *(DOK Level: 2–3; Content Topic: R.8.3)* Only Option D states a fact—the size of the player. The other options state opinions or persuasive comments.

14. Responses will vary. Students should include the name of the product, the information that inspired the purchase, and an opinion about whether the advertising claims were true. *(DOK Level: 2–3; Content Topic: R.8.3)*

15. Responses will vary. Students should express an opinion and include reasons for the opinion. Some might state that watching a lot of television is bad for adults because it takes time away from more worthwhile activities. The quick cuts and flashing lights may shorten an adult's attention span in the same way that they can shorten a child's. Others might not think watching a lot of television is bad for adults. *(DOK Level: 2–3; Content Topic: R.2.7)*

LESSON 24

PAGE 107

   B.

PAGE 108

1. B.
2. B.

PAGE 109

1. A.
2. A.

PAGES 110–111

1. constitute *(DOK Level: 2; Content Topic: R.3.5)*

2. references *(DOK Level: 2; Content Topic: R.3.5)*

3. specify *(DOK Level: 2; Content Topic: R.3.5)*

4. introductory *(DOK Level: 2; Content Topic: R.3.5)*

5. authorize *(DOK Level: 2; Content Topic: R.3.5)*

6. certify *(DOK Level: 2; Content Topic: R.3.5)*

7. This question must be answered by applicants who are under 18 years old. *(DOK Level: 2; Content Topic: R.3.5, R.5.1)*

8. The purpose of box 2 is to find out how the patient is related to the employee who has the dental insurance. *(DOK Level: 3; Content Topic: R.3.5, R.5.2)*

9. Box 13 requires a signature so that information about treatment and dental history can be released to the insurance company. *(DOK Level: 3; Content Topic: R.3.5, R.5.2)*

10. The interest rate will increase to 19.9% if the cardholder is late paying his or her bill twice during a six-month period. *(DOK Level: 3; Content Topic: R.3.5, R.3.3)*

11. C. *(DOK Level: 2; Content Topic: R.5.1)* Section 2 is where you would list your previous work experience. The salary you received at your last job is part of the information you would include in this section.

12. B. *(DOK Level: 3; Content Topic: R.2.2)* Line 4 of the instructions tells the employee to sign and date line 14 in order to have the payment sent directly to the dentist.

13. D. *(DOK Level: 3; Content Topic: R.5.1)* These words introduce the information about cash advances in section E. They make it clear that the credit card can also be used to get cash.

14. Sample response: Always read the instructions on a form carefully; provide all the information the form requires; print neatly; and make sure all answers are true and complete. *(DOK Level: 3; Content Topic: R.2.5)*

15. Responses will vary. Students should express an opinion about how legal documents should be written and include reasons or personal experiences to support the opinion. *(DOK Level: 3; Content Topic: R.4.1/L.4.1)*

LESSON 25

1. **A.**
2. **B.**

1. **A.**
2. **B.**

1. **B.**
2. **B.**

1. **malfunction** *(DOK Level: 1–2; Content Topic: R.4.1/L.4.1)*
2. **probationary** *(DOK Level: 1–2; Content Topic: R.4.1/L.4.1)*
3. **affix** *(DOK Level: 1–2; Content Topic: R.4.1/L.4.1)*
4. **contaminated** *(DOK Level: 1–2; Content Topic: R.4.1/L.4.1)*
5. **eligible** *(DOK Level: 1–2; Content Topic: R.4.1/L.4.1)*

6. **reinstated** *(DOK Level: 1–2; Content Topic: R.4.1/L.4.1)*
7. **The supervisor will give the employee a written evaluation.** *(DOK Level: 1–2; Content Topic: R.2.1, R.3.5)*
8. **An employee can use sick leave for any illness, for pregnancy, for doctor or dentist visits, or for illness in the employee's immediate family.** *(DOK Level: 1–2; Content Topic: R.2.1, R.3.5)*
9. **The disks may become warped.** *(DOK Level: 1–2; Content Topic: R.2.1, R.3.5)*
10. **D.** *(DOK Level: 2–3; Content Topic: R.5.2)* If your friend is going to need to take more than a few days off, she will need some type of leave. Family Leave allows an employee to take off up to four months.
11. **C.** *(DOK Level: 2–3; Content Topic: R.2.1, R.3.5)* The second paragraph of the manual describes how to properly insert batteries into the remote control. One of the steps is matching the plus and minus signs on the batteries with those inside the battery compartment.
12. **D.** *(DOK Level: 2–3; Content Topic: R.2.1, R.3.5)* Step 2 of the safety procedures on page 114 has two parts. The first gives the instruction to wipe up the fluids with paper towels. The second part tells the worker to dispose of the paper towels in a red trash bag.
13. **Responses will vary. Students should include reasons to support the yes or no response. Some might say it is important to read the entire employee handbook as soon as possible after starting a new job because the handbook may contain information that your supervisor has forgotten to tell you. In addition, once an employee is given a handbook, it becomes his or her responsibility to know what is in it.** *(DOK Level: 2–3; Content Topic: R.2.7)*

14. Responses will vary. Students should include a description of the features of the perfect instruction manual and an explanation of how these would make the manual easy to understand. *(DOK Level: 2–3; Content Topic: R.2.7)*

LESSON 26

PAGE 117

B.

PAGE 118

1. B.
2. B.

PAGE 119

1. B.
2. B.

PAGES 120–121

1. **exempt** *(DOK Level: 1–2; Content Topic: R.4.1./L.4.1)*

2. **incur** *(DOK Level: 1–2; Content Topic: R.4.1./L.4.1)*

3. **liability** *(DOK Level: 1–2; Content Topic: R.4.1./L.4.1)*

4. **retained** *(DOK Level: 1–2; Content Topic: R.4.1./L.4.1)*

5. **prospective** *(DOK Level: 1–2; Content Topic: R.4.1./L.4.1)*

6. **summoned** *(DOK Level: 1–2; Content Topic: R.4.1./L.4.1)*

7. Answers should include two of the following: Jurors would have to abandon a person under their care or supervision because they could not find a caregiver during jury duty. Jurors would incur costs that would make it difficult to pay daily living expenses or support others. Jurors would suffer physical hardship that would result in illness or disease. Jurors would not get paid because an employer is not required to compensate them. *(DOK Level: 2–3; Content Topic: R.5.2)*

8. The car dealer can change his or her mind if the value of the trade-in is diminished as a result of physical damage, alteration, or deterioration in mechanical condition of the vehicle. *(DOK Level: 2–3; Content Topic: R.5.2)*

9. The landlord could spend the security deposit if the tenant does damage to the premises or defaults on the agreement. *(DOK Level: 2–3; Content Topic: R.5.2)*

10. **C.** *(DOK Level: 1–3; Content Topic: R.4.1/L.4.1)* The context clues are often the words or phrases surrounding the unfamiliar word. In this case, the clue for the meaning of "compensation" appears after the word—"Juror will receive $40 for each day's attendance."

11. **D.** *(DOK Level: 2; Content Topic: R.2.2)* This is the only option that correctly summarizes what the section says.

12. **A.** *(DOK Level: 1–2; Content Topic: R.2.1)* Based on the passage, the tenant needs to agree to allow the landlord to enter the apartment, but the tenant cannot be unreasonable about this. The landlord will want to check with the tenant in advance to be sure he or she has permission to enter.

13. Responses will vary. Some people have bought or sold a used car. In some cases there may not have been any written agreement (if the car was bought from a friend, for example). Those who have signed a written agreement can explain their experiences. *(DOK Level: 2–3; Content Topic: R.2.7)*

14. Responses will vary. Most people will have experience with signing an apartment lease and can discuss their concern or displeasure with parts of the agreement. For example, they may have wanted to have pets, but the lease did not allow it. Or, the rent was higher than they'd hoped. Or, perhaps, the landlord included additional requirements on the lease that

displeased them, such as no overnight guests, no subletting, or no parking in the driveway. *(DOK Level: 2-3; Content Topic: R.2.7)*

UNIT 3 REVIEW

PAGE 123

1. **A.** *(DOK Level: 2; Content Topic: R.3.5, R.5.1)* The name of your cat belongs in the section about current pets. The other sections are about people and the home.

2. **B.** *(DOK Level: 2; Content Topic: R.3.5, R.5.1)* A neighbor who knows you would be a reference.

3. **Sample response: If there are children in the home, the adoption agency wants to be sure that the dog they place in the applicant's home will be comfortable around children. Some dogs do not do well with children; some do OK with older children, but not younger children.** *(DOK Level: 3; Content Topic: R.3.5, R.5.2)*

4. **Sample response: The adoption agency wants to know how often the dog may be left alone and that the applicant has a plan for the dog while he or she is traveling.** *(DOK Level: 3; Content Topic: R.3.5, R.5.2)*

5. **Responses will vary. Students should indicate responsibility for the dog.**

6. **Sample response: The people listed as references should be ones that respect me, and I should contact the people to tell them that I plan to list them as references.**

UNIT 3 MINI-TEST

PAGES 124-125

1. **B.** *(DOK Level: 2; Content Topic: R.2.1)* The main idea of the passage is that the Silk Road was used for trade between China and the West.

2. **C.** *(DOK Level: 2; Content Topic: R.3.4)* The final sentence tells how sea travel affected the Silk Road, which supports Option C.

3. **D.** *(DOK Level: 1; Content Topic: R.2.1)* The Silk Road was also used to trade political, social, artistic, and religious customs.

4. **D.** *(DOK Level: 2; Content Topic: R.7.2)* According to the diagram, waxing gibbous comes just before a full moon.

5. **B.** *(DOK Level: 3; Content Topic: R.7.2)* A second full moon in one month is a Blue Moon. The cycle takes 29.5 days, so the first phase would have to be a full moon.

6. **D.** *(DOK Level: 2; Content Topic: R.7.2)* According to the diagram, waning gibbous comes just after a full moon. Since a Blue Moon is a full moon, it would be followed by a waning gibbous, too.

7. **A.** *(DOK Level: 3; Content Topic: R.7.2)* According to the diagram, the lighted side of the moon is facing the sun during a new moon.

UNIT 4: WRITING

LESSON 27

PAGE 129

Sample responses:
1. Topic 2: Keeping Score in Bowling
2. Topic 1: My Dream Job; Topic 2: Good Bosses and Bad Bosses
3. Topic 1: My Favorite Movie of All Time; Topic 2: My Favorite Movie Character
4. Topic 1: Adopt an Animal; Topic 2: Hunting Should Be Outlawed *(DOK Level: 2; Content Topic: W.2)*

PAGE 130

Sample response: Advantages of a Large Family: never lonely, learn to get along with others, support one another

Sample outline:

Topic: Advantages of a Large Family

I. Never lonely

    A. When young you have someone to play with

    B. When older you have someone to go out with

II. Learn to get along with others

    A. Learn to share

    B. Learn to solve arguments

    C. Learn to compromise

III. Support one another

    A. Have people to call on when you need help

    B. Have people to borrow money from

    C. Have people to talk to about your problems *(DOK Level: 2; Content Topic: W.2)*

Sample idea map:

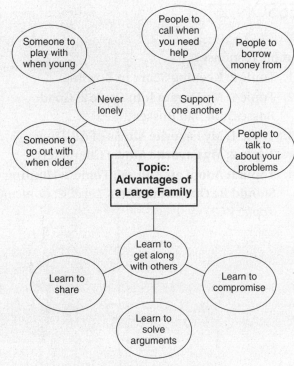

(DOK Level: 2: Content Topic: W.2)

PAGE 132

1. **A.** *(DOK Level: 1–2; Content Topic: W.2)* Sentence A is the best opening statement. Sentence B is not clear about which view the writer is taking. Sentence C is too general.

2. **A.** *(DOK Level: 1–2; Content Topic: W.2)* Sentence A is the best opening statement. It makes a strong statement about the main idea. Both Sentences B and C are vague statements that do not clearly support the topic.

3. **B.** *(DOK Level: 1-2; Content Topic: W.2)* Sentence B is the best opening statement. It clearly introduces the author's topic. Sentence A does not clearly support the topic. Sentence C is a supporting detail.

PAGE 133

Practice

    Check 1, 3, 4, and 6. *(DOK Level: 1–2: Content Topic: W.2)*

Write

    Responses will vary. Students should write a paragraph about sports with a topic sentence and at least three supporting details. *(DOK Level: 2: Content Topic: W.2)*

PAGE 134

Practice A

    Paragraph 1: 1, T, 3, 2, 4

    Paragraph 2: 4, 3, T, 2, 1 *(DOK Level: 1–2; Content Topic: W.2)*

Practice B

    Paragraph 1: time order

    Paragraph 2: facts/reason, cause/effect *(DOK Level: 1–2; Content Topic: W.2)*

Write

Sample paragraphs:

1. **Morning people and night people are very different. Morning people wake up with the sun, smile, and start talking. When night people have to get up early, they grumble and refuse to talk. Night people come alive at the end of the day. They are ready to party just as morning people are about to turn in for the night. (organization:**

compare/contrast) *(DOK Level: 2; Content Topic: W.2)*

2. Learning to organize your time will change your life. You can begin by writing down how you spend every hour of the day. Do this for one week and you will begin to see where your time is going. Next, make a list of the time wasters you can avoid. Then figure out how much time you have left for the things you have been putting off. (organization: time order) *(DOK Level: 2; Content Topic: W.2)*

3. Friendship is one of the most important things in life. If you know how to be a good friend, then you know how to be loyal. Friendship also teaches you how to keep secrets and how to make sacrifices for someone else. Friendship is supposed to be a two-way street. If this is true, then all the good you give will come back to you. (organization: facts/reasons) *(DOK Level: 2; Content Topic: W.2)*

PAGE 135

Practice

Responses will vary. Students should write a conclusion that provides a summary, makes a prediction, makes a recommendation, or asks a question.

PAGE 138

Practice A

Students should make at least three of the following revisions:

1. Revise the first sentence, which is too broad. A good revision could read, "Kingston Heritage Chorus goes on a rehearsal retreat every spring."

2. Delete the fifth sentence. The concert outfits are not related to the topic here.

3. Begin a new paragraph with the sentence "Organizing the retreat is a big job."

4. Move the sentence "The Retreat Coordinator needs a committee of at least six people" to follow the sentence "Organizing the retreat is a big job." *(DOK Level: 1–2; Practice Topic: W.3)*

Practice B

Students should write a new version of the paragraph that incorporates their edits.

Write

Students should use editing marks to revise their conclusions and write a new version that incorporates their edits. *(DOK Level: 1–2; Practice Topic: W.3)*

PAGE 139

Practice A

I can achieve success and improve my reading by making some easy changes in my daily life. Reading is essential to success. At first, I thought it might be hard to become a better reader, but after careful thought, I realized it doesn't have to be. *(DOK Level: 1–2; Practice Topic: W.3)*

Practice B

Students should use editing marks to edit their conclusions.

UNIT 4 REVIEW

PAGE 146

1. Prewriting. This step means planning before you write. It involves defining a topic, generating ideas, and organizing those ideas.

2. Writing a first draft. This step involves writing the first version of a piece of writing. The main goal of this step is to put ideas on paper in an organized way.

3. Revising and Editing. This step involves reviewing and evaluating the first draft. Revising means reviewing the content of the writing. Editing means looking carefully at the sentences, words, and mechanics.

4. Writing the final draft. This step involves incorporating all the changes that came about while revising and editing and making a clean, final copy.

5. Publishing the final draft. This step involves sharing the final draft with others. *(DOK Level: 1–2; Content Topic: W.2)*

6. Sample response: Topic 1: How to recycle at home and work; Topic 2: How we can help prevent global warming *(DOK Level: 1–2; Content Topic: W.2)*

7. Sample response: Topic 1: What are the planets?; Topic 2: What is it like to be an astronaut? *(DOK Level: 1–2; Content Topic: W.2)*

PAGE 147

8. Response will vary. The opening should clearly state whether students agree or disagree with the old saying. Each Roman numeral should list a reason why students agree or disagree, and the supporting details for each reason should be listed on the A., B., C. lines under each Roman numeral. Finally, the conclusion should summarize the points students have made. *(DOK Level: 2–3; Content Topic: W.2)*

PAGE 148

Students should make at least three of the following revisions:

1. Revise the second sentence of the first paragraph, which is a run-on sentence. A good revision could read, "You can buy it at any hardware store, and you can use it for almost anything."

2. Insert a comma and clean up the last sentence of the first paragraph. If you use duct tape to seal a leaky window frame, it will probably outlast your house!

3. Delete the third sentence of the second paragraph. What the study does not cover is not related to the topic here.

4. Add more explanation and a conclusion to the second paragraph. *(DOK Level: 2; Practice Topic: W.3)*

UNIT 4 MINI-TEST

PAGE 149

Students should show evidence of prewriting, drafting, and revising/editing. The final draft of the response should clearly identify which argument is better supported and cite specific evidence from the text. Refer to the Scoring Rubric on page 140.

UNIT 5: LANGUAGE SKILLS
LESSON 29

PAGE 152

1. who's *(DOK Level: 1; Content Topic: L.2.3)*
2. I've *(DOK Level: 1; Content Topic: L.2.3)*
3. wasn't *(DOK Level: 1; Content Topic: L.2.3)*
4. weren't *(DOK Level: 1; Content Topic: L.2.3)*
5. didn't *(DOK Level: 1; Content Topic: L.2.3)*

Sample responses:

6. I can't dance the tango. *(DOK Level: 1–2; Content Topic: L.2.3)*
7. I won't answer the phone at night. *(DOK Level: 1–2; Content Topic: L.2.3)*

PAGE 153

1. week *(DOK Level: 1–2; Content Topic: L.1.1)*
2. fair *(DOK Level: 1–2; Content Topic: L.1.1)*
3. capital *(DOK Level: 1–2; Content Topic: L.1.1)*
4. aisles *(DOK Level: 1–2; Content Topic: L.1.1)*
5. know *(DOK Level: 1–2; Content Topic: L.1.1)*
6. lessen *(DOK Level: 1–2; Content Topic: L.1.1)*
7. close *(DOK Level: 1–2; Content Topic: L.1.1)*
8. whole *(DOK Level: 1–2; Content Topic: L.1.1)*

Sample responses:

9. I accept your apology. *(DOK Level: 1–2; Content Topic: L.1.1)*
10. He tried to brake the car in time but couldn't. *(DOK Level: 1–2; Content Topic: L.1.1)*

PAGE 154

1. who *(DOK Level: 1–2; Content Topic: L.1.1)*
2. then *(DOK Level: 1–2; Content Topic: L.1.1)*
3. well *(DOK Level: 1–2; Content Topic: L.1.1)*
4. among *(DOK Level: 1–2; Content Topic: L.1.1)*
5. to *(DOK Level: 1–2; Content Topic: L.1.1)*
6. too *(DOK Level: 1–2; Content Topic: L.1.1)*

LESSON 30

PAGE 155

1. **appears** *(DOK Level: 1; Content Topic: L.1.2, L.1.7)*
2. **glow** *(DOK Level: 1; Content Topic: L.1.2, L.1.7)*
3. **is** *(DOK Level: 1; Content Topic: L.1.2, L.1.7)*
4. **are** *(DOK Level: 1; Content Topic: L.1.2, L.1.7)*

Sample responses:

5. **Cars clog the roads in my town.** *(DOK Level: 1–2; Content Topic: L.1.2, L.1.7)*
6. **The city buses or the train is a convenient way to go to work.** *(DOK Level: 1–2; Content Topic: L.1.2, L.1.7)*

PAGE 156

1. **is** *(DOK Level: 1; Content Topic: L.1.2, L.1.7)*
2. **wants** *(DOK Level: 1; Content Topic: L.1.2, L.1.7)*
3. **are** *(DOK Level: 1; Content Topic: L.1.2, L.1.7)*
4. **are** *(DOK Level: 1; Content Topic: L.1.2, L.1.7)*
5. **seem** *(DOK Level: 1; Content Topic: L.1.2, L.1.7)*

Sample responses:

6. **Here is the money you asked for.** *(DOK Level: 1–2; Content Topic: L.1.2, L.1.7)*
7. **The jury has not reached a verdict yet.** *(DOK Level: 1–2; Content Topic: L.1.2, L.1.7)*

LESSON 31

PAGE 157

1. **We** *(DOK Level: 1; Content Topic: L.1.3)*
2. **He** *(DOK Level: 1; Content Topic: L.1.3)*
3. **She** *(DOK Level: 1; Content Topic: L.1.3)*
4. **They** *(DOK Level: 1; Content Topic: L.1.3)*

Sample responses:

5. **They are nice.** *(DOK Level: 1–2; Content Topic: L.1.3)*
6. **We have a lot in common.** *(DOK Level: 1–2; Content Topic: L.1.3)*

PAGE 158

1. **me** *(DOK Level: 1; Content Topic: L.1.3)*
2. **him** *(DOK Level: 1; Content Topic: L.1.3)*
3. **us** *(DOK Level: 1; Content Topic: L.1.3)*
4. **her** *(DOK Level: 1; Content Topic: L.1.3)*
5. **them** *(DOK Level: 1; Content Topic: L.1.3)*

Sample responses:

6. **Please listen to me.** *(DOK Level: 1–2; Content Topic: L.1.3)*
7. **I don't want the tickets, so I am giving them to you.** *(DOK Level: 1–2; Content Topic: L.1.3)*
8. **Our boss gave the tickets to us.** *(DOK Level: 1–2; Content Topic: L.1.3)*

PAGE 159

1. **his** *(DOK Level: 1–2; Content Topic: L.1.3)*
2. **His** *(DOK Level: 1–2; Content Topic: L.1.3)*
3. **your** *(DOK Level: 1–2; Content Topic: L.1.3)*
4. **mine, yours** *(DOK Level: 1–2; Content Topic: L.1.3)*
5. **our** *(DOK Level: 1–2; Content Topic: L.1.3)*

Sample responses:

6. **Mine is neat.** *or* **My home is neat.** *(DOK Level: 1–2; Content Topic: L.1.3)*
7. **Mine is small.** *or* **My hometown is small.** *(DOK Level: 1–2; Content Topic: L.1.3)*

PAGE 160

1. **Cities** *(DOK Level: 1; Content Topic: L.1.3)*
2. **snowstorms** *(DOK Level: 1; Content Topic: L.1.3)*
3. **newspaper** *(DOK Level: 1; Content Topic: L.1.3)*
4. **mayor** *(DOK Level: 1; Content Topic: L.1.3)*
5. **police chief** *(DOK Level: 1; Content Topic: L.1.3)*
6. **brother** *(DOK Level: 1; Content Topic: L.1.3)*

Sample responses:

7. **My car had been sitting in the snow for three days, and it was dead.** *(DOK Level: 1–2; Content Topic: L.1.3)*
8. **Although he was already late for work, Joe offered to jump-start the car.** *(DOK Level: 1–2; Content Topic: L.1.3)*

PAGE 161

1. **our** *(DOK Level: 1; Content Topic: L.1.3)*
2. **they** *(DOK Level: 1; Content Topic: L.1.3)*
3. **she** *(DOK Level: 1; Content Topic: L.1.3)*
4. **their** *(DOK Level: 1; Content Topic: L.1.3)*
5. **his** *(DOK Level: 1; Content Topic: L.1.3)*

Sample responses:

6. The actress was good in her first movie role. *(DOK Level: 1–2; Content Topic: L.1.3)*
7. Take the beef or chicken out of the freezer and thaw it. *(DOK Level: 1–2; Content Topic: L.1.3)*

PAGE 162

1. **are** *(DOK Level: 1; Content Topic: L.1.3)*
2. **has** *(DOK Level: 1; Content Topic: L.1.3)*
3. **take** *(DOK Level: 1; Content Topic: L.1.3)*
4. **gives** *(DOK Level: 1; Content Topic: L.1.3)*
5. **are** *(DOK Level: 1; Content Topic: L.1.3)*
6. **have** *(DOK Level: 1; Content Topic: L.1.3)*

Sample responses:

7. Everyone in my family is going to the reunion. *(DOK Level: 1–2; Content Topic: L.1.3)*
8. No one in my family has a van. *(DOK Level: 1–2; Content Topic: L.1.3)*
9. All of my friends are wonderful people. *(DOK Level: 1–2; Content Topic: L.1.3)*
10. Several of my coworkers have the flu. *(DOK Level: 1–2; Content Topic: L.1.3)*

LESSON 32

PAGE 163

Sample responses:

1. Our city is considered to be one of the best in the world. *(DOK Level: 1–2; Content Topic: L.1.4)*
2. We have a great zoo and lively nightlife. *(DOK Level: 1–2; Content Topic: L.1.4)*
3. There is always something happening in our city. *(DOK Level: 1–2; Content Topic: L.1.4)*

4. No other city can compare to ours. *(DOK Level: 1–2; Content Topic: L.1.4)*

PAGE 164

1. **I** *(DOK Level: 1–2; Content Topic: L.1.4)*
2. **C** *(DOK Level: 1–2; Content Topic: L.1.4)*
3. **I** *(DOK Level: 1–2; Content Topic: L.1.4)*
4. **C** *(DOK Level: 1–2; Content Topic: L.1.4)*
5. **I** *(DOK Level: 1–2; Content Topic: L.1.4)*
6. **I** *(DOK Level: 1–2; Content Topic: L.1.4)*
7. **C** *(DOK Level: 1–2; Content Topic: L.1.4)*
8. **I** *(DOK Level: 1–2; Content Topic: L.1.4)*

LESSON 33

PAGE 165

1. **M** *(DOK Level: 1–2; Content Topic: L.1.5)*
2. **C** *(DOK Level: 1–2; Content Topic: L.1.5)*
3. **M** *(DOK Level: 1–2; Content Topic: L.1.5)*
4. **C** *(DOK Level: 1–2; Content Topic: L.1.5)*
5. **C** *(DOK Level: 1–2; Content Topic: L.1.5)*
6. **M** *(DOK Level: 1–2; Content Topic: L.1.5)*
7. **M** *(DOK Level: 1–2; Content Topic: L.1.5)*
8. **M** *(DOK Level: 1–2; Content Topic: L.1.5)*

Sample response:

One night a tremendous windstorm ripped through our town. All night long the wind howled around our house. At one point I heard a crunching sound, followed by a loud snap. The next morning we found our small tulip tree uprooted, lying across our garden. *(DOK Level: 2; Content Topic: L.1.5)*

PAGE 166

Sample responses:

1. While I was passing a large rock, a clap of thunder made me scream. *(DOK Level: 1–2; Content Topic: L.1.4)*
2. Sailing up the harbor, we saw the pier. *(DOK Level: 1–2; Content Topic: L.1.4)*
3. As we flew over the town, the cars and houses looked like toys. *(DOK Level: 1–2; Content Topic: L.1.4)*
4. While I was putting the chair together, I lost the screw. *(DOK Level: 1–2; Content Topic: L.1.4)*

5. When I opened the jar, the sauce spilled all over the floor. *(DOK Level: 1–2; Content Topic: L.1.4)*

6. As he was walking up the steps, the package fell. *(DOK Level: 1–2; Content Topic: L.1.4)*

Sample responses:

7. Going to my class, I met an old friend. *(DOK Level: 2; Content Topic: L.1.5)*

8. Angry at her husband, the woman stormed out of the house. *(DOK Level: 2; Content Topic: L.1.5)*

9. Already hungry, the dog sat by his empty food bowl. *(DOK Level: 2; Content Topic: L.1.5)*

10. Without thinking, I left the garage door up. *(DOK Level: 2; Content Topic: L.1.5)*

PAGE 167

1. I *(DOK Level: 1–2; Content Topic: L.1.5)*
2. I *(DOK Level: 1–2; Content Topic: L.1.5)*
3. L *(DOK Level: 1–2; Content Topic: L.1.5)*
4. I *(DOK Level: 1–2; Content Topic: L.1.5)*
5. I *(DOK Level: 1–2; Content Topic: L.1.5)*

LESSON 34
PAGE 168

1. CS *(DOK Level: 1–2; Content Topic: L.2.4)*
2. CS *(DOK Level: 1–2; Content Topic: L.2.4)*
3. S *(DOK Level: 1–2; Content Topic: L.2.4)*

Sample responses:

4. James watches reality TV every day, but his roommate only watches the news. *(DOK Level: 2; Content Topic: L.2.4)*

5. Some reality TV shows have been on the air for many years, yet others have just started their run. *(DOK Level: 2; Content Topic: L.2.4)*

PAGE 169

Sample responses:

1. My first week on the job was a disaster, and my boss told me so. *(DOK Level: 2; Content Topic: L.2.4)*

2. I was really upset, yet I knew things had to get better. *or* I was really upset, but I knew

things had to get better. *(DOK Level: 2; Content Topic: L.2.4)*

3. I tried as hard as I could, for I really wanted to keep the job. *(DOK Level: 2; Content Topic: L.2.4)*

4. My coworker gave me good advice, so I felt more confident. *(DOK Level: 2; Content Topic: L.2.4)*

5. Next week has to be better, or I'll think about quitting! *(DOK Level: 1–2; Content Topic: L.2.4)*

PAGE 170

1. Although I have a car, I usually take the bus. *(DOK Level: 1–2; Content Topic: L.1.6, L.2.4)*

2. I prefer the bus because I care about the environment. *(DOK Level: 1–2; Content Topic: L.1.6, L.2.4)*

3. If we don't help to reduce pollution, the problem will only get worse. *(DOK Level: 1–2; Content Topic: L.1.6, L.2.4)*

4. Let's act before it's too late. *(DOK Level: 1–2; Content Topic: L.1.6, L.2.4)*

Sample response:

Walk one block south on Andrews Street until you get to Anchor Lane. Turn right on Anchor. Continue west on Anchor, crossing Hyridge and Mesa. Keep walking until you get to Washington. Turn right and walk one block to the community swimming pool. If you keep going straight on Anchor, there is an easy shortcut. If you cut through the first parking lot on your right, you'll see the pool. You can't miss it! *(DOK Level: 2; Content Topic: L.1.6, L.2.4)*

LESSON 35
PAGE 171

1. NP *(DOK Level: 1–2; Content Topic: L.1.6)*
2. P *(DOK Level: 1–2; Content Topic: L.1.6)*
3. NP *(DOK Level: 1–2; Content Topic: L.1.6)*
4. P *(DOK Level: 1–2; Content Topic: L.1.6)*
5. P *(DOK Level: 1–2; Content Topic: L.1.6)*

6. NP *(DOK Level: 1–2; Content Topic: L.1.6)*

7. NP *(DOK Level: 1–2; Content Topic: L.1.6)*

Sample responses:

8. You can buy food at a grocery store, a snack shop, and a restaurant. *(DOK Level: 1–2; Content Topic: L.1.6)*

9. When you are sick, you should stay home, drink fluids, and rest. *(DOK Level: 1–2; Content Topic: L.1.6)*

PAGE 172

1. Writing helps people think, speak, and learn. *(DOK Level: 1–2; Content Topic: L.1.6)*

2. Those who can write well will be leaders in the community, state, and nation in years to come. *(DOK Level: 1–2; Content Topic: L.1.6)*

3. By writing frequently, reading often, and seeking feedback, writers can improve. *(DOK Level: 1–2; Content Topic: L.1.6)*

4. Learning to write clearly, correctly, and effectively is a goal. *(DOK Level: 1–2; Content Topic: L.1.6)*

Sample responses:

5. I can write letters, messages, and lists. *(DOK Level: 1–2; Content Topic: L.1.6)*

6. Three qualities of good writing are precise words, vivid details, and correct grammar. *(DOK Level: 1–2; Content Topic: L.1.6)*

LESSON 36

PAGE 173

Sample responses:

1. The baseball game took place on Saturday at 3 p.m. *(DOK Level: 1–2; Content Topic: L.1.8)*

2. When the game started, the players relaxed. *(DOK Level: 1–2; Content Topic: L.1.8)*

3. The pitcher did not know where to throw the ball. *(DOK Level: 1–2; Content Topic: L.1.8)*

4. After each inning, they repeated their signals. *(DOK Level: 1–2; Content Topic: L.1.8)*

5. The game ended with a home run with the bases loaded. *or* The game ended with a grand slam. *(DOK Level: 1–2; Content Topic: L.1.8)*

6. No one knows where the next game will be held. *(DOK Level: 1–2; Content Topic: L.1.8)*

Sample response:

Solitaire is a card game I can happily spend hours playing. This game has two advantages over the other games I play. First, solitaire is played by one person, so I don't need a partner to play. Also, solitaire has many versions. Some are simple games using only one deck of cards. Other versions are complicated and require two decks. The more complex games can continue for a long time. Maybe that's why solitaire is also called "Patience." *(DOK Level: 2; Content Topic: L.1.8)*

PAGE 174

1. B.

2. A.

3. Sample response: You can probably find things that you don't need or just don't want anymore in your own home. *(DOK Level: 2; Content Topic: L.1.5, L.1.6, L.1.8)*

PAGE 175

1. A.

2. B.

3. Sample response: The witness said last Sunday's accident involved a red sports car and a bike. *(DOK Level: 1–2; Content Topic: L.1.8)*

LESSON 37

PAGE 176

First, go north to the corner. Second, turn right at the food store. Look for the sign for Smith Street. When you see the sign, walk a block more. Then turn left. Last, stop at the dress shop. Our apartment is on the second floor. *(DOK Level: 1–2; Content Topic: L.1.9)*

Sample response:

First, walk one block to Price Street. When you pass the gas station, turn left. Next, turn right at the train tracks. After you see the post office, pass the bank and walk four more blocks. The grocery store will be on the northwest corner. *(DOK Level: 1–2; Content Topic: L.1.9)*

PAGE 177

1. **finally** *(DOK Level: 1; Content Topic: L.1.9)*
2. **nevertheless** *(DOK Level: 1; Content Topic: L.1.9)*
3. **furthermore** *(DOK Level: 1; Content Topic: L.1.9)*
4. **thus** *(DOK Level: 1; Content Topic: L.1.9)*
5. **however** *(DOK Level: 1; Content Topic: L.1.9)*

Sample responses:

6. **My hairdresser cut my bangs too short; moreover, she dyed my hair the wrong color.** *(DOK Level: 1–2; Content Topic: L.1.9)*
7. **I have only three dollars in my bank account; indeed, I need a job!** *(DOK Level: 1–2; Content Topic: L.1.9)*
8. **She forgot to add the yeast; consequently, the dough did not rise.** *(DOK Level: 1–2; Content Topic: L.1.9)*

PAGE 178

We should begin a recycling program in the office. There are many ways we could recycle. For example, we could provide a bin for recycled paper near the copier. In addition, we could make changes in the cafeteria. We could encourage people to bring their lunches to work in reusable bags. Similarly, we could encourage recycling by adding bins for people to recycle cans and bottles. On the other hand, we could do nothing and simply contribute to the polluting of Earth. In summary, I care about the Earth, and I would like to see us do something about it by starting a recycling program in the office. *(DOK Level: 1–2; Content Topic: L.1.9)*

LESSON 38

PAGE 180

1. writer ed j. smith reports that people are taking cheaper trips in the Summer.
2. mr. and mrs. mott drove to orlando, florida, and went camping.
3. last year, the Motts went to sea world.
4. this year, dr. ortega and his family went hiking instead of going to mt. rushmore in south dakota.
5. ms. wills visited her friend in Wisconsin rather than flying to the Island of st. kitts.
6. miss e. k. link from newtown, long island, spent two days in maine.
7. she went to lake mead last year.
8. busch gardens in tampa, florida, is still very busy, though.
9. My Doctor wants to go to israel and see the dead sea.

Sample responses:

10. My dentist is Dr. Lou Graham. *(DOK Level: 1–2; Content Topic: L.2.1)*
11. I would love to go to Jamaica. *(DOK Level: 1–2; Content Topic: L.2.1)*
12. I was born in Mexico. *(DOK Level: 1–2; Content Topic: L.2.1)*

PAGES 181–183

1. Last year I worked on Senator Smith's campaign. *(DOK Level: 1–2; Content Topic: L.2.1)*
2. The campaign office was on Fifth Avenue in the Chrysler Building. *(DOK Level: 1–2; Content Topic: L.2.1)*

3. **A debate was sponsored by a group called Independent Voters of America at their building on the Hudson River.** *(DOK Level: 1–2; Content Topic: L.2.1)*

4. **Laura Washington, vice president of the organization, made a speech.** *(DOK Level: 1–2; Content Topic: L.2.1)*

5. **This year, monday, january 18, dr. martin luther king jr. day will be a paid holiday.**

6. **This holiday is in the place of columbus day, which we took as a day off on october 10.**

7. **The plant will, of course, be closed for the usual Fall and Winter holidays— thanksgiving, christmas, and new year's eve.**

8. **If any of these holidays fall on a monday or a friday, you will have a long weekend.**

9. **This year the Company's independence Day picnic will be on sunday, july 7.**

10. **I will be back at work on Tuesday, september 6, the day after labor day.**

11. **Some people want to have the party on Flag day, june 14, instead.**

12. **There has also been talk of a halloween party for october 31, which is a thursday this year.**

13. **We could hold the party on friday, october 25, if that is a better time.**

Sample responses:

14. **My favorite holidays are Thanksgiving and Valentine's Day.** *(DOK Level: 1–2; Content Topic: L.2.1)*

15. **The best day of the week for me is Sunday.** *(DOK Level: 1–2; Content Topic: L.2.1)*

16. **My favorite season is spring.** *(DOK Level: 1–2; Content Topic: L.2.1)*

harriet quimby was the first woman to earn a pilot's license. she was a writer in new york before she flew a plane. she fell in love with airplanes in 1910 when she saw her first flying meet. harriet became a pilot and toured in mexico with a troupe of pilots. she decided she would be the first woman to cross the english channel. she took off on april 16, 1912, sitting on a wicker basket in the cockpit. after a scary flight, she landed on a french beach.
(DOK Level: 1–2; Content Topic: L.2.1)

Sample responses:

17. **I live in Austin, Texas.**

18. **I like to shop at Whole Foods, Book People, and Waterloo Records.** *(DOK Level: 1–2; Content Topic: L.2.1)*

may 20, 2014

supreme computer, inc.
958 alexander street
river tower
Columbus, oh 43221
dear mr. Potter:

my supervisor, doris healy, director of sales here at bradley associates, asked me to send you the enclosed brochure detailing the services our company provides to computer stores like yours. If interested, you can take advantage of our free trial offer by calling before may 31. We are closed next Monday because of memorial day.

Sincerely,

James Hobson

james hobson
sales assistant
(DOK Level: 1–2; Content Topic: L.2.1)

LESSON 39

PAGE 184

1. **C** *(DOK Level: 1–2; Content Topic: L.2.2)*
2. **F** *(DOK Level: 1–2; Content Topic: L.2.2)*
3. **F** *(DOK Level: 1–2; Content Topic: L.2.2)*
4. **F** *(DOK Level: 1–2; Content Topic: L.2.2)*
5. **F** *(DOK Level: 1–2; Content Topic: L.2.2)*
6. **C** *(DOK Level: 1–2; Content Topic: L.2.2)*
7. **C** *(DOK Level: 1–2; Content Topic: L.2.2)*

Sample responses:

8. **The minimum driving age in this state is 16.** *(DOK Level: 1–2; Content Topic: L.2.2)*
9. **Many drivers simply drive too fast.** *(DOK Level: 1–2; Content Topic: L.2.2)*

PAGE 185

1. **The verb is missing.** *(DOK Level: 1–2; Content Topic: L.2.2)*
2. **The subject is missing.** *(DOK Level: 1–2; Content Topic: L.2.2)*
3. **The verb is missing.** *(DOK Level: 1–2; Content Topic: L.2.2)*
4. **The subject is missing.** *(DOK Level: 1–2; Content Topic: L.2.2)*

Sample responses:

5. **My older sister is still living with our parents.** *(DOK Level: 1–2; Content Topic: L.2.2)*
6. **She enjoys spending time with them in the evenings.** *(DOK Level: 1–2; Content Topic: L.2.2)*

PAGE 186

1. **RO** *(DOK Level: 1–2; Content Topic: L.2.2)*
2. **RO** *(DOK Level: 1–2; Content Topic: L.2.2)*
3. **RO** *(DOK Level: 1–2; Content Topic: L.2.2)*
4. **RO** *(DOK Level: 1–2; Content Topic: L.2.2)*
5. **C** *(DOK Level: 1–2; Content Topic: L.2.2)*
6. **RO** *(DOK Level: 1–2; Content Topic: L.2.2)*
7. **C** *(DOK Level: 1–2; Content Topic: L.2.2)*
8. **C** *(DOK Level: 1–2; Content Topic: L.2.2)*

PAGE 187

Sample responses:

1. **The Special Olympics started in 1968. It is a sports competition for people with disabilities.** *(DOK Level: 1–2; Content Topic: L.2.2, L.2.4)*
2. **More than 7,000 athletes attend, and they come from 150 nations.** *(DOK Level: 1–2; Content Topic: L.2.2, L.2.4)*
3. **Each nation competes in 19 sporting events, but athletes do not have to enter every event.** *(DOK Level: 1–2; Content Topic: L.2.2, L.2.4)*
4. **Everyone is a winner, for each athlete gets a ribbon or a medal.** *(DOK Level: 1–2; Content Topic: L.2.2, L.2.4)*
5. **Many people come to watch, and they are impressed by the athletes.** *(DOK Level: 1–2; Content Topic: L.2.2, L.2.4)*

Sample responses:

6. **I enjoy watching the Olympic Games, and I'm looking forward to seeing the next games on TV.** *(DOK Level: 1–2; Content Topic: L.2.2, L.2.4)*
7. **Winning a gold medal must be a thrill. The athletes work so hard for it.** *(DOK Level: 1–2; Content Topic: L.2.2, L.2.4)*

LESSON 40

PAGE 189

1. **Tran's** *(DOK Level: 1; Content Topic: L.2.3)*
2. **children's** *(DOK Level: 1; Content Topic: L.2.3)*
3. **friends'** *(DOK Level: 1; Content Topic: L.2.3)*
4. **factory's** *(DOK Level: 1; Content Topic: L.2.3)*
5. **bodies** *(DOK Level: 1; Content Topic: L.2.3)*

Sample responses:

6. **Mr. Tillis's sweater is too small for him.** *(DOK Level: 1–2; Content Topic: L.2.3)*
7. **Sarah and Emma's cousin came to visit.** *(DOK Level: 1–2; Content Topic: L.2.3)*
8. **My boss's desk is always neat.** *(DOK Level: 1–2; Content Topic: L.2.3)*
9. **My brothers-in-law's football tickets are free if someone wants them.** *(DOK Level: 1–2; Content Topic: L.2.3)*

10. Dr. Reyna's schedule is very busy. *(DOK Level: 1–2; Content Topic: L.2.3)*

LESSON 41

PAGE 191

1. The picnic was ruined by ants, flies, and gnats. *(DOK Level: 1–2; Content Topic: L.2.4)*

2. Dogs howl, whine, or bark when they need to go out. *(DOK Level: 1–2; Content Topic: L.2.4)*

3. My favorite restaurant serves breakfast, lunch, and dinner. *(DOK Level: 1–2; Content Topic: L.2.4)*

4. C *(DOK Level: 1–2; Content Topic: L.2.4)*

5. Sang Lee has traveled to New York City, Boston, and Pittsburgh on business. *(DOK Level: 1–2; Content Topic: L.2.4)*

6. Carrie directed, acted, and sang in the community play. *(DOK Level: 1–2; Content Topic: L.2.4)*

7. I wrote, edited, proofread, and printed my article for the newspaper. *(DOK Level: 1–2; Content Topic: L.2.4)*

8. C *(DOK Level: 1–2; Content Topic: L.2.4)*

9. Scout likes her tacos hot, spicy, and crunchy. *(DOK Level: 1–2; Content Topic: L.2.4)*

10. You have to rest, eat well, and drink plenty of water to get over a cold. *(DOK Level: 1–2; Content Topic: L.2.4)*

11. C *(DOK Level: 1–2; Content Topic: L.2.4)*

12. We gazed in awe at the huge, majestic, snowy mountain. *(DOK Level: 1–2; Content Topic: L.2.4)*

13. C *(DOK Level: 1–2; Content Topic: L.2.4)*

Sample responses:

14. While in Washington, D.C., we visited the White House, the Capitol, and the Washington Monument. *(DOK Level: 2; Content Topic: L.2.4)*

15. I love to sit on my large, comfy, orange couch in the morning. *(DOK Level: 2; Content Topic: L.2.4)*

16. Mom planted, weeded, and pruned in her garden. *(DOK Level: 2; Content Topic: L.2.4)*

17. The beautiful building was ancient, massive, and imposing. *(DOK Level: 2; Content Topic: L.2.4)*

18. Dad added basil, tomatoes, and bay leaves to my spaghetti sauce. *(DOK Level: 2; Content Topic: L.2.4)*

PAGE 193

1. We will handle this legally, of course, by going to the zoning board. *(DOK Level: 1–2; Content Topic: L.2.4)*

2. C *(DOK Level: 1–2; Content Topic: L.2.4)*

3. C *(DOK Level: 1–2; Content Topic: L.2.4)*

4. My mom, who is eighty years old, ran a marathon last year. *(DOK Level: 1–2; Content Topic: L.2.4)*

5. Before you donate Pooky, your favorite stuffed animal, think about keeping it. *(DOK Level: 1–2; Content Topic: L.2.4)*

6. C *(DOK Level: 1–2; Content Topic: L.2.4)*

7. The cell phone should be returned to Mr. Brown, the owner. *(DOK Level: 1–2; Content Topic: L.2.4)*

8. The plane, a Boeing 747, landed safely in Los Angeles. *(DOK Level: 1–2; Content Topic: L.2.4)*

9. The developer, however, will likely put up a fight. *(DOK Level: 1–2; Content Topic: L.2.4)*

10. I walk my dogs, Marley and Bailey, around the park every day. *(DOK Level: 1–2; Content Topic: L.2.4)*

Sample responses:

11. I walked with Harvey, my friend, to school today. *(DOK Level: 1–2; Content Topic: L.2.4)*

12. You will, however, have to show your ID at the door. *(DOK Level: 1–2; Content Topic: L.2.4)*

LESSON 42

1. **Would you like to get a dog?** *(DOK Level: 1–2; Content Topic: L.2.4)*

2. **I love my dog!** *or* dog. *(DOK Level: 1–2; Content Topic: L.2.4)*

3. **Owning a dog is a big responsibility.** *(DOK Level: 1–2; Content Topic: L.2.4)*

4. **Puppies are so darn cute!** *or* cute. *(DOK Level: 1–2; Content Topic: L.2.4)*

5. **But, boy, can they chew!** *or* chew. *(DOK Level: 1–2; Content Topic: L.2.4)*

6. **If you rent, you have to ask your landlord if it's okay to have a dog.** *(DOK Level: 1–2; Content Topic: L.2.4)*

7. **To adopt a dog, you have to answer a lot of questions.** *(DOK Level: 1–2; Content Topic: L.2.4)*

8. **Do you have a fenced-in yard?** *(DOK Level: 1–2; Content Topic: L.2.4)*

9. **Where will the dog stay?** *(DOK Level: 1–2; Content Topic: L.2.4)*

10. **Owning a dog can be very expensive.** *(DOK Level: 1–2; Content Topic: L.2.4)*

11. **You will have to ask your vet how much shots cost.** *(DOK Level: 1–2; Content Topic: L.2.4)*

12. **Do you still want a dog?** *(DOK Level: 1–2; Content Topic: L.2.4)*

Sample responses:

13. **There are different breeds of dogs.** *(DOK Level: 1–2; Content Topic: L.2.4)*

14. **What kind of dog is your favorite?** *(DOK Level: 1–2; Content Topic: L.2.4)*

15. **Dogs are the best pets ever!** *(DOK Level: 1–2; Content Topic: L.2.4)*

LESSON 43

1. **The skies opened up, and lightning streaked across the clouds.** *(DOK Level: 1–2; Content Topic: L.1.9, L.2.4)*

2. **Last year we had floods, but this year was not as bad.** *(DOK Level: 1–2; Content Topic: L.1.9, L.2.4)*

3. **The storm caused severe damage, and several people were injured.** *(DOK Level: 1–2; Content Topic: L.1.9, L.2.4)*

4. **Windows were shattered by the wind, so we went into the basement.** *(DOK Level: 1–2; Content Topic: L.1.9, L.2.4)*

5. **We read books, or sometimes we played cards.** *or* books, and *(DOK Level: 1–2; Content Topic: L.1.9, L.2.4)*

Sample responses:

7. **The street was deserted, and the stores were closed.** *(DOK Level: 1–2; Content Topic: L.1.9, L.2.4)*

8. **The couch was new, so we tried not to get it dirty.** *(DOK Level: 1–2; Content Topic: L.1.9, L.2.4)*

9. **The soldiers marched bravely, but their mission failed.** *(DOK Level: 1–2; Content Topic: L.1.9, L.2.4)*

10. **The sky looked threatening, so we left the beach early.** *(DOK Level: 1–2; Content Topic: L.1.9, L.2.4)*

11. **The fruit was ripe, so we picked as much as we could.** *(DOK Level: 1–2; Content Topic: L.1.9, L.2.4)*

12. **I should get gas soon, or I will run out.** *(DOK Level: 1–2; Content Topic: L.1.9, L.2.4)*

13. **We could see this movie, or we could see a different one.** *(DOK Level: 1–2; Content Topic: L.1.9, L.2.4)*

Sample responses:

2. **When you drive on the Blue Ridge Parkway, you can stop at many overlooks.** *(DOK Level: 1–2; Content Topic: L.1.9, L.2.4)*

3. **Most people stop at Mt. Mitchell because that's the most spectacular view of all.** *(DOK Level: 1–2; Content Topic: L.1.9, L.2.4)*

4. **Although you'll want to take pictures, it's hard to get those mountain ranges on film.** *(DOK Level: 1–2; Content Topic: L.1.9, L.2.4)*

5. **Stay on the parkway until you reach the city of Asheville.** *(DOK Level: 1–2; Content Topic: L.1.9, L.2.4)*

UNIT 5 REVIEW
PAGES 200–201

1. **I'm** *(DOK Level: 1; Content Topic: L.2.3)*
2. **didn't** *(DOK Level: 1; Content Topic: L.2.3)*
3. **We've** *(DOK Level: 1; Content Topic: L.2.3)*
4. **She'll** *(DOK Level: 1; Content Topic: L.2.3)*
5. **won't** *(DOK Level: 1; Content Topic: L.2.3)*
6. **clothes** *(DOK Level: 1; Content Topic: L.1.1)*
7. **than** *(DOK Level: 1; Content Topic: L.1.1)*
8. **accept** *(DOK Level: 1; Content Topic: L.1.1)*
9. **week** *(DOK Level: 1; Content Topic: L.1.1)*
10. **between** *(DOK Level: 1; Content Topic: L.1.1)*
11. **are** *(DOK Level: 1; Content Topic: L.1.2, L.1.7)*
12. **know** *(DOK Level: 1; Content Topic: L.1.2, L.1.7)*
13. **breaks** *(DOK Level: 1; Content Topic: L.1.2, L.1.7)*
14. **gives** *(DOK Level: 1; Content Topic: L.1.2, L.1.7)*
15. **is** *(DOK Level: 1; Content Topic: L.1.2, L.1.7)*

Sample responses:
16. **They buy a red sports car.** *(DOK Level: 1–2; Content Topic: L.2.2)*
17. **It is on the corner of Main and Ridge.** *(DOK Level: 1–2; Content Topic: L.2.2)*
18. **He says he is happy to help.** *(DOK Level: 1–2; Content Topic: L.2.2)*
19. **He gives his parents a ride to the farmers' market every Saturday.** *(DOK Level: 1–2; Content Topic: L.2.2)*
20. **Walking home from school, Jake saw a bird land on a white fence.** *(DOK Level: 1–2; Content Topic: L.1.5)*

21. **While I was watching TV, the comedian made me laugh.** *(DOK Level: 1–2; Content Topic: L.1.5)*
22. **As I was making my bed, a mouse ran across the room.** *(DOK Level: 1–2; Content Topic: L.1.5)*
23. **While I was cooking dinner, my dog begged me for food.** *(DOK Level: 1–2; Content Topic: L.1.5)*
24. **As Suki was taking a shower this morning, the water turned freezing cold.** *(DOK Level: 1–2; Content Topic: L.1.5)*
25. **Jen walks her dog at night, unless it's raining.** *(DOK Level: 1–2; Content Topic: L.1.6)*
26. **It's also pleasant in the morning whenever the sun is shining.** *(DOK Level: 1–2; Content Topic: L.1.6)*
27. **Because she loves animals, she treats her dog like a person.** *(DOK Level: 1–2; Content Topic: L.1.6)*

UNIT 5 MINI-TEST
PAGES 202–203

Finding your way around Chicago is not easy. If you decide to take a train, first you need to decide which train line you need. Second, you need to find a station along that train line. Then you need to buy a ticket. When you see a train coming, be ready to get on. Last, get off the train at the right stop. You can then take the bus or walk to your final destination. *(DOK Level: 1; Content Topic: L.1.6)*

1. **Rob went to New York in September to visit his uncle.** *(DOK Level: 1; Content Topic: L.2.1)* New York is a state, so it should be capitalized.
2. **Because it was autumn, sights like the Statue of Liberty weren't crowded.** *(DOK Level: 1; Content Topic: L.2.1)* Autumn is a season, so it should not be capitalized. The Statue of Liberty is a monument, so it should be capitalized.

3. **On Labor Day, Rob walked through Central Park and up Fifth Avenue.** *(DOK Level: 1; Content Topic: L.2.1)* The first word of a sentence should be capitalized. Labor Day is a holiday and Rob is a proper name, so both should be capitalized. Central Park is a landmark and Fifth Avenue is a street, so both should be capitalized.

4. **He ate French food and saw a game at Yankee Stadium.** *(DOK Level: 1; Content Topic: L.2.1)* French is a proper adjective and Yankee Stadium is a tourist attraction, so both should be capitalized.

Sample responses:

5. **The apartment on the fourth floor is vacant.** *(DOK Level: 1–2; Content Topic: L.2.2)* The verb is missing from the original item.

6. **S** *(DOK Level: 1–2; Content Topic: L.2.2)* The sentence has a subject and verb and expresses a complete thought.

7. **Thinking about it on the way home from work, he decided to take it.** *(DOK Level: 1–2; Content Topic: L.2.2)* The original item does not express a complete thought.

8. **Craig has an unusual job. He is a chef.** *(DOK Level: 1–2; Content Topic: L.2.2)*

9. **He used to work in a store. He was a cashier.** *(DOK Level: 1–2; Content Topic: L.2.2)*

10. **Then he went to cooking school for two years. It was a long program.** *(DOK Level: 1–2; Content Topic: L.2.2)*

11. **Did you come to our wedding?** *(DOK Level: 1–2; Content Topic: L.2.4)* Questions should end with question marks.

12. **My husband and I were married at a Catholic church in Chicago, Illinois.** *(DOK Level: 1–2; Content Topic: L.2.4)* Catholic is a proper adjective, so it should be capitalized. A comma is needed between a city and state. Illinois is a state and should be capitalized. Statements should end with periods.

13. **It was the best wedding ever!** *(DOK Level: 1–2; Content Topic: L.2.4)* Exclamatory sentences should end with an exclamation mark.

14. **His brothers Ed, Hal, John, and Joe stood on his side.** *(DOK Level: 1–2; Content Topic: L.2.4)* Hal and Joe are proper names, so they should be capitalized. Items in a list should be separated by commas.

15. **I, on the other hand, had only my sister Amy stand by me.** *(DOK Level: 1–2; Content Topic: L.2.4)* Parenthetical expressions should be set off by commas. Amy is a proper name, so it should be capitalized. Statements should end with a period.

16. **The wedding was beautiful, and all the guests had a good time.** *(DOK Level: 1–2; Content Topic: L.2.4)* The first word of a sentence should be capitalized. A comma is used before a coordinating conjunction in a compound sentence. Statements should end with a period.

17. **Do you know where we went for our honeymoon?** *(DOK Level: 1–2; Content Topic: L.2.4)* Honeymoon is a common noun, so it should not be capitalized. Questions should end with a question mark.

18. **We went to Atlantic City, Niagara Falls, and New York City.** *(DOK Level: 1–2; Content Topic: L.2.4)* Atlantic City, Niagara Falls, and New York City are all place names and should be capitalized. Items in a list should be separated by commas. Statements should end with a period.

19. **Then we visited Millie, my aunt on my mother's side, for a few days.** *(DOK Level: 1–2; Content Topic: L.2.4)* Nonessential appositives should be set off with commas. Statements should end with a period.

20. **I was absolutely exhausted!** *(DOK Level: 1–2; Content Topic: L.2.4)* Exclamatory sentences should end with an exclamation mark.

21. **Sam's** *(DOK Level: 1–2; Content Topic: L.2.3)* Use an apostrophe and *s* to form the possessive of singular nouns.

22. **twins'** *(DOK Level: 1–2; Content Topic: L.2.3)* To show plural possession, make the noun plural first, then add an apostrophe.

23. **Manny's** *(DOK Level: 1–2; Content Topic: L.2.3)* Use an apostrophe and *s* to form the possessive of singular nouns.

24. **His** *(DOK Level: 1–2; Content Topic: L.2.3)* Possessive pronouns, such as *his,* do not have apostrophes.

25. **waitress's** *(DOK Level: 1–2; Content Topic: L.2.3)* Use an apostrophe and *s* to form the possessive of singular nouns.

POSTTEST

PAGE 207

1. **B.** *(DOK Level: 2; Content Topic: R.2.2)* The last sentence of paragraph 6 refers to the feelings of hope in youth, supporting Option B.

2. **A.** *(DOK Level: 2–3; Content Topic: R.4.3/L.4.3)* No one wants to kill the children (Option B), and the phrase means the opposite of Options C and D.

3. **Sample response: He would thank her and follow her plan, because he responds to her crying with kindness and friendship. He does not belittle her or decide to leave her or show frustration. It is likely that he would respond to her with kindness and friendship under other circumstances as well.** *(DOK Level: 2–3; Content Topic: R.3.2, R.2.7)*

4. **D.** *(DOK Level: 2–3; Content Topic: R.3.2, R.2.7)* Tom is saving the candle for later use, which supports Option D.

5. **B.** *(DOK Level: 1–2; Content Topic: R.2.6)* The two stories describe the adventures of young people.

6. **Responses will vary but should be supported with details from the selection and background knowledge.** *(DOK Level: 1–2; Content Topic: R.2.7)*

PAGE 209

7. **D.** *(DOK Level: 1–2; Content Topic: R.3.3)* The purpose of paragraph 3 is to explain why Nuttel's sister gives him letters of introduction, which supports Option D.

8. **D.** *(DOK Level: 1–2; Content Topic: R.2.6)* Nuttel is uncomfortable in the scene, which supports Option D.

9. **Sample response: Framton Nuttel is visiting Mrs. Sappleton's house because he is spending some time in the country. His sister wants him to meet the neighbors, so she gives him some letters of introduction, one of which is to Mrs. Sappleton.** *(DOK Level: 1–2; Content Topic: R.3.2)*

10. **travel** *(DOK Level: 1; Content Topic: R.4.1/L.4.1)*

11. **swallowed up** *(DOK Level: 1; Content Topic: R.4.1/L.4.1)*

12. **hurried, moved briskly** *(DOK Level: 1; Content Topic: R.4.1/L.4.1)*

13. **the death of her husband and brothers** *(DOK Level: 1–2; Content Topic: R.2.1)*

PAGE 211

14. **C.** *(DOK Level 2; Content Topic: R.3.2)* Roosevelt states, "I know it will make very little difference to you whether I resign," which supports Option C.

15. **A.** *(DOK Level 2–3; Content Topic: R.2.3)* According to the introduction to the letter, the organization discriminated based on race, which supports Option A.

16. **B.** *(DOK Level 1–2; Content Topic: R.6.1)* Roosevelt is disappointed in the organization and determined not to be associated with their work, which supports Option B.

17. **D.** *(DOK Level 2–3; Content Topic: R.4.3/L.4.3)* Roosevelt does not want to be associated with the organization's decision, which supports Option D.

18. **Sample response: Eleanor Roosevelt meant that if the DAR had allowed Marian Anderson to play at Constitution Hall, the organization would have been setting an example to others that discrimination is not acceptable. The DAR could have shown an enlightened or new attitude toward**

African Americans not often seen at this time in American history. *(DOK Level 2; Content Topic: R.2.2)*

19. **Sample response: She could have written the DAR a mean-spirited letter, chastising them for their decision. She could have gone to talk to them in person to let them know how she felt about their decision. She could have expressed her opinion to the media.** *(DOK Level 2–3; Content Topic: R.2.7)*

PAGE 213

20. **C.** *(DOK Level: 1–2; Content Topic: R.3.1)* The first sentence of the selection refers to the failure of the Roanoke colony, which they are trying to avoid with their settlement.

21. **A.** *(DOK Level: 2; Content Topic: R.2.2)* A summary gives the main ideas of a selection, and the main ideas of the selection are given in Option A.

22. **D.** *(DOK Level: 1–2; Content Topic: R.4.1/L.4.1)* The second-to-last sentence discusses the need for better housing, or shelter, which supports Option D.

23. **B.** *(DOK Level: 1–3; Content Topic: R.2.6)* The quotation helps show that the selection is factual, or informative.

24. **A.** *(DOK Level: 2–3; Content Topic: R.4.3/L.4.3)* The advertisement described the land as beautiful and wealthy to attract settlers.

25. **Sample response: The men were adventurers more focused on making a fortune than settling a colony. They also did not have farming experience or carpentry skills.** *(DOK Level: 2; Content Topic: R.2.2)*

PAGE 215

26. **chromosome** *(DOK Level: 1; Content Topic: R.4.1/L.4.1)*

27. **genome** *(DOK Level: 1; Content Topic: R.4.1/L.4.1)*

28. **DNA** *(DOK Level: 1; Content Topic: R.4.1/L.4.1)*

29. **gene** *(DOK Level: 1; Content Topic: R.4.1/L.4.1)*

30. **allele** *(DOK Level: 1; Content Topic: R.4.1/L.4.1)*

31. **A.** *(DOK Level: 2; Content Topic: R.2.2)* The three parts of a nucleotide are listed in the second sentence of paragraph 2.

32. **When organisms reproduce, they pass copies of their DNA to their offspring. This passing of genetic materials is heredity.** *(DOK Level: 2–3; Content Topic: R.2.2)*

33. **Genes are specific segments of DNA at specific locations on specific chromosomes. The expressed traits of an organism result from protein production based on the specific nucleotide sequence of genes.** *(DOK Level: 2–3; Content Topic: R.2.8)*

34. **The nucleotide sequence of a gene is very important because it provides the information for the synthesis of specific proteins, which in turn affects the traits expressed by an organism. If the nucleotide sequence changes, the correct protein may not be produced.** *(DOK Level: 2–3; Content Topic: R.2.7)*

PAGE 217

35. **matter, energy** *(DOK Level: 2; Content Topic: R.2.2)*

36. **conversion** *(DOK Level: 2; Content Topic: R.2.2)*

37. **theory** *(DOK Level: 2; Content Topic: R.2.2)*

38. **created, destroyed** *(DOK Level: 2; Content Topic: R.2.2)*

39. **The Law of Conservation of Energy states that energy cannot be created or destroyed during ordinary chemical and physical changes.** *(DOK Level: 2; Content Topic: R.2.2)*

40. **A.** *(DOK Level: 1–2; Content Topic: R.2.1, R.4.1/L.4.1)* The first sentence of paragraph 4 defines an open system.

41. **C.** *(DOK Level: 2–3; Content Topic: R.2.7)* The entire selection is about the conservation of energy, which supports Option C.

PAGE 218

42. **C.** *(DOK Level: 1–2; Content Topic: R.2.1)* The third bullet in the guidelines supports Option C.

43. **B.** *(DOK Level: 1–2; Content Topic: R.2.1)* The first sentence of the guidelines supports Option B.

44. **D.** *(DOK Level: 2–3; Content Topic: R.2.7)* The second bullet in the guidelines supports Option D.

45. **Sample response: I always liked "Row, Row, Row Your Boat." Even though it is a silly song, I like how it sounds when people sing it in rounds, with singers starting the song at different times. Yes, Happy Lands Day Care Center would accept this song because it is appropriate for children with nothing that would scare them.** *(DOK Level: 2–3; Content Topic: R.2.7, W.2)*

PAGE 219

46. **A.** *(DOK Level: 1–3; Content Topic: R.2.5)* The second sentence of the introductory paragraph can be used to support Option A.

47. **Let Me Hear It Again** *(DOK Level: 2; Content Topic: R.2.2)*

48. **Sample response: I enjoy reading horror stories the most. I love the way they grab and play with my emotions. Some parts of the book make me shiver and shake. A really good horror story can make me so scared that I leave the lights on when I go to bed.** *(DOK Level: 2–3; Content Topic: W.2)*

PAGE 220

49. **C.** *(DOK Level 1–2; Content Topic: W.1)* The letter acknowledges the problems and explains how they will be fixed.

50. **B.** *(DOK Level 1–2; Content Topic: W.1)* The first sentence of the letter supports Option B.

51. **D.** *(DOK Level 1–2; Content Topic: W.1)* The last sentence of the first paragraph supports Option D.

PAGE 223

52. **Responses will vary. Students should clearly identify which argument is better supported and cite specific evidence from the text. Refer to the Scoring Rubric on page 140.**

PAGE 224

53. **D.** *(DOK Level 1–2; Content Topic: L.1.2, L.1.7)* In the second part of the compound sentence, the verb needs to agree with the subject *options*.

54. **A.** *(DOK Level 1–2; Content Topic: L.1.2, L.1.7)* This sentence does not relate to the overall topic and should be removed.

55. **C.** *(DOK Level 1–2; Content Topic: L.2.4)* The original sentence is a fragment. The revision supplies a subject (the understood *you*) and a complete verb.

56. **D.** *(DOK Level 1–2; Content Topic: L.2.4)* Sentence 7 is punctuated correctly.

57. **B.** *(DOK Level 1–2; Content Topic: L.2.4)* A comma is needed after each item in a series.

PAGE 225

58. **D.** *(DOK Level 1–2; Content Topic: L.2.4)* The paragraph as a whole is in the present tense, so the verb in this sentence should be too.

59. **A.** *(DOK Level 1–2; Content Topic: L.2.4)* *However* is not the appropriate connecting word to use here. *When* makes the meaning of the sentence clearer.

60. **B.** *(DOK Level 1–2; Content Topic: L.2.1)* Because the specific name of the company is not used here, the word *company* should not be capitalized.

61. **A.** *(DOK Level 1–2; Content Topic: L.1.1)* If you substitute *They are* in the sentence, it makes sense, so the contraction is correct.

62. **C.** *(DOK Level 1–2; Content Topic: L.2.4)* There is a shift in the main idea beginning with sentence 9, so a new paragraph is needed here.

PAGE 226

63. **B.** *(DOK Level 1–2; Content Topic: L.2.2)* These two independent clauses should be separated by a comma and a coordinating conjunction.

64. **D.** *(DOK Level 1–2; Content Topic: L.2.2)* Sentence 6 clearly continues the same thought as sentence 5, so there should not be a paragraph break between them.

65. **A.** *(DOK Level 1–2; Content Topic: L.2.4)* A comma is needed after the introductory dependent clause.

66. **D.** *(DOK Level 1–2; Content Topic: L.2.2)* The list of actions should be parallel in structure: *learn, solve,* and *work.*

PAGE 227

67. **C.** *(DOK Level 1–2; Content Topic: L.2.2)* The names of months are always capitalized.

68. **A.** *(DOK Level 1–2; Content Topic: L.2.2)* Paragraph B needs a topic sentence. Option A is broad enough to introduce the whole paragraph.

69. **C.** *(DOK Level 1–2; Content Topic: L.1.8)* The sentence contains two independent clauses. The most meaningful conjunction to join these clauses is *so,* and a comma is needed as well. The conjunction *and* is not needed.

70. **D.** *(DOK Level 1–2; Content Topic: L.1.3)* It is not clear enough what the pronoun *them* refers to in this sentence. In the context of the passage, *voters* makes the most sense.

PAGE 228

71. **B.** *(DOK Level 1–2; Content Topic: L.1.5)* The phrase *Around a large area* is misplaced. It needs to follow the word it modifies, *distances.*

72. **D.** *(DOK Level 1–2; Content Topic: L.2.2)* This paragraph is written in the present tense, as is the first part of the sentence. It describes the current situation with building security.

73. **B.** *(DOK Level 1–2; Content Topic: L.2.4)* Option B shows a logical relationship between the ideas. The others do not.

74. **C.** *(DOK Level 1–2; Content Topic: L.1.3)* Read the sentence without *you and* to test which pronoun is correct.

PAGE 229

75. **C.** *(DOK Level 1–2; Content Topic: L.1.1)* Try reading the sentence with *you are* instead of *you're.* It doesn't make sense, so the contraction must be incorrect.

76. **A.** *(DOK Level 1–2; Content Topic: L.1.3)* Read the sentence without *and I* to test which pronoun is correct.

77. **B.** *(DOK Level 1–2; Content Topic: L.1.3)* The pronoun refers to *people.*

78. **B.** *(DOK Level 1–2; Content Topic: L.1.3)* The verb must agree with the subject *expressions,* which is plural.

adjective a word that modifies, or helps describe, a noun or a pronoun. A **proper adjective** is made from a proper noun.

adventure a story in which the characters take risks

adverb a word that modifies a verb, an adjective, or another adverb

advertisement a public notice designed to attract attention or customers

antecedent the noun to which a pronoun refers

apostrophe a mark of punctuation (') used to show possession or a contraction

application taking information from one situation and using it in another situation

appositive words or groups of words that rename or provide more information about a noun or pronoun. **Essential appositives** are necessary to the meaning of a sentence. **Nonessential appositives** are not necessary to the meaning of a sentence.

audience the person or person for whom you are writing

biography the true story of a real person's life written by another person

body the middle paragraphs of an essay, which develop and support the main idea; the contents or main portion of a letter

brainstorm to generate ideas about a topic by listing everything you can think of about it

brochure a pamphlet containing informative or advertising material

cause a person, thing, or event that brings about a result

cause and effect a way of organizing details showing how one thing (the cause) makes another thing (the effect) happen

character a person in a story or a play

classic a story that has set a high standard of excellence, remains meaningful, and continues to be read after many years

clause a group of words with its own subject and predicate. An **independent clause** can stand alone as a sentence; it is a complete thought. A **dependent clause** cannot stand alone as a sentence because it is not a complete thought.

clichés overused or overworked words or expressions

closing a parting phrase in a letter

comma a mark of punctuation (,) used to indicate a pause or separation

compare to find the ways things are alike

compare and contrast a way of organizing details that shows how they are similar and different

complex sentence a sentence with an independent clause and a dependent clause

compound sentence a sentence with two or more independent clauses, or complete thoughts

conclusion a judgment or opinion based on facts and details; the last paragraph of an essay, which signals the end and highlights the points the reader should remember

conflict a struggle or problem between characters or forces

conjunctive adverb adverbs that connect ideas

context clues the words and sentences surrounding a word or phrase. The context of a word helps show what the word means.

contraction a word formed by joining two other words using an apostrophe to show where a letter or letters have been left out

contrast to find the ways things are different

coordinating conjunction a connecting word that may be used with a comma to join two independent clauses, or complete thoughts, in a compound sentence

court case a legal case or dispute brought before a court for resolution

detail a fact about a person, place, thing, event, or time

diagram a drawing of an object, concept, or process

dialogue conversation between characters

direct object the noun or pronoun that receives the action of the verb in a sentence

document a piece of writing designed to communicate official or legal information

edit to check the content, style, and grammar of a piece of writing

effect the result of a cause

essay a short piece of nonfiction writing that gives the author's thoughts or opinions about something

evidence supporting facts, words, dialogue, or details that support an author's purpose

fact a statement that can be proven true

fantasy a story that involves unreal or unbelievable places, events, or creatures

fiction writing that is about people, places, and events invented by the author

final draft the final version of a piece of writing, prepared after editing and revising

first draft the first version of a piece of writing

form a printed document with blank spaces to be filled in with specific information

handbook a concise reference book covering a particular subject

head a headline; an important main caption or title

homonym a word that sounds like another word but is spelled differently and has a different meaning

idea map a way of organizing ideas by putting them in groups that are related

implication not directly stating something

indirect object the noun or pronoun that tells to whom or for whom an action is done in a sentence

inference an idea that the reader figures out based on clues an author presents and what the reader already knows

informal language language used in casual speech and writing, including clichés and slang

informational writing nonfiction writing that informs the reader about a topic or idea or explains something

legal documents documents that spell out agreements between parties or grant a right

main idea the most important point in a paragraph or passage

manual a reference book used to give instructions on how to do something or operate something

map pictures or charts that show geographical regions. Maps can also show political boundaries, historical changes in population or ideas, information about climate, routes traveled by people, or the distribution of resources.

modifier a descriptive word or phrase. A **misplaced modifier** is one that is in the wrong place in a sentence. A **dangling modifier** is one that does not modify a word in the sentence.

mood the atmosphere the author creates in a written work

mystery a story about solving a puzzle. The main character of a mystery is usually a detective who has to figure out who committed a crime.

narrator the character telling the story

nonfiction writing that is about real people, places, and events

noun a word that names a person, place, or thing. A **common noun** names a person, place, or thing. A **proper noun** names a specific person, place, or thing.

object of a preposition the noun or pronoun that follows a preposition such as *in* or *from* in a sentence

opinion a belief or judgment that cannot always be proved

outline a way of organizing ideas by putting them in numbered and lettered lists

parallel structure words or phrases that are in the same form

period a mark of punctuation (.) used to end a statement or command.

persuasive techniques using language to get the reader to think or act a certain way

photograph an image of people, places, things, or events that has been captured by a camera and printed

plot the series of events that create the action of a story

plural a form of a word that shows more than one

point of view the way the action is seen by the narrator or author of a piece of writing

possessive the form of a noun or pronoun that shows something is owned and to whom it belongs

predicate the part of a sentence that tells what the subject does or is, or what is being done to the subject

predict to tell what you think will happen in the future

prewriting planning before you begin to write. It includes defining your topic, generating ideas about it, and organizing those ideas.

pronoun a word that can take the place of a noun in a sentence

publishing sharing your final draft with your audience

punctuation the set of symbols used in writing to guide the reader

purpose your or an author's reason for writing—for example, to tell a story, to describe, to explain, or to persuade

question mark a mark of punctuation (?) used to end a question

restate to say something again using different words

revise to change writing in order to improve or correct it

run-on sentence two or more independent clauses, or complete thoughts, that are not correctly separated by punctuation

scan to look over text quickly to find specific information, such as a date, key word, or name

scientific method series of logical steps that can be used to solve problems. Steps usually include asking questions, making observations, testing ideas, and formulating conclusions.

sentence a group of words that expresses a complete thought

sentence fragment a group of words that does not express a complete thought

sequence the order in which events occur; time order

setting the time and place in which the events of a story take place

skim to read something quickly, looking for main ideas

slang informal or "trendy" language most often used between friends that changes from year to year

subhead a heading or part (as in an outline); a caption, title, or heading of less importance than the main heading

subject the person or thing that a sentence is about

subject-verb agreement when a subject and verb agree in number

subordinating conjunction a connecting word used before a dependent clause to connect it to an independent clause

summarize to state briefly the most important ideas of a longer piece of writing

synthesize to put together several elements to form a whole idea

tense the form of a verb that shows time, or when an action takes place

theme a general truth about life or human nature that is suggested in a work of literature

time order a way of organizing events in the order in which they happened; sequence

tone the author's attitude or feeling about a subject

topic sentence a statement of the main idea that will be developed in a paragraph

transition word a connecting word that signals the way ideas are related

writing process a five-step process that helps writers express their ideas in a cohesive, organized manner. The steps include prewriting, writing a first draft, revising and editing, writing a final draft, and publishing.

writing prompt a set of instructions for a writing assignment

verb a word that shows action or state of being

visualize to form a picture in your mind